BOB, AFGHANISTAN, AND ME

A war story about friendship,
love, and tragedy.

Brad Drake

This book has been approved and the material within cleared for publishing by the Department of Defense. The views expressed in this publication are those of the author and do not necessarily reflect the official policy or position of the Department of Defense or the U.S. government.

Merchandise related to this book can be found at:
www.r-249.com

All media inquiries can be directed to:
www.braddrake.net
815-290-9087

This book is dedicated to the memory of

Sergeant First Class Robert T. Allen
1981-2018

"Walking tall, machine gun man."
Alice in Chains, "Rooster"

This book is also dedicated to the memories of

Staff Sergeant James D. Mowris
1966-2004

Specialist Jacob A. Warner
1979-2004

Staff Sergeant Terry J. Scofield
1966-2020

FOREWORD
BY JEFF DRAKE

For as long as I can remember, my brother Brad always did things differently than my older brother and me. We grew up playing baseball and basketball. I used to beg him to play wiffle ball with me in the summer. Eventually he would agree, only to immediately mess with me enough during the game to get me to stop playing. He was smart enough to know that I would then not bug him to play anymore. In high school, Brad wrestled and was in gymnastics which were completely the opposite of what Chris and I did. It was no surprise to me that Brad enlisted in the Army when he was a senior because my older brother and I both had chosen to go to college. Deep down inside, I always knew it was a great path for him. Brad thrives on routine, order, and structure; which he found in the Army. I was away at school when he left for Basic Training, so it wasn't as hard on me as it was on my parents. I must admit, however, I was still worried about him. I had spent a lot of my life looking after him, since he was only 3 years younger than me, and now I could not protect him anymore. He was on his own. When he was in Basic Training and AIT, I would print out the weekly pro wrestling results and send them to him. I looked forward to his letters back and I still have them 21 years later. This was my way of still connecting and keeping tabs on him, but he would be growing into his own man.

When 9/11 happened, I was sure he would be activated and started to worry. Like Brad says in this book, the men of our family, and extended family, had a habit of fighting this country's wars. It was going to be this generation's turn. He was not activated right away, and, in all honesty, I became so busy with my own life, that the thought escaped me after a while. That was until 2003. I remember I was in the Police Academy and had to have my uniforms pressed in a certain military style. I had no idea what the hell that meant so I went to Brad for help. He did his best in pressing my uniforms like requested. He was close in his efforts, and I passed inspection. He, along with my Dad, laughed at me when I came home and said that I passed but had to do pushups anyway because of another recruit's mistake. They knew that the instructors were breaking us down to build us back up. Brad knew that no matter how well my uniforms looked that we would have had to do pushups anyway. The two of them were soldiers, no matter what they were doing as civilians. That is what always impresses me about people that have served. The soldier is never gone in them. Old men saluting always makes me smile. They never lose that mentality.

Right as I was getting ready to graduate, Brad's unit got activated. It was nerve-racking but I remember talking to Brad about it. I was talking to him in a brotherly fashion and reminding him that I told him to go to college instead of enlisting. He responded that "This is what I signed up for." It was that mentality that will always stick with me. It was almost like he was excited to go because finally he would be able to put his training to use. He left with his unit in early March. His 21st birthday was a few weeks later and my brother Chris and I drove up to Wisconsin where he was stationed before heading overseas. We took him out that night. I will save you the details, but the punch line is that we only stayed one night. The next day when we were leaving, my parents were showing up to celebrate with him. They spent the day waiting for him to recover from his hangover! It was a great time although my parents didn't think so.

Brad's 21st birthday was the first time I met Bob Allen. Bob struck me as kind of quiet, until we were out for a while that night. He dressed like the punk rock kids in high school. I liked him immediately. Bob was a fun guy and from moment one I could tell he and Brad had a special bond. They fed off of each other. That kind of connection is hard to find. Bob was a unique person, like Brad. They did not conform to what was cool or what the world thought they should be. They knew who they were and what they wanted to be. It is no surprise to me that Bob was a great soldier, and it is no surprise to me that Bob and Brad worked so well together. I could see their chemistry the first day I met him and that is a very rare thing in this life. I am glad Brad got to experience it, even for such a short time. Bob became a comfort to me in that he was with my brother when I couldn't be. He was watching out for him, Brad was watching out for Bob, and for that I am thankful.

Brad spent over two years of his life fighting a war. It was the longest two years of my life, worrying about him. I probably haven't said it enough, or at all to him, but I couldn't be prouder. He was born to be a soldier. He left my little brother but came back a man I respect. Bob Allen was a part of that process. This book is obviously a tribute to Bob but also is a story of a man. Like his father, grandfathers, cousins, and great uncles, Brad went to war and made it home to tell the story. Like all of them, his love for his country was greater than his love for himself. Brad, Bob, and all veterans have seen and done things that most won't ever understand. They are truly heroes.

After his first tour from 2003-2004, Brad gave me a combat American flag from one of his uniforms. For 18 years, that flag has been in my left pocket of my vest every day at work. Call it superstitious or call it crazy, but in my mind that flag, and my brother, have protected me for 18 years. They will protect me until I retire. If my son becomes an officer, it will go in his vest too. The tables have turned, you see. The boy I once protected, now protects me. My kid brother, Brad, became my hero.

FOREWORD
BY RYAN SUTHARD

September 11th, 2001 - This isn't when I met Bob, but it was definitely the day that confirmed he was a special breed. Anybody who is old enough to remember this day knows that this was not your average Tuesday morning. For the soldiers of C Company, 787th Military Police Battalion (Basic Training) however, this started as a special morning. We had graduated Basic Training the Friday before, had the weekend off, then started our Advanced Individual Training, or AIT, on Monday. Monday was basically an introduction to the Military Police Academy. Tuesday was the first real day....our first real day as soldiers.

We stood in formation with our uniforms starched and ironed to the extent that the creases in our sleeves could cut skin. Our boots shined in the early morning sun like glass. Our drill sergeants were all still with us, but rumors had gone around that they would treat us like professionals now. We weren't so sure. It was this uncertainty that kept anybody from noticing the base coming alive with activity and our drill sergeants frantically running around concerned with something. Looking back, the signs were there that something big had happened, but we were unable to focus on anything else than a professional appearance and the unknown of AIT.

Eventually our company commander came to the front of the formation to address us. He began explaining how the county had just been attacked by terrorists and that both World Trade Centers and the Sears Tower were now, "this tall", as he held his hand parallel to the ground about waist high. Yes, he told us the Sears Tower had been taken down as well. There was an odd feeling that

9

hovered over the silent formation. Bob was in the platoon next to me and as I tried

to process the information, I looked over at him. He didn't look at me. He stared

straight forward as one is supposed to do in a formation. He did not look

concerned. He was not sweating. Bob was still just waiting for class to start.

Throughout the day, rumors spread that the "attack" was fake and was

presented to the unit to reinvigorate us and sharpen our focus for AIT. Other

soldiers said their friends had similar experiences when they went through basic

and AIT, and the timeframe sure was a coincidence. Due to the rules of no TV in

training, they would not show us the videos, so we could not confirm anything.

After training, we were allowed to talk to our families and learned that this was

not some elaborate hoax by our drill sergeants. I sat near my locker in the

barracks contemplating what this had met when Bob came and found me. "You

gotta see this!", he stated excitedly. Now, I should mention that Bob and I met at

the processing center where you are picked up to leave for basic training. Most

new soldiers were wearing polo shirts and nice pants, with the occasional jeans.

Then there was Bob. Bob had black jeans and a KMFDM t-shirt that, if memory

serves correctly, had a tear in it. As a fan of metal and hard rock, I gravitated

toward him. In basic training during what little free time we had, we would sit and

listen to Pantera and share stories of nearly being arrested or doing idiotic things

while drunk. We were friends right off the bat.

Bob grabbed me and demanded I come to the drill sergeants' office.

When we arrived, I saw about 25 cots with sleeping bags strewn about the hallway

directly outside their office. Soldiers were sitting on their cots and looking

somber. Bob went on to explain that all of these soldiers were on "suicide watch" due to the fact that the country was inevitably going to war. "APPARENTLY THE ARMY'S ABOUT MORE THAN FREE COLLEGE MONEY" Bob said to me loud enough to ensure they all heard it too.

From there, Bob and I would go on to be in the same unit and do three deployments together. I was best man in his wedding and he is my daughter's Godfather. Along the way our brotherhood grew with Brad Drake, Lester Dodson, and many others. The pages ahead describe the adventures of us four, and how a bunch of wide-eyed, rarely-sober, Midwestern boys became men while navigating one of the most uniquely underrated moments in modern history.

This book takes place during an era of our country's modern history that has so-far gone overlooked. To truly understand the feeling of the time, imagine for a moment that you are between the ages of 19 and 23 (I was 17 in basic, 20 on my first deployment). The country had been peaceful during our lifetime and the only "experience" in the ranks was rare and came from Desert Storm or Somalia. There was no social media, and no cell phones to speak of. We knew what the internet was, but nobody really used it for much. Then, all of a sudden, the country is attacked at a level not seen since 1941. The Army was now an all-volunteer force and decided to heavily rely on the National Guard and Reserves. In order to get us trained up for the Middle East and ready to fight, the Army activated a few HUNDRED THOUSAND of us late teen-early 20s scumbags and jammed us together on a military base in Wisconsin. Now, Fort McCoy in Wisconsin was crawling with hordes of horny, drunk kids who were told they were going to war. Since there was relatively no experience in the leadership, our sergeants essentially told us they had no idea if any of us were going to make it home.

We spent hours in the freezing cold training on Vietnam and WWII tactics to go to the desert and fight an insurgency we knew little about. Then, in the evenings, we would drink until nearly blind. There were fights, arrests, and lots of pregnant women. This went on for months as they decided what they wanted to do with us. Then, when you finally get over there, you experience things that could never be described to the average American. Some good, some great. Some bad, some horrible. Near-death experiences stopped being scary or uncommon. Then, you're expected to come home and blend back in as though you were at a weekend retreat that nobody wants to hear about. Everyone handled these feelings and experiences differently. Some became better people and used the experience as a spring-board to success on the civilian side. Some took their own lives trying to cope with it all.

Bob stayed the same. The Bob I knew on the afternoon of September 11th was the same Bob I knew in the middle of an Afghan prison riot in 2006. He was the same Bob I knew getting promoted to Sergeant First Class and working as a career counselor at the US Military Academy in West Point, NY. He was just Bob. He was a soldier, a professional. He was my friend. These are some of his stories.

A SPECIAL INTRODUCTION
BY KARI KARUBAS, EDITOR

You will never meet anyone like him. He's surprising. At first, he seemed to only be a one-dimensional acquaintance. I was wrong. We worked together for the same employer though in different departments. I knew who he was. I thought that I had maybe seen him from a distance once, but I wasn't all that sure. Occasionally, there would be an email from him sent to the entire faculty listing alerts, announcing new systems, coaching us through upgraded operations, and offering helpful reminders to the many of us who needed to be reminded. Afterall, old buildings can be tricky.

My coworkers described him as stoic and maybe a bit removed. I think you'd have to have one of those stone-cold poker faces or maybe one of those "Always-bringing-the-A-Game" gazes to be in that role. It helps that he's got a build on him. And a few biker tattoos. He walks like a cop.

His role at work was no joke. Old buildings can be tricky. And the precious cargo sitting inside the classrooms, walking through the hallways, swimming in its pools, lighting the Bunsen burners, and running towards the end zones of athletic and academic dreams must be promised a high standard of quality. Just ask their parents. They must also be guaranteed an even higher amount of safety. The lists of demands from any institution are countless and copious, but this one in particular serves over 4,000 students, over 400 staff members, and the surrounding community. Brad carries around with him a work phone 24/7.

I get that rising up of acid in the back of my throat just thinking about what a list like that would look like. The list that needs to be addressed *today*.

The list that needs to be addressed today but covers *next year's needs.* The list that someone threw at you because there's an *emergency.* And to turn one's back on any corner or closet of those buildings - even if for one accidental or distracted second - would be an unforgiving and irrevocable mistake. His back never turns. He works harder than most people in never making a mistake. Brad's attention to detail, even the smallest detail, is at an Olympic - Five Star level.

His role is an intense one. Unofficially, and off the record, I believe the demands of the job he does today took years off the life of the man who held it before him and who died suddenly at 65 years young.

His office is located at one building and he directs and operates both buildings: boilers, electricity, contractors, pavement, asbestos abatement, pipes, wires, vents, deliveries, set-ups, tear-downs, and most importantly: people. These people. Those people. The very necessary people needed in servicing and maintaining the structure and operations of a school. That's a lot of personalities. More than a melting pot. That delicate balance of human resource colliding with those demanding lists all peppered with emergencies and smashed down daily by the grind. And that's where he is an expert.

So now there's a dimension. He's far from one-dimensional. I never knew this until we began this editing journey together. My coworkers, like me, were wrong. That stoic look and removed demeanor was a hyper focus of respect, a commitment he held dear in his heart in promising to care for the people he promised to care for. He was being loyal to what was being asked of him.

Should he not know something; he would research it vigorously. Should someone know more than he; he would defer to their expertise; taking notes in his own learning every step of the way. There is no such thing as being too tired or exhausted to him. If anything, he doesn't fear fatigue or exhaustion. What motivates this man to be and do what is required of him, are other people. It matters to him that they are treated well and cared for. Not just certain people; but all people.

In editing his manuscript and in speaking closely with him, I was lucky enough to learn a better definition of loyalty, respect, and commitment. Brad's definition is the one I'd like to teach my own children. It's the one Webster should use. Americans are lucky that we have people like Brad, with his better definitions, fighting for our freedoms and privileges. You will see that for yourself in the grace and grandeur of his platoon and fellow soldiers as you read his book: it was a selfless harmony of soldiers who worked so well together despite obstacles and hardships. And because of that harmony, they all became smarter, stronger, and better in every capacity of their adult lives. Working closely. Working together. Working with cohesion. Working without conflict other than the one they were fighting for. What makes them so rare is how much they all still stay close with each other to this very day. And those that were lost, are honored and still living on through the retelling of stories and in rehashing memories of the good old days that maybe weren't always so good. Lost, but never forgotten. I had a chance to meet many of these fine soldiers. Everything Brad took the time to emblazon in his novel about them is true. Their jokes are hilarious. They are all protective of each other. The drinks flow. The dancing is endless. They fill, pack, nurture, harvest each of their individual and collective lives with *loyalty*, *respect*, and *commitment*. And what I loved most about this group was their honesty and vulnerability with one another. It ran deep and showed such an organically beautiful bond.

Brad has scripted his life and career today with those same definitions of *loyalty*, *respect*, and *commitment* that he initially wrote while a young soldier. I'm certain that his amazing family helped with his earlier drafts in their unconditional love and support of him.

In January, 2021 my department chair reached out. I had been teaching English via zoom to juniors from my kitchen table for almost a year. COVID and our "stay at home" order certainly changed the way teaching and learning transpired. My days were flat. My mind was numb. I eagerly responded to her email with a brain hungry for editing work. Brad and I connected, and our zoom-editing sessions commenced. I had no idea the complexity of this journey I was about to embark upon.

I learned so much! I learned that I prefer hearing this amazing story of friendship, love, and tragedy from a primary source and in a conversational voice. It was as if we sat across from each other over coffee some Sunday afternoon and barroom antics from the night before were being recalled. There's something special about the ease of Brad's delivery. His necessary details weren't didactic and could comfortably speak to a mass audience. Either a military audience or someone like me - a military-idiot. I appreciated the time he took in unraveling everyone's personalities - those little details that made Schlitz such an ass or the way he made you respect Papa Sco as if he were your own father. Brad took some risks in sharing with you those *not so glorious* micro-moments of what stress, pressure, urgency, duty, and responsibility can do to someone. That human vulnerability was appreciated. How truly fragile even the strongest and bravest person might be that one day and under that final ounce of weight. He also shared with us his own *not so glorious* moments from the past that no one is free from and most haven't yet the courage to face. I know I have many of those. And many I have yet to still face. His book is relatable on so many levels. It is a cathartic experience. A real one. An honest one. One that shows the glory of being on the same page, sharing the same values, working hard for a cause, sacrificing for each other, and constantly working towards peace and improvement.

In spending time with Brad, I also learned that he isn't all stoic looks, removed demeanor, and demanding lists. He will start singing randomly a song. Any song. A song about pretty much anything: red lights, eating hamburgers, using your belt for self-defense, the kid on the playground that had to get tackled by the principal for making a get-away during lunch, etc. Nothing is off limits. Nothing is safe from one day not becoming a song. He also has a thing for professional wrestling, Chewbacca T-shirts, 1980's movie quotes, and has an incredible ear for creating exceptional playlists. And if you're lucky enough to be sitting near him when a jam comes on, you're going to be sitting next to Google-meets-Wikipedia-meets a historical recollection of the artist's/band's tour information and whatever their most recent scandal might be.

I also learned that Brad would do anything for his family. They are people with the biggest hearts who want to love and be loved.

I also learned that every day spent in his world without Bob Allen is a bit of an empty one. I get to hear more stories about this incredible friendship made out of all the right ingredients. Two kids who grew up in the same town; went to war together; had the same interests; the same passions; entered into adulthood together; never stopping loving each other. If you can make it in life with just one of those - you're a lucky person. Brad's left him too soon. Shakespeare gave eternal life in Sonnet 18 to his subject. I'd like to think that Brad gives eternal life to Bob and Bob's memory in the publishing of this book. You, the reader, will fall in love with Bob. He says everything the rest of us aren't brave enough to say. He does things the rest of us wish we were courageous enough to do.

I didn't know much about Brad, or his job, or his time as a soldier, or anything about him prior to working with him on the manuscript. We had worked for the same employer for several years. He was at one point a one-dimensional acquaintance that sent out emails with important words in them like "priority", "urgent", "precautionary", and I think one even had something in there about "voltage inspection." And in our time spent editing; I never saw his face. We would spend hours in our editing sessions and guess who didn't have his camera on? He didn't even know it. And yes, not having his camera on was turned into a song a while back. You will never meet anyone like him. He's surprising.

Enjoy this remarkable story about friendship, love, and tragedy written by a soldier, best friend, and author who has defined better than anyone else; loyalty, respect, and commitment.

We read to understand.

FROM THE AUTHOR

First off, I apologize for the language used throughout this book. Unfortunately, it's the way we talked.

This book is written by memory from a span of time covering 18 years. I did not keep a journal or take notes during any of my time in the military or the years after. I have done my best to recall names, dates, and events accurately. I have often called and texted with friends and fellow former soldiers to try and get exact details right. Unfortunately, I know that details will be wrong in some points of the book. Please know that I did my best to get it right and as close to accurate as possible.

I have changed the names of people and places, when necessary, to protect privacy and to protect operational security.

This is the story of the best, and in some cases the worst, times of my life. I have put my whole heart into this project, which started out as a series of social media posts in July, 2018. I have attempted to give you the full story, in all its rawness and reality, as seen through my eyes. I have gone through a roller coaster of emotions while writing this book, sometimes having to step away for days at a time to bounce back from memories that I never wanted to revisit again.

I hope you enjoy this story. It's Bob's story, it's my story, and it's the story of 2.7 million other young men and women that served in Iraq and Afghanistan from 2001-2021. May God bless you all.

BRAD DRAKE - MARCH, 2022

ACKNOWLEDGEMENTS

Thank you to….

Megan Folkerts, for helping me initially edit. Your time, patience, and encouragement are most appreciated.

Bridget Keane Nagarajan, for helping me through the initial process and being my top supporter of this project.

Jean Drenth, for being an example to all of perseverance and strength.

Jamie Hasenfang Allen, for being the epitome of grace and class and for being a devoted and loving wife. May your heart one day mend.

Tom Allen, for all of your encouragement. May this book bring laughter and joy to memories of your boy.

David Drenth, for listening to my stories, laughing, and taking an interest in learning about the adventures your brother and I shared. There are a few new ones in here.

Emily Drenth, for being a good little sister and growing up into a delightful, young woman. May these pages show you how good of a man your big brother was.

Joe Allen, for spending time with me on a Saturday night at Q and reminiscing about your brother. That was a special night and something we both needed to heal – just a bit.

Jim and Linda Drake, my parents, who have supported me in everything I've ever done. Without you, I wouldn't be who I am today. I can never show enough gratitude to you.

Chris Yaccino, an old friend, and the man who designed the cover to this book. Thank you, Chris, for putting into an image what has been in my head for a very long time.

Kari Karubas, my editor, I can never thank you enough for your tireless and endless work with this project. You have helped bring memories back to life and bring light to darkness once again. Without your great efforts, this project would have never been possible.

DET 4 and the HHC 327th MP BN, for you are this story; you are the best of friends I've ever had. May the world now see what brought us together and what keeps us together to this very day.

MAP OF AFGHANISTAN

This map is used with free use policy regarding education
from the Nations Online Project.
http://www.nationsonline.org

CONTENTS

PART 1: THE FIRST RUN

PART ONE:

THE FIRST RUN

CHAPTER 1

ARMY GREEN

When I was a small child, we kept our toys in a closet that was built under the stairs in the basement of our home. When I would open the door to the closet, I was always fixated by the clothing hanging on a closet pole overhead. These weren't just any clothes; they were a small collection of my Dad's military uniforms from the late 1960s. They were neatly pressed and hung-up with obvious pride as they were spaced apart so as not to run into each other and compromise their creases.

As I got older, taller, and stronger, I was able to pull up a folding chair and get closer to the uniforms hanging. There was one uniform that I hadn't seen yet and it was covered in plastic – the type you'd see from the dry cleaner. One day I stepped up on the chair and reached high enough to remove the plastic cover over this particular uniform. What I found was my Dad's dress-green uniform coat. I was in awe of the patches, campaign ribbons, gold sergeant's rank on the sleeves, and the blue infantry collar pieces. It made me so proud to know that my Dad once wore it.

Although my Dad rarely talked about his service in the Army, if I asked him about his uniforms in the "toy closet", he would explain what they were and what purpose each uniform had. I was so impressed by these uniforms and by my

Dad that I made my mind up by the age of ten that I was going to wear a uniform of my own someday.

I didn't know it at the time, but when I made up my mind at ten years old that I was going to be a soldier, there was an eleven year old living only blocks away from me named Bob Allen who had the exact same ambitions. Bob and I were ten years away from becoming friends, but we were obviously wired on the same wavelength since birth.

On December 19, 1999 I joined the U. S. Army Reserve at the age of seventeen. All I ever wanted to do was be a soldier and I finally took the first steps toward becoming one that day. A family friend had talked me out of going active duty Army like I had originally wanted. This man had served for four years in the Marine Corps. and he insisted that I join the Reserve. His logic was that if I didn't like it, I could ride it out one weekend a month. If I did like it, I could always go active duty. This way of thinking may have been the right way of thinking at the time, but boy did things change in just a few short years!

Like most high school kids joining the military, I was unprepared when I went to MEPS (Military Entrance Processing Station.) I wasn't exactly sure what I wanted to do in the military, but I knew I could type really fast. In fact, when taking the placement test at MEPS all the NCOs (Non-Commissioned Officers) gathered around as I smashed the typing record at over 160 words per minute.

My career as a clerk in military administration lasted about five minutes. When I sat down with the counselor to select a job (MOS - Military Occupational Specialty) she gave me a list of dozens that my ASVAB (Armed Service Vocational Aptitude Battery) score had qualified me for. I scored well and this led me to have opportunities in many different fields, but those fields were still limited when it came to the Army Reserve. I had to select a job that was in a unit close to home. At that point, the counselor pointed out a job called 54B which was a Chemical Operations Specialist. I knew absolutely nothing about what a Chemical Operations Specialist was, but it offered a bonus, so I signed on immediately.

With this job, I was assigned to the Headquarters and Headquarters Company of the 327th Military Police Battalion out of Arlington Heights, Illinois. Again, I didn't quite know or understand what any of that meant; I just knew that once I completed my training I would be assigned to that unit.

Before I left for basic training, I trained with the unit a couple of times as a civilian. I didn't really understand what was going on, I didn't quite fully understand the rank system, and I could tell that I was mostly a nuisance there to those that had work to do.

On August 1, 2000, I left for basic training. I took this very seriously and for months prior to leaving, I worked out hard. In high school I was an outstanding athlete, setting a school record in gymnastics and being nationally ranked on the still rings. I was also an accomplished wrestler. I knew what it took to get in shape and I worked hard. I did dozens of sets of pushups, sit-ups, and pull-ups each day. I also ran at least two miles per day, usually in the middle of the day when it was hottest. Needless to say, when I left for basic training I was five-feet-seven inches and 150lbs. I didn't have an ounce of fat on me and I was very strong for my age and size.

When my family dropped me off at the recruiter's office, that was the first time I had ever seen my stoic; Vietnam Army artilleryman father show emotion. For a second it looked like he might cry as he hugged me goodbye. An instant later that look vanished and he returned to his stoicism as he led my mother and grandmother, both in tears, back to the car.

The recruiters brought us to a hotel where we would stay the night before getting up bright and early the next day to be taken back to the MEPS. I recall rooming with two other kids from my area that night. One was going to Ft. Benning, Georgia where he would eventually become an infantryman. He had about a dozen rolls of toilet paper in his luggage. This kid had an older brother that was already in the Army and the brother had insisted to his younger brother that there wouldn't be any toilet paper available, so he'd better take some from home. I thought it was an odd thing, but it made sense at the time.

The other kid was going to Ft. Leonard Wood, Missouri with me where he would become a truck driver. He was a pudgy kid with glasses and wore a look of terror on his face about what was coming his way. His name was Eric. Obviously, I didn't know much about what was coming my way either, but I knew well enough to physically prepare. This poor kid hadn't prepared at all, and he didn't look like he'd been much of an athlete either. Basic training is very hard for those who are starting from behind physically. Not only will all the physical tasks be more difficult for those out of shape, but it can also be dangerous as the risk for injury is much higher. I felt bad for him. I can still remember to this day the look of terror on the face of Eric.

Early next morning, they fed us breakfast in the hotel and we climbed aboard busses that took us to the MEPS station. The exact details of this are cloudy, but I can recall that they made us strip down to our underwear in order to look us over from head to toe. I received a new tattoo just a few weeks prior and this lady doctor rubbed, poked, and prodded the tattoo. She asked me several times how old the tattoo was, and I told her it was a few weeks old. After a while, she seemed okay with that answer, and I was cleared to proceed. Showing up there with a fresh tattoo was a risk and fortunately mine was healed up enough to get through.

Again, I can't remember the exact details of that day, but I do recall being given paperwork in a large envelope and bussing to the airport in groups. My group was flying into St. Louis from Chicago and there were about a dozen of us eventually heading to Ft. Leonard Wood, Missouri. I think the oldest of us was twenty-two and it was a very diverse group from every different ethnicity and background. We all got along and were friendly with each other.

When we eventually landed in St. Louis it was nighttime. We were met at the gate by an army specialist from Ft. Leonard Wood and brought to an area in the airport where we all had the opportunity to eat. Shortly after dinner we were put on another bus, this time for the couple of hours ride to Ft. Leonard Wood. Strangely, and I can't explain why, I never once felt homesick or scared. I was excited about what was coming. Across from me in the bus aisle was the pudgy kid, Eric, from my hotel with the terrified expression. He was seated next to a little blonde girl, and they were holding hands. They both looked like they were ready to crack from fear. Inside my head I thought, "These two don't stand a chance."

When we arrived at Ft. Leonard Wood it was late at night. Our bus was met with yelling and screaming as we walked single file into a processing building. There was mass confusion as drill sergeants and NCOs were yelling at us from a multitude of directions. The first thing we had to do was line up in alphabetical order, but we weren't permitted to talk or make noise. Imagine the confusion as a couple of hundred kids were trying to look at each other's paperwork to get in proper order. There were mess-ups all over, of course, and the drill sergeants and NCOs blew their lids, hollering and arranging us in the proper order. From there they broke us down into smaller groups and marched us outside. They put us in a formation, in the middle of the night, and I remember a staff sergeant standing at the front of the formation and asking if anyone wanted to quit right then and there and go home. I was surprised as I saw a few hands go up. Specifically, I remember this red-headed kid with a potbelly putting his hand up. I remember hearing this kid talk big on the bus ride yet now he wanted to go home. I felt bad for those kids. They were quitting on something that they hadn't even given a chance yet. After the quitters were pulled out of the formation, they read off our names and the barracks numbers we were assigned to. Inside the barracks, we were issued a wall locker and a bed. We were told to lock up our stuff and then go to sleep.

Reception was strange. For the next two weeks we did a lot of nothing. We sat around waiting, we ate three meals a day, we did some medical checks, and we also received our shots. After a few days we were issued military clothing, and I felt a lot of pride putting on the uniform for the first time. Sadly, with all this sitting around, I felt my fitness levels starting to drop. I was itching to work out, but we were prohibited from doing any kind of physical exercise. I assume they didn't want anyone getting injured before they left for their training unit.

The day we were issued our clothing, we received our duffel bags to put our clothing in. The duffel bags were stenciled by a selected group of kids who were also in reception. We had to stand in a line and wait for our bags to get done. I waited, and waited, and waited, and waited for my bags. Every kid around me had been called and picked up their bags except for me. After hours of waiting, my name was finally called. I sprinted to pick up my bags and bring them back to my wall locker in the building. Once in the building and while locking up my bags, our reception drill sergeant called a formation. I ran as fast as I could from the building, but I was too late. The drill sergeant took me aside and ran me through fifteen straight minutes of pushups and sit-ups. Fortunately, I was in good shape and the exercise didn't even phase me; though, conducting the movements in the dirt left me filthy. After the drill sergeant finished letting me have it, I was dismissed back to the formation.

On my way back to the formation these two kids, that I didn't even know, ran over to help me up. They dusted me off while shaking their heads and said, "That's bullshit what happened to you." One kid had a New York accent and his name was Lopez. I never saw or heard from him again. He and the other kid had been on the detail of stenciling the bags. They had run over to just be decent people, I guess. They probably felt bad about the punishment I received in being late due to their stenciling taking too long.

I had to sprint to catch up with the formation that had already begun marching to the chow hall. I decided right then and there that I'd never be late for anything the rest of my life - even if it was out of my control. A fear of being late was stained on my brain right then and there that still exists to this day.

A few days later, they had us take a fitness test, otherwise known as a PT (Physical Training) test. Our reception drill sergeant and the assisting NCOs explained how the exercises worked. First, we did pushups; second, we did sit-ups; and lastly, we did a two-mile run. I remember I didn't have the slightest of issues with any of the exercises, I was just pissed that I felt that I wasn't at my best after sitting around for two weeks.

When I finished the PT test and was catching my breath after the run, a drill sergeant called me over and read off my scores to me. He asked me if I knew what those numbers meant, I told him no, and he told me my PT scores were outstanding. He went on to say that if I progressed further, I could even qualify to earn a bonus. That was the first and only time I had ever heard anything like that in the military. I don't know if that drill sergeant was BSing me in order to try and improve my fitness even more, or if he was sincere about some kind of bonus program that existed that nobody else seemed to know about.

CHAPTER 2

THE BEGINNING OF IT ALL

The day finally came when the cattle trucks arrived to take us to our basic training companies. We loaded into the cattle trucks as tightly as we could with all of our bags and gear. It was mid-August now and it was hotter than sin. We were howled at and told to keep our heads down by a drill sergeant. It was a silent fifteen minute or so ride to the new barracks. When the cattle trucks finally stopped, the doors opened, and we were being screamed at and herded into a formation.

I did exactly as was told and ran as fast as I could get my 150-pound ass into that formation. I stood as straight as possible at the position of attention and stared at the back of the head of the kid in front of me. The drill sergeants were like sharks with blood in the water. They would look for weakness and then swarm to it. I saw several duffel bags ripped open and clothing dumped out. Duffle bags were to be locked. I also saw dozens of kids who hadn't moved quickly enough for the drill sergeant's liking doing pushups and sit-ups. The words used and the names called to make fun of and humiliate these young privates were very funny when looking back on them now, but at the time there was absolutely nothing humorous about the words exchanged.

This was it. This was the beginning of my 21 weeks in becoming a chemical soldier. In those 21 weeks, I had learned how to do just about anything and to do it in under five minutes. I learned how to take care of myself and how to take care of others. I learned how to complain with the best, and I learned how to pull pranks and issue demeaning ribs to bring anyone out of a bad mood.

You make some good friends while in basic training and I made a few. There was a kid named Craig Bernard who was from Oswego, Illinois. He had a natural "up" personality and we nicknamed him "El Bernardo." There was another guy from Minnesota whose name was Mark Johnson. The three of us were in the same platoon, we were the same age, and we became good friends. We learned quickly that when the weather became cold, a good place to find yourself was in volunteering for kitchen duty (KP). Sure, you worked a 16-hour day, but at least you weren't freezing outside in training! The three of us volunteered for KP often.

Basic training itself is exactly what it sounds like, you are there to learn the basics of being a soldier. The very first thing you learn to do is how to march. If you have any type of natural rhythm, this is not an issue. Even if you don't have rhythm, when you get yelled at enough, you will develop it. You march everywhere with your platoon in basic training. Your platoon consists of 25-30 soldiers and four platoons then feed into an entire company which is a total of 120 soldiers or more.

Eating is difficult in basic training. At my training area of Ft. Leonard Wood, there were four chemical training companies that ate together in the same chow hall. This means that over 480 soldiers had two hours to eat in the same building that sat only 80 at a time. The seating arrangements in this chow hall only had room for eight soldiers per table. By the time the last soldier sat down, you had one minute to eat your food. If you were the last soldier, you were going to end up hungry. For the rest of the soldiers at the table, you had about a total of four minutes to put down your meal. Needless to say, you never had enough time to finish your food.

This system of eating caused a calorie deficit to take place. Since we were on our feet marching everywhere and training for 18 hours a day, calories were being shed at a remarkable rate. If you came into basic training overweight, it was not uncommon to lose 25 pounds in those eight weeks. If you came to basic training in good shape, you were now underweight.

I was one of the soldiers that was now underweight and I was ravishingly hungry 24 hours a day. After the first four weeks in training, a doctor came in and they separated the males and females into our respective barracks areas. The doctor made us strip down and stand on towels in our underwear. He walked by each soldier and checked our bodies for injury, skin diseases, and general welfare. The doctor then had us step forward one at a time and step onto a scale that had been brought into the room. When I stepped on the scale, I was down to 130lbs. In just six weeks of being at Ft. Leonard Wood, I had lost 20lbs. The doctor raised concern at my weight loss at first, but then he shrugged his shoulders and told me I'd gain it all back and to not worry about anything.

Basic training is not just physical, in fact the physical part of it is very small. It is mostly mental. The drill sergeants intend to break you of all bad habits and then turn you into a disciplined, orderly, machine.

You are screamed and yelled at all day and every day. Sometimes you could be doing absolutely everything right, but you would still be yelled at and forced to do push-ups or other physical exercise. In my case, this happened several nights a week. I stayed in a room with seven other young men and one of the young soldiers in our room would forget to lock up his wall locker. Not locking up your property in the Army is a cardinal sin. Drill sergeants would come in, find the wall locker unlocked, and would then push it over. Naturally, this would wake us all up and then we'd be forced to help the soldier clean up his mess. Then, while being screamed at, we'd all be punished with push-ups and sit-ups for allowing this to have happened in the first place. It was a terrible cycle and that kid finally figured it out by the end of the eight weeks.

Army basic training in the year 2000 meant that you had to learn a lot of different subjects in order to become a soldier. We learned basic radio operation, basic first aid, basic chemical defense procedures, basic hand-to-hand combat, basic rifle marksmanship, drill and ceremony, and much more. Every subject was broken down into days or weeks of training. Each subject was also treated as the most important training that you'd ever receive in your life, and it all concluded with a pass or fail. If you failed subjects, they could send you with another company later on to redo something you failed. If you failed again, you'd be *recycled* and get put with a company one or two behind you. It was extremely important to avoid failure.

Physical training is critical while in basic training. Every morning at 4:30am we arranged into our first formation for PT. They broke us down into ability groups; A, B, and C, and then our groups would be marched to conduct training independently from the whole company. Strength training and cardio alternated each day. I was in the A group for PT and by the end of basic training, we were doing eight-to-ten mile runs. Sometimes we did even more.

At the conclusion of basic training, there was a small ceremony where we were finally recognized as soldiers. For my company this meant very little because not very much changed; we would stay in the same housing; we would stay with the same people, and we would train together in the same company and platoons.

My MOS for advanced individual training (AIT) was chemical. At the time, this meant that we were trained in nuclear, biological, and chemical warfare defense. We learned how to operate detectors and equipment. We learned how to decontaminate areas that had already been attacked. We also learned how to operate smoke machines to put up massive smoke screens and generate smoke signals. We had to learn mathematical formulas for the operation of these machines and equipment. And we had to learn their effects on the human body in order to recognize and understand the impact of a chemical attack on a human.

Being a chemical soldier was a complicated MOS to have in the military and it carried a lot of smaller, different sectors you could specialize in. All of our training and tactics were still based on Cold War enemy information. In short, we were training to defend against a Russian nuclear, biological, or chemical attack.

During the 13 weeks of advanced individual training, two things stand out to me the most. The first was an anti-terrorism series of instruction that we received. This was in September of 2000 and we were given several briefings on Osama bin-Laden, al-Qaeda, and other terrorist groups working and operating around the world. We learned all about their capabilities, their financing, their structure, and their tactics. It was a very interesting class and it all became reality just a year later.

The other major thing that I'll always remember is that we had to go through the Chemical Defense Training Facility (CDTF.) For years after, I was convinced that this was a hoax, and that we hadn't actually been exposed to real chemicals and radiation. In reality, it was very real, as was confirmed later by one of our fellow trainees. That fellow trainee ended up working at the CDTF for years while on active duty in the Army. When the day came for us to have our day in the CDTF, we were broken down by our platoons and then loaded onto two-ton trucks. The trucks were covered so we couldn't see where we were going. The trucks drove us around for a long time before finally coming to a halt. Once stopped, the cover was folded up in the back and the gate dropped so we could unload. We found ourselves at a series of buildings that were surrounded by high walls, barbed wire, and observation posts staffed with soldiers with automatic machine guns.

We spent the entire day and night in this facility conducting operations that we had been trained in. We were fully suited up in chemical suits and masks, broken down into small groups, with each group entering different chambers and rooms. While in these rooms, we were given a series of tasks to do including decontaminating equipment, decontaminating each other, and calibrating machines properly to read what chemical we were exposed to and how dangerous its impact was. After we completed our tasks in one room, we would then move onto the next room where we were given a fresh list of tasks to do. That day we were exposed to radiation, nerve agents, and several other forms of chemical warfare.

We successfully reacted to each issue and conducted successful decontamination operations.

At the end of this training, we were stripped down piece by piece in our equipment and decontaminated with heavy duty bleach-water. Our undergarments were taken off and thrown into trash cans which we later learned would be safely incinerated. Once we were naked, we were herded into a large shower room where we were given a final decontamination and then showered.

After the shower was completed, we dressed and celebrated. We knew that this was our final major task before we would graduate from AIT.

We had a final medical check about a week before graduation from AIT. I'm sure this was to see if any of us had injuries that had to be reported to the units we were going to. It was the same doctor and he was doing the same checks. When I stepped on the scale, I was 157lbs. The doctor had been absolutely correct.

Those 21 weeks were difficult and challenging not only physically, but also mentally. In the end, on December 19, 2000, nothing made me prouder than to put on that Army green uniform and have my drill sergeant shake my hand and say to me, "Good job, Private Shithead." I had a lot of respect for our drill sergeants in that company. 90% of them had combat patches and were Gulf War veterans. Most had previously served as infantry or artillery and transferred into Chemical Defense later in their careers.

This particular drill sergeant that shook my hand was Drill Sergeant Garrett. Drill Sergeant Garrett's favorite names for his soldiers were "shithead," "big head," "dumb ass," and my personal favorite, "mother fucker." Previously, I had seen Drill Sergeant Garrett snap when a soldier in my room complained about not passing inspection.

In retaliation to the complaining soldier and while trashing our room, Garrett yelled out, "You don't even know what an inspection is, Private Dumb Ass! When I was coming up we had white glove inspections. Mother fuckin' white gloves!"

Another time I heard Garrett incorrectly refer to a soldier who was the rank of specialist as a "private." The specialist corrected Drill Sergeant Garrett by saying, "…but Drill Sergeant, I'm a specialist."

Drill Sergeant Garrett answered quickly with, "Okay then, Specialist Shithead."

I was thrilled to finally be done with this training. After the graduation ceremony, I loaded into my parent's SUV and we made the six hour drive back to Darien, Illinois just slightly ahead of a horrible, blinding snowstorm.

After 21 weeks, stepping into our house that night was the best feeling I had experienced in my young life at that point.

CHAPTER 3

REPORTING IN

I reported to my company for my first drill weekend in January, 2001. As stated before, my company was a headquarters company for a military police battalion. We had two sister line companies with us in our battalion that were all MPs, but our company was a headquarters company which meant that we were established to support the operations of our two sister companies. Naturally, our company carried soldiers from many different fields. My company had four platoons of mechanics, medical personnel, confinement MPs, clerks, cooks, construction workers, and much more.

Since I had gotten home from advanced training a few weeks earlier, I had been prepping for this day. I read as much information as I could get my hands on regarding the daily operations of the Army. I had my uniform pressed as well as I knew how to and I had my boots polished brightly. I had followed all the instructions given to me about what to bring to the unit, and I had everything ready the night before. This first drill back was a special drill night that started on a Friday night. Terrified to be late, I was at the unit two hours before the first formation.

I checked in with the company clerk as protocol dictated and, while there,

I met a few of the other new soldiers. Specifically, I remember meeting Dennis Rolke and Jake Warner and they were both MPs. Dennis Rolke was a tall, slim guy with light features from the northside of Chicago. He was around my age and from the minute I met him I knew he had a great sense of humor and was a little goofy. Jake Warner, on the other hand, was slightly shorter than me with a stocky, powerful build. He was three years older than me and carried himself with confidence and a touch of arrogance. All three of us exchanged introductions and checked in with the clerk and the supply sergeant at the same time.

I was the only chemical soldier assigned to the company at that time and did not have an NCO to answer to. I was put in a mixed platoon with mechanics and other support staff soldiers. I remember during that very first formation the first sergeant called me to the front of the formation where I was promoted to private E-2. I operated with military precision when called to the front, exactly the way I had been taught in basic training. After the formation was dismissed, the other soldiers were giving me a hard time, chuckling, and calling me a "kiss ass." It was then that I started looking them over and seeing un-pressed uniforms, un-shined boots, flabby bellies, and haircuts that were borderline out of regulation. I immediately realized that the Reserves were not going to be what I had hoped for. I was disappointed, to say the least.

Despite the appearances and lack of military professionalism, I quickly made friends in the unit. There turned out to be quite a few soldiers in the unit that were high speed, focused, and squared away. I did my best to run with them and to stay away from the others.

In the months to come I was told that the open NCO slot for my job hadn't been filled in a long time. This was the position of the sergeant I was supposed to answer to. I was told that I would fill the slot as an E-2. The operations master sergeant, who was not a nice guy in the least, threw all the chemical handbooks at me and told me that I was the NBC NCO until another one was brought in. He also tossed me a set of keys to the cage where our NBC equipment was kept. Without being told, I quickly went to work organizing the cage, testing and cleaning equipment, and doing what I was trained to do. Other platoons' sergeants would walk by my cage as I was hard at work and look at me strangely mumbling under their breaths. I was concerned and thought maybe I was doing something wrong. I couldn't figure out what it was until my own platoon sergeant told me that I was doing good work and going above expectations. The other sergeants were mumbling and puzzled, apparently. I again realized how torn up the Reserves were. I was doing what I was taught to do, looking like I was taught to look, and acting like I was taught to act. To me I was simply following regulations, but in the Reserve system in those days, I apparently was acting like a super soldier.

I can't recall his name, but my platoon sergeant was a staff sergeant and his last name started with a B. He was a tall, very slim guy with glasses and looked to be in his early 50s. He was some kind of a mechanic on the civilian side and his personal vehicle was a pick-up truck loaded with parts, tools, and equipment. He was nice to me and encouraging to me as a young private. Although he was a mechanic and couldn't help me in my field, he helped answer any questions I had to the best of his ability. I learned quickly that it was up to me to figure things out for myself, and I worked really hard to do so. Fortunately, the military has a manual for everything and I was able to seek out the answers to questions that I had and successfully work alone.

Time went on like this through 2001. I read the training manuals and learned everything I could about my job. I had no problem with teaching classes at 19 years old and doing all the duties of an NBC (Nuclear, Biological, Chemical) NCO. In June of that year, we went to annual training at Ft. McCoy, Wisconsin. Annual training in the Reserve is where you go to a training area for two weeks and accomplish whatever tasks are assigned. This was my first AT and I once again saw how disorganized and messed up the Reserves were. In the span of five months, this was my third red flag. I knew this AT was going to be doomed when I was told to be at the unit at 6 o'clock in the morning to be in the convoy traveling up to Ft. McCoy; a three-hour drive from Arlington Heights. I arrived early at 5 o'clock and nobody was there. Do you know what time we finally hit the road? It was after 3 o'clock in the afternoon. There was a litany of issues that led to this. Soldiers were late. The NCO didn't have the fuel cards. Nobody was there to unlock the arms room so we could draw our weapons. Everything that could go wrong did because the planning and coordination was a joke. The only thing that went right was the initial drawing of our vehicles. The motor pool sergeant in charge of the vehicle draw in those days was a sharp guy. He was a total jerk, but he always had his shit straight. Eventually he took a liking to me and I learned a lot from him.

When we finally got to McCoy, the disaster just continued. If it could be messed up, our unit at that time could really mess it up. I was almost relieved when the company first sergeant loaned me out to another company in the field.

They were needing someone to work as a radio operator for their company. I was told to get into a Humvee and they drove me out to a training site in the middle of nowhere.

As part of my chemical training, our drill sergeants and training NCOs spent a lot of time teaching us the fundamentals of radios and radio communication. Everyone in the Army is taught the basics, but as chemical soldiers we were told that most males would be assigned to infantry units. In those infantry units, chemical soldiers would be used as radio operators in the field and would rarely actually do chemical work. My training had been above average and I felt pretty confident in radio operation.

When I was taken to the unit I was loaned to, I was given a cot, and then brought to the operations tent where I was introduced to the radio operators. The lead operator's name was Specialist Jones. He was about 40 years old, 40 pounds overweight, and I was immediately concerned about what kind of half-assed, Reserve-style instruction I was going to get. To my surprise, this guy was an absolute wizard and I immediately liked him. I worked with him stringing out wire and making connections. I also worked with him for a few hours learning how to operate the different systems of the radios. We had two systems while in training there. One was for the actual post and one was for the training exercise. Each had different code systems that you had to know. This was all deep Cold War type stuff, but you had to know it in order to successfully operate a radio. It wasn't easy. You had to be alert, sharp, and aware of when the codes changed. There were also field phones coming into the tent. As a radio operator, you had to run all this action along with keeping logbooks. It was a complicated and busy job, but I enjoyed the work.

On that first AT, I spent several days in the field with that company. I worked 12 to 16 hour shifts on the radio and I became quite good with it. SPC Jones not only taught me the hardware part of radio operations, but he also taught me how to operate radios correctly. This was way beyond anything I had learned in basic training. I left there feeling that I could control any radio situation. This would come in handy later down the road in my military career.

A few months later I would be given my first Army Achievement Medal and a promotion to private first class after a special training session we had in Smyrna, Tennessee. I had served as the radio operator for our battalion and I handled it like a fat kid handles cake: efficiently and aggressively. I was rewarded with the decoration.

Right around this time period, when attending a routine drill, I remember seeing a group of civilians. These were kids that hadn't gone through basic training yet and were getting ready to leave soon. I remember I saw this one guy that I had gone to high school with. He was a year older than me in school. I remembered seeing him in the halls of our school. Back then he had a blue Mohawk and wore heavy leather boots and leather jackets. I never met the guy while in school, but I recall seeing him and thinking he must have been a wild child. He was about 6 feet tall with a slim build, he had blonde hair, and he had heavy German features. While recognizing him at drill, I saw him look over at me and recognize me too. I thought, "Oh boy, this wild man is going to be in the unit!"

His name was Bob Allen.

CHAPTER 4

MILITARY POLICE

After September 11, 2001, everything changed. I remember receiving a call that along with other Reserve units, our unit had been placed on alert. I remember immediately how much security had drastically improved at the unit during this first drill back. There were now checkpoints and things felt a lot more serious. At that first drill, I recall we had a battalion formation and it was announced that one of our sister companies, an MP line company, had been activated. The company was being sent to Ft. Hood, Texas to relieve an active-duty MP company. Our sister company would be activated for at least one year and they would take over the post police duties for the active duty unit that was being sent overseas.

The deploying company did not have enough numbers yet, so they asked for volunteers from the two other companies in the battalion to supplement their force. I volunteered along with about a dozen others, but I was rejected because I was not an MP. That wouldn't last long.

I was working in my cage later that afternoon when the First Sergeant stepped in. I immediately snapped to parade rest.

The First Sergeant said, "PFC Drake, you're a good soldier so I'm going to make you a better soldier. Starting next month, you're beginning 95B school."

At that time, 95B was the designation for military police. I had no desire to be an MP and I asked the first sergeant if it was possible that I could go to another school for further chemical training instead of MP school.

"No," he responded. "You need to pick up another MOS in order to rise through the ranks." He then turned around and walked out of the cage. That was it. I was going to MP school whether I liked it or not.

I would start MP school the next month and fortunately for me, it was still on the same drill weekends I was already scheduled for. It was also a major plus that the school was being held in Arlington Heights, where my company was based out of.

For the next eight drill weekends I attended 95B school at Arlington Heights. I was completely away from my old unit and rarely got to mix it up with my friends. I wasn't alone in this training, though. A sergeant from my company was also placed in this training. His name was SGT John Wiley, he was around thirty years old, and he had joined our unit not too long before. We hit it off right away and became friendly.

While in MP school I was exposed to a whole new world in the Army, and I liked it. As MPs our grooming standards were higher, our uniform standards were higher, our boot polishing standards were higher, and every standard was higher. Our instructors drilled into us that being an MP meant setting the standard for the Army in not just appearance, but also in morality and composure. I really liked this, and I took it quite seriously.

It was at this training where I first met MSG Holder. He was a SFC back then and he had a positive impact on me from the first time I met him. MSG Holder was around five feet ten inches tall, but he was powerfully built, and sported a Chicago-style mustache. He was a police officer on the civilian side, had over 25 years in the regular Army and Army Reserve at this point, and he almost always had a wad of chewing tobacco in his mouth. When MSG Holder ran a class, and he did dozens in that school, he taught out of experience and not just by the book. He knew what he was talking about because he had been there and done it already. He shared his knowledge and experience with us every class and we learned not only what the book said, but also how things would really be done in the real world. He was an excellent teacher and a senior soldier that I admired and aspired to be like.

The MPs in my company were the 95C designation, but the training I was going through in this school was 95B training. This can get confusing, so stick with me here. To put it simply, even though both designations were military police, B was street police and C was prison guards. Although some of the training was similar, they were two entirely different jobs and classes.

I took to this new MP training and I really liked it. We learned how important it was to keep paperwork and keep records straight. That made another profound impact on my life. To this day, I keep tidy records and write down everything that I think is important and should be recorded. I can't even begin to tell you how many times this has come through and helped me in my life. Going through this MP training was like someone turned on a light in a dark room for me. I absorbed this training like a sponge and I enjoyed my new, although forced, military occupation.

In the summer of 2002, I started a new civilian career as a pipefitter apprentice. I didn't fully understand what a pipefitter did at that time, but I knew that they made a lot of money. That was very attractive to me, so I applied and was accepted into the apprenticeship. After a week of indoctrination into the union, I was assigned to work for a company that operated out of downtown Chicago. I worked at the shop of this company from five o'clock in the morning until one-thirty in the afternoon each day. The union and the company knew that I was in the Army Reserve, so they weren't upset in the least when, a month after my hire, I had to take two weeks off of work in order to finalize my MP training at Ft. McClellan, Alabama.

Alabama in August is hotter than hell and the two weeks I spent there, along with SGT Wiley, were absolutely miserable. This training threw up my fourth red flag about the Reserves. The training company running the school screwed up absolutely everything they could possibly screw up. For example, we attended a flashlight signal course where the instructor didn't have a flashlight. He kept making hand motions and telling us how he *could* show us how to signal with the flashlights, *if he only* had his flashlight. Several of us offered this staff sergeant the use of one of our flashlights, but he declined. The fact of the matter was that this was all too much the norm in the Army Reserve back then; this staff sergeant and the others doing the training had no idea what they were doing because they never had to do it for real.

Another highlight of this training was when we had a range day where we had to qualify with our M-9 pistols. After having a difficult time qualifying in basic training with a rifle, I felt embarrassed and ashamed. When I got home from basic training, I purchased a .22 caliber rifle. I used to take that rifle to the range 2 to 3 times a week. I re-taught myself how to shoot. While in MP school, knowing that pistol qualification was coming, I used to rent a 9mm pistol at the same range and fire it. I was determined to never qualify anything less than sharpshooter again. My training paid off and I shot expert on the pistol. While I was thrilled with qualifying expert, my enthusiasm quickly vanished as our transportation vehicles never showed up to the range to pick us up. We stayed in the hot Alabama sun all day and then waited half the night until transportation finally came to pick us up and take us back to the barracks. Someone that was helping to run the school had forgotten to schedule a pickup for us from the range. It still baffles me how disorganized this school was.

I made friends with a guy at this school and his bunk was next to mine. I remember the first words he said to me were, "Damn, boy, I hope you like women because I can tell you're making love to weights!" This was his way of paying me a compliment on my physique. This guy was from somewhere in the south and he was a loudmouth - I liked him right away. After his compliment we shook hands and introduced ourselves. His name was Donovan O'Shea and he was a specialist E-4 in his early 30s. He was also a firefighter on the civilian side. From what I could gather, he had been on active duty for years, had gotten out, and now he had come back into the system through the Reserves. O'Shea was going through MP school because he was assigned to an MP unit after previously being infantry on active duty.

Later that night as I was brushing my teeth in the latrine, O'Shea walked up next to me to begin brushing his own teeth. He wasn't wearing a shirt. I saw his chest looked like someone took chunks out of it and his back looked like someone took a fork and stabbed him a thousand times. His chest and back were badly disfigured with scar tissue. I didn't say a word to him about his scarred-up body, but I'd be lying if I didn't tell you I was incredibly curious. The next morning when we were getting dressed my questions were answered when he put on his uniform shirt. O'Shea had a combat infantryman's badge, a 10th Mountain Division combat patch sewn on his right shoulder, and airborne and air assault tabs on his chest. Through conversation, I learned that O'Shea had been in Somalia and he had been shot up pretty badly. This was a time in the Army Reserve when you rarely saw anyone with a combat patch, not to mention have a story like this guy. O'Shea was the real deal, a good guy, and I always wondered how things turned out for him once the wars kicked off.

The ridiculous training in Alabama dragged on and culminated with a field exercise for the last few days of the course. While in the field they decided that we would do a road march one late morning. While we did this road march the heat was over 100 degrees. In the Army, training is supposed to be substantially halted with weather this hot, but that wasn't the case here with this training group. I jokingly said to O'Shea, who was in front of me during the march, "One of these overweight guys is going to go down here. This is heart attack weather." Sure enough, about an hour later they ceased our road march. An older, overweight soldier, had keeled over and had a heart attack during the road march. I'm not certain if he survived or not, but they had to medivac him out. I participated in a lot of stupid, unnecessary things in the Army, and this road march was near the top of the list.

After this genius of a road march was done, the trainers decided that we were going to have a tactical vehicle driving course and that we would be tested

54

out on it. They gave us a map with points on it and we were supposed to navigate ourselves to these checkpoints. An NCO was supposed to be stationed at each of these checkpoints to sign off on our sheet to verify that we made it.

O'Shea and I partnered up with two other guys in our canvas covered Humvee and hit the course. This was 2002 and there were no up-armored Humvees yet. We did absolutely nothing that we were instructed to do and O'Shea took us joy riding instead. O'Shea gunned the engine and took us into valleys, gunned it over natural jumps, did donuts in the middle of dusty fields, and the best part came when he tried to pass through a stream. About two feet into the stream, we realized it was about five feet too deep and our Humvee was stuck. We were dying laughing as the vehicle filled up with water up to our armpits. O'Shea stood up in the truck and called for assistance through the dying radio which was shooting sparks and smoking as it fried underwater. The instructors showed up demanding to know what had taken place. O'Shea, who had been around a long time and was a certified badass, said, "Sergeant, we completed the course. We took it upon ourselves to drive back through the course to check on the other vehicles."

The staff sergeant looked at O'Shea and said, "Check on the other vehicles for what?"

O'Shea answered quickly and convincingly, "Sergeant, it's heat category 5 out here and over 100 degrees. We filled up two extra jerry cans of water because we knew how hot it was going to be. We were checking on the other vehicles to make sure the other soldiers had enough water. When we got to this stream here, it seemed shallow enough to cross, but it turned out to be deeper than expected."

The staff sergeant, and the other NCOs with him, bought O'Shea's explanation and then thanked him for being a good soldier and looking out for others. Little did they know that we hadn't done one bit of the assigned course and had been screwing around the entire time. A wrecker showed up eventually, the Humvee was toast, and we caught a ride back to the tent area laughing the whole time.

Eventually, this ridiculous experience was over. The last day at McClellan, however, they gave us the afternoon and evening off. O'Shea, myself, and a few others went out and bought a case of beer. O'Shea drove us back on post to a giant parking lot. It was the first time I had ever seen a legit southern headlight party. All the vehicles in the lot were in a circle with their headlights on and they were all tuned into the same radio station. There were about fifty of us total at this party standing in front of the headlights, drinking, and having a great time. O'Shea and I left and went back to the barracks around midnight. When we got back there were drunk bodies scattered in beds and passed out all over the floor. One guy never made it to his bunk. There were shoes, there were his pants, and then there he was naked and face down on the floor in front of his bunk. It was a disaster!

The next morning, I woke up and found myself duct taped to my bed. I don't know if it was O'Shea or one of the other guys, but it was a pretty funny thing to wake up to. With great struggle, I was finally able to break the tape loose. I got cleaned up, and then shook hands goodbye with O'Shea and the other guys that were in my bunk group. John Wiley, my sergeant from the unit back home, several others, and I did not have to attend the graduation ceremony since our flights were scheduled to leave early that morning. We caught a bus and got the hell out of there. Ft. McClellan was a miserable experience, but we were now certified 95Bs.

CHAPTER 5

MY NEW PLATOON

When I returned to the unit that fall, I was now placed with the MPs. There were no NCOs in the platoon, and SGT Wiley was made the acting platoon sergeant. From my understanding, a lot of the NCOs had transferred out of the company. The NCOs who hadn't transferred out were with our sister company in Texas and they had yet to return from their duty there. It was a strange set up having all E-4s and under in a platoon led by an E-5. Despite this, I made quick friends with this group of MPs. Many of the soldiers in this platoon had not been in the unit long and had attended basic training and AIT together. They were all tight already. This group of soldiers were 95Cs, what the platoon was designed for in the headquarters company. John Wiley and I were newly coined 95Bs, but at this stage it really didn't matter.

I met, for the first time, Ivan Beal. Ivan was a tall, powerfully built guy from the north side of Chicago. He was a friendly, fun-loving guy who also talked with a lot of grunts and groans. He was close friends with Jake Warner and Dennis Rolke, the two other MPs that entered the unit when I did. When it comes to someone you want with you when things get bad, Ivan is one of the first that comes to mind.

I also met Alan Garretson, who was from northwest Indiana. Alan was a tall, slim guy who, like me, was in his early 20's, but already married with a child. He was always calm and cool and I never saw him rattled. We called him Garretjerk as a nickname.

Although I had met him when he was drilling as a civilian, Eddie Balderas had gone through training with this group also. Eddie was a tall, slim kid who was from Little Village in Chicago. He was a bright guy with a great personality. We got along right away.

Ryan Suthard was there also that day and I met him for the first time. Ryan was two years younger than me, a bit taller, and was a stocky guy. He also was the hairiest human being I'd ever met. His chest and back were like a sweater. We would nickname his chest and back hair his "pelt." Ryan would also be known, affectionately, as "Fluffy." Fluffy had one of the greatest senses of humor I'd ever seen in a person and he had a very likable personality. He was also freakishly intelligent. We were fast friends.

There was a tall skinny kid that was newer to the unit also. His name was Matt Bender. Matt was a smart guy, a smooth talker, and you could tell that he was going places in life. I'm pretty certain he was still enrolled in college at this point. On the civilian side he worked security at a swanky five-star hotel in downtown Chicago and he had some interesting stories of what went on with actors and actresses in the wee hours. Matt and I also got along well right away and he was great with impersonations.

There was a strange bird in this platoon, well a few of them, but this one in particular was named Stephen Oldham. He was quite older than all of us, in his late-20s or so. There was just something off about him that I can best describe as maybe someone who did too many drugs in their youth. There was a bit of a hesitation in his responses to things and his face always had a bit of blank look on it. He was slightly taller than me, he had child-sized feet, and he had excessively wide hips for a man. He was very oddly built. I liked him, we got along, but there was just something not right about him.

Last, but definitely not least, was the guy I had gone to high school with and had never talked to in my life: Bob Allen. He had changed quite a bit from high school, obviously. We shook hands and immediately talked about high school and about people we knew. To my surprise, Bob knew a lot about me. He knew where I lived, he knew who I hung around with, and he knew what sport's teams I was on in high school. I don't know how he knew all this, but he did. We quickly found out we had a lot in common when it came to movies and music. We also had a mutual interest in making fun of people. We quickly came up with nicknames for the other MPs such as SGT Walrus, Fluffy, Stupid Little Fat Hands, the Red Monster, and many others. Here I'd lived just a few blocks away from this guy for most of my life, and this was the first time we were getting to know each other!

Before the next drill, there was a message on the answering machine at my parents' house where I still lived. It was Bob telling me that he had just gotten a new pickup truck and asking if I'd like to ride with him and Stephen Oldham together for the drill. I declined as I didn't know Bob that well yet. I was terrified of being late since the incident in basic training and I always liked to drive myself to drill because I knew I'd be early. Sure enough, that Saturday at drill I saw that Bob and Oldham were also early. The next day I agreed to ride with them.

Bob came by the next morning and picked me up and we rode to drill with Oldham. Bob jammed his music loudly. It was the type of music I was also into, and we were at drill nice and early – the way I liked it. After drill that day, Bob asked me if I wanted to come with him and Oldham for beers. I was only twenty years old at the time, but Bob told me not to worry about it. We drove the forty miles from the unit back home to Darien and we went to a bar called Q. The bar was under a mile from where Bob and I lived and I was excited when they served us without carding me. This was the first time Bob and I ever drank together. Even at twenty years old I knew how much I liked drinking, more than most people at that age, and it felt good to meet someone that felt the same way. We had a terrific time that day blasting the jukebox and putting away pitcher after pitcher. Bob and I laughed ourselves silly, making fun of people, quoting movies, and making tough decisions about what to play next on the juke. I knew right then and there that I had made a great friend and that we were cut from the same cloth.

Bob had one of the greatest senses of humor I'd ever known. He had a witty, dry sense of humor that most today would probably find offensive. Bob, like me, liked to make fun of absolutely everyone and everything. For example, if you had a mole on your face, he'd nickname you Mole Face and call you that to your face. Once we had a soldier who had real bad acne scars all over his face. Bob appropriately nicknamed the soldier Scar Face.

Another time we had an instructor for a class who had a distinct, familiar look as a famous television star from the 1980s. Bob was quick to nickname the instructor Sergeant ALF. It was this style of humor, this endless style of humor, that remains forever engrained in my brain from Bob.

After that drill weekend when we rode together for the first time, Bob and I rode together for every drill, every month. Sometimes Oldham was with us, other times he wasn't.

One time I was driving the three of us to drill in my white F-150 pick-up truck. I had to fill up at the gas station before we hit the expressway. It was first thing in the morning, so Bob and Oldham ran into the convenience store at the gas station to grab something to eat while I pumped gas. After I'd finished topping off the tank, I put the nozzle back in place and then hopped back into my truck, ready to leave. Bob came out of the store a few moments later and hopped into the passenger seat.

A few moments after Bob came out, we saw Oldham come out of the store. He was scanning the lot with a blank look on his face. It was obvious that he couldn't remember which vehicle was mine. Instead of flagging him down or helping him in any way, Bob and I just watched him to see what he would do next.

A few fuel pumps behind my truck was a small, red Ford Ranger pick-up truck. It looked absolutely nothing like my full-sized truck. The owner had finished fueling up and had walked inside the station to pay his bill. Bob and I watched as Oldham walked over to the passenger side of the Ranger, opened the door, and sat down in the cab. We were laughing loudly as the owner came out, freaked out about why Oldham was in his truck, and started yelling at him to get out of his truck.

Oldham got out of the truck confused as ever, and we let him walk around a little longer until we finally called him over to my vehicle; the correct vehicle.

Whether I was driving or Bob was driving, he'd always bring a freshly made CD with music on it to jam loudly to while on the 40-mile drive to the unit. I discovered Bob really liked industrial music, classic rock, and he also enjoyed trance music. I had secretly been a trance fan for years, but it wasn't exactly a popular thing to proclaim in those days. The first time I heard a trance song come on from one of Bob's mix CDs, I quickly gave him a high five and yelled out "Yes!" This was a definite step in further cementing our friendship. After most drills we would usually stop out for beers at Q. We would put away pitcher after pitcher and dump endless money into the jukebox. You have to keep in mind that in 2002 there weren't downloadable jukeboxes yet, so your selection of music was based on what was loaded into the box. Fortunately for us, Q had the *Alice in Chains* Unplugged album. Bob and I would constantly play that album and we always agreed that it was the greatest Unplugged album ever made.

Bob and I continued to find that we had more and more in common and we were both enamored with the same 1980s movies and '80s pop culture. I could quote any movie from 1980-1989 and Bob would know it. Bob could quote just about any movie from that era and I'd also know it. We also both really enjoyed the Army and we took it very seriously. Each of us admitted that we would have been better off going active duty from day one, but Bob had taken similar advice as was issued to me and decided to join the Reserves thinking he'd have the option to go active duty if he wanted to. What we learned quickly, in those days, is that it was easier to catch a space shuttle to Mars than it was to be released from the Reserves in order to go active Army. There was no chance for us to go active duty and we were just going to have to gut it out despite how torn up and disorganized things were. We both had a similar disdain for how unprofessional things were in the Reserves, but we did have hope with the present war going on that things would quickly improve.

We weren't too far off either. Our unit started getting new equipment every time we went to a drill and, very quickly, we were modernizing and shedding our Vietnam era gear.

CHAPTER 6

THE DRUMS OF WAR ARE BANGING

In late January, 2003 on the civilian side of life, I had been working on a natural gas pipeline in Palatine, Illinois. I was an apprentice pipefitter, as previously stated, and my duties on this job were to be the right-hand man for a welder. On our crew was a back-hoe tractor that would dig large trenches next to a road. Next, another tractor would bring over 21-foot lengths of gas pipe. The welder and I would guide the pipe into stands, and then I would assist him welding out the lengths of the pipe together. Next, another tractor would come over and we'd strap up two to three lengths of welded pipe to the rigging on the tractor. The tractor would then travel with the pipe to the proper location and then drop the pipe into the trench. I would already be there waiting to guide the pipe home after placing wooden blocks on the ground of the trench. The welder and I would then make sure the pipe got into place properly, we'd unhook the straps, and then we'd move to our next task which was welding the pipe to the other pipe that was already in the hole. This could be very brutal, dangerous work, and the winter elements were tough to be out in for ten to twelve hours a day. It was January in Illinois which means the ground was filled with snow and water and it was very easy to slip and fall. It was a tough job, but I showed up every day and worked hard and earned the respect of the foreman and the welder I worked for. I guess you could say I took their shit and kept coming back so they had no choice but to accept me as one of their own.

On this particular January day, I happened to not be working because I had been laid off, which was not uncommon. The company I was working for would usually lay me off for a few days every couple of weeks and then they'd call me right back. It was a seniority thing, I guess, and I was the man with least seniority because I was an apprentice. The trades can be very seasonal, and I was lucky to be getting this amount of hours in the dead of winter in the first place. This day, which happened to be a Wednesday, I was sitting in a cigar shop in the town right next to mine in the early afternoon. I was there with my lifelong friend, Matt Goodwin, who joined the Reserves only days after me, but had decided to enroll in ROTC - the Reserve Officer Training Corps. He was a cadet at this time. Matt and I were smoking cigars and watching a special on the shop's television about North Korea when my cell phone rang. When I answered, it was SGT John Wiley, our former platoon sergeant who had been replaced at the last drill by an E-6 that had transferred in. John told me that he had gotten word from our platoon sergeant and was instructed to inform me that our battalion had been activated. I wasn't surprised; I had a feeling that it was only a matter of time since the Afghanistan war was now entering its second year. Also, the war drums were starting to bang about a potential Iraq invasion.

That weekend at drill, all three companies in the battalion were issued official active-duty mobilization orders. The one MP line company had only been back from Texas for about a month or two and they were already being mobilized again with my company and the other sister company. We would officially start

66

active duty on Monday, February 3. This was the real thing and to a lot of soldiers in the unit it came as a harsh reality.

Fortunately for me, I was a young, single guy who still lived at home. I was out-of-work anyway, so it was quite easy for me to head down to my union's apprenticeship coordinator office and hand over a copy of my orders. By law, they had to hold my spot in the apprenticeship. Luckily for me, Local Union 597 went above and beyond with their support. For most others in my unit, the sudden activation put a great deal of strain on their professional and personal lives. There was a lot of life they needed to organize and there wasn't a whole lot of time to do it in. I felt bad for them. The worst part is that we had no idea where we were going or how long we would be gone for. Everything was a mystery.

Bob Allen was ecstatic about this activation. His job at the time was working for his step-father as an electrician's helper. It was not a difficult transition for him into active duty either as he still lived at home also. Boredom could be Bob's worst enemy and I know he felt his life was boring at this time. He had a smile from ear to ear and was totally ready for whatever was coming our way. Most of us in the platoon felt the same way, but most of us were not as overjoyed as Bob was.

One of the first things we had to do as an activated company was to travel to Ft. Snelling, Minnesota. We were supposed to take busses, but the busses never showed up that morning to transport us. Someone, somewhere forgot to order the busses. About six hours later, our entire company was transported to the airport where we were flown out to Minnesota. Fortunately, there were busses on the other end that took us to a hotel.

The next morning, we reported to Ft. Snelling and we spent a few days there going through medical checks and updating all of our personnel records. It was a very long and very boring process. We stood in line for hours only to find out when we got to the front of the line, that we were now actually in line to get into the real line. Our battalion was one of dozens that had been activated, so there were thousands of soldiers at Ft. Snelling all doing their pre-deployment checks at the same time. All of us felt the same wrath towards long lines and the pain of waiting in them. It was a miserable experience.

We were all glad to get back to the unit once the checks at Ft. Snelling were over. Once back at the unit, we began packing up all the company's things to be transported to our mobilization site, which we found out was going to be Ft. McCoy, Wisconsin. Fortunately for us, Ft. McCoy was only a few driving hours away. To prepare for this move of equipment, our battalion spent thousands of dollars on wood and building materials. We set up a workshop in the motor pool and we began building hundreds of crates of all sizes and fastening them on top of pallets. Not all soldiers were assigned to this duty, but there were about thirty of us mixed in from all three companies working together on it. Once the crates were built, we then painted and labeled them. It was a lot of work and we kept at this for twelve to sixteen hours a day. Bob and I worked side by side with most of our platoon doing this type of work day and night.

I had experience using a forklift and so did Jake Warner, my friend that I met when I first came to the unit. Warner had been down in Texas with the other MPs for over a year and it was good to have him back. Warner and I were now in the same platoon and every morning he and I showed up at least an hour before the first formation. We'd get together in a classroom where he would shine his boots or press his uniforms. Most of the time I sat there drinking my coffee, reading the paper, and chatting with him. One thing he and I had in common was our appreciation for the band the *Red Hot Chili Peppers*. Our favorite album of theirs was "Californication" and he'd play it often on his computer.

Once the crates we were making were completed, Jake or I would use the forklift to transport the newly built crates back to the main building of the unit to be filled with the items being transported.

Soon enough, civilian tractor trailers began showing up to the unit's loading dock. We had a second forklift at the loading dock and either Jake Warner or I would hop in the forklift and load the empty trailers. This tended to take a very long time because in typical Reserve fashion, there would be confusion with the crates. Every crate had a packing slip that matched a manifest that was given to the driver. This was really an easy process and should have been a simple task to carry out. Leave it up to Reservists, however, to over-complicate and mess it up. After the first day of dealing with this debacle, Jake and I figured out the best way to get the job done was to not ask any questions, take over the manifest paperwork ourselves, and just load the trucks. It helped move things along much quicker. I fear if we had not done this, we might still be there today.

Most of us in our platoon became good friends during this time because we were working hard together seven days a week. When you work side by side with people, take all your meals together, and spend the majority of your time with one another; a bond develops. Our bond as a group was definitely growing here and what was shocking to me was that nobody was getting on each other's nerves or having issues with each other. That's a rarity. I also don't remember anyone ever complaining about the work, in fact I think we all rather enjoyed it. Building these crates and doing this kind of manual labor was certainly better than being back in the main building doing boring inventories and getting our asses chewed by superiors. In the military it's better a lot of the time to fly under the radar and to just do your work in peace.

Someone with us who was on the detail had brought a really nice stereo into the motor pool and we mounted speakers up around our whole work area. That stereo jammed out all day and night. One of the oddest things I remember in that time period was hearing "War Pigs" by *Black Sabbath* playing one afternoon. Fellow MP Pete Orlowski said out loud, "Boy, how appropriate is this?" He was right. It was a song about politicians and their pawns.

The hours spent doing heavy labor went on for weeks at the unit: for seven days a week. Bob and I would still go out for beers occasionally, but most nights we weren't getting back home until after nine o'clock at night after being at the unit since five o'clock in the morning. Looming in our thoughts all the while were the questions "when and where"? Nobody knew anything about when our companies would officially leave for Ft. McCoy. The only thing we knew was that we were heading there at some point.

As I said earlier, bonds were developing and great friendships were being formed. Since Bob and I lived closer to the reserve center than fifty miles, the Army would not put us up in a hotel like all the other soldiers who came from great distances. Bob and I had to commute every day. Quite a few times Bob stayed at the hotel where the unit was lodging hundreds of soldiers and I stayed there myself a few times. We didn't stay there for convenience, however. We stayed to party. I can tell you that those were some fun hotel room parties!

It was interesting to see things developing beyond the friendship barrier among the soldiers. Young men and young women were becoming more than friends. Our battalion was made up of three fully staffed companies, and there were a lot of young men and women looking for a good time. I was twenty years old at this point, in great shape from bodybuilding training, and I was a pretty sharp dresser. Believe it or not, but I really enjoyed female companionship too! I wasn't interested in the long-term type, but the short-term type of companionship. I had a few flings with ladies of the battalion during this time.

During one of these parties one night, I was getting quite a bit of attention from one of the most beautiful girls in our company. I had had a thing for her for over a year. She was stunningly gorgeous with jet black hair, dark brown eyes, and a beautiful dark Hispanic complexion. As the drinks were flowing, this girl became friendlier and friendlier toward me. I remember I was wearing this all-white Abercrombie stocking cap and she took my hat and was wearing it around. She kept getting me drinks and eventually was sitting on my lap while I was playing cards with the other soldiers. As the night was getting late, I asked her if she wanted to leave the party. She said yes. I told her I was going to head down to the vending machine to get something to drink and I asked her if she wanted anything. She told me to come straight to her room, she had Gatorades on ice there. She then told me not to worry, her roommate was staying in someone else's room that night. I was super excited as I walked into the room with her, completely certain it was my lucky night. When I went inside, I took my sweater off and she told me to sit on the bed. When I sat on the bed, she brought me a Gatorade and she had one herself. I laid back on the bed and she then laid with her head on my chest. After a few minutes of this I put my move on her. I tried kissing her and she pulled away. She then stood up and got upset with me that I had tried to kiss her. In response, I got up, grabbed my sweater, and headed for the door. I asked her, "Did I miss something? Did we come back here to play cards?" She answered that she didn't like me like that. I walked out the door. This wasn't the last time this girl would play her games with me, but it was the last time that I fell for it. Meanwhile, the rumor around the unit for the next month was that she and I were an item because people saw us leave the party together.

After this experience, I never got involved romantically with other female soldiers again. It caused unnecessary drama and, in some cases, very serious problems. I learned my lesson from this experience and took to heart that I got lucky with just some rumors being spread.

We were finally given a date that we would leave for Ft. McCoy and it was March 5, 2003. When the last crate was packed and loaded, when the last tractor trailer hit the road, and when all our personal and military gear was packed up, the send-off day finally arrived. I will never forget that day for the rest of my life. For our send-off, our families were invited to the unit. We also had a general from the regional command come in to give us well wishes. Our whole battalion was heading to McCoy without a mission, without dates, and without any knowledge of anything that was going to take place. We knew nothing. I'm certain that all of us felt that this would be the last day we would see our families until we returned home from the deployment.

I'm a strange guy, I guess. I never once got homesick during my time in the military. Sure, there were things I missed about home such as good food or the feeling of togetherness combined with a holiday meal, but it never overcame me, and I never got depressed or lonely over it. I was fortunate to grow up with a very loving family that always supported me. I think knowing that I had the support from my family helped me to compartmentalize my emotions when it came to leaving them for periods of time. I always accepted where I was, who I was with at the time, and tried to make the best of it. This send-off day, I felt a similar hardness. I felt it was my time to do my duty just as my Dad, my grandfathers, and my great grandfathers had done. My family has had a tradition of fighting in this country's wars since the Civil War. It was simply my time now.

The Drake men have an ability to mask emotion with a stoic face and I was no exception. When the ceremony and breakfast were over, it was time to say goodbye to our families for the last time. That was the first, and only, time I ever saw my Dad close to crying. My mother was a big crier over the years and very emotional and I was used to seeing her cry, but this was the first time I ever saw my Dad this upset. Being a Vietnam veteran, I think my Dad was overcome with emotion knowing that this was for real, this was a war, and he knew firsthand the risks associated. I can't begin to imagine how tough that had to be for a veteran father to send his son off to war. Needless to say, that was the hardest goodbye I've ever had to say. Mentally, it wasn't hard for me because I knew I was doing what I was meant to do, but it was hard for me emotionally because I could see how much stress and pain this put on my parents. When we parted from each other, I locked those emotions up and quickly went back to business mode.

An hour later our battalion loaded up on busses headed to Ft. McCoy. It was a cold day and there was a pretty bad snowstorm taking place. When I climbed on the bus, I focused on what was ahead. My best friend Bob Allen had left earlier that morning on the convoy hauling all our trucks up to McCoy, so I had an empty seat next to me when I sat down. Within seconds, Matt Bender sat down next to me. Without saying a word, I knew Matt felt the same way I did even though he had recently gotten married and was leaving behind a pretty, young wife. Matt stared straight ahead with his headphones on. As our bus drove out onto Central Road on the way to the expressway, I remember seeing a soldier's father holding up a young child. Jessie Antia, a female MP with our platoon, was the mother of this baby girl. That was a tough thing to see. If Jessie cried on that bus, which she had every right to do, none of us heard it. That bus remained dead silent for hours and not a single soldier said a word.

The long, quiet bus ride was over three hours in duration to Ft. McCoy. I will never forget what I saw when we were driving on the final road to get to the gates of the post. We were miles out from the post and our highway ran right next to a rail line. There were hundreds and hundreds of tanks, helicopters, Humvees, trailers, trucks, etc. being shipped on the line. This line went on for miles. I had never seen so much equipment being moved at once. I knew right then and there that this Iraq thing must not be a bluff, our country was going to take on a second front in the War on Terror.

When we finally got into the post, our busses stopped in front of some old two-floor barracks buildings and dropped us off. We all worked hard in the snowstorm unloading gear and loading it into the buildings. What we found inside the buildings was a time machine back to the 1940s. Our toilets were open toilets, no stalls, and the barracks were open bay except for three rooms at the end of the top floor reserved for NCOs. Each bunk had a foot locker and a small shelf with a clothes rack to hang clothes on. There also wasn't a floor. The barracks floor was red underlayment where old tile had obviously been stripped, but new tile had never been put back down in its place. The red produced a chalky substance that coated your boots and anything that touched it was eternally coated with a red film. Some soldiers would accidently drop wet towels on this floor and then have to throw the towels out – the red would never wash out!

We male MPs were placed on the second floor of the barracks with some other male personnel mixed in on the first floor. On my end of the barracks Alan Garretson took the closest bunk to the wall and I took the next bunk. Bob Allen took the next bunk after me and Oldham set up next to Bob. Each side had roughly 12 bunks, leading to 24 bunks total with the three larger NCO rooms at the end. Our barracks were primitive at best, but we quickly got used to them.

The toilet situation was interesting. I had seen these in movies, but I'd never experienced a setup like this in person. The first morning Bob Allen broke the ice. A bunch of us were on the toilets doing our business and Bob yells out to the guy across from him, "Hey! Are you done with that newspaper? Why don't you pass it over to me?" He wasn't kidding. Bob was serious. The guy passed the newspaper. After that it was no big deal anymore to use the latrine with several others gathered around you.

As you will find with any group of young men, porn magazines started showing up in the latrine. They were neatly cared for and stacked behind the toilets with other literature such as newspapers and other magazines. Pete Orlowski one day stormed out of the latrine holding up one of the porn magazines. He was very upset and yelled out, "I will not be subjected to this filth!" and he threw the magazine in the garbage can. I remember I was shaving when this happened and MSG Bellington was shaving next to me. MSG Bellington was in his late 40s, was a powerfully built black man well over 6 feet tall who had spent most of his life in the Army. He was all-business, all the time, and a man I had a great deal of respect for. Bellington yelled out in response to Orlowski, "Man, that's just too much college. Just too much damn college." I almost cut myself I was laughing so hard!

CHAPTER 7

TRAINING AND RANGES

That initial time spent at McCoy was very interesting. We did our official in-processing which included making sure that all of our paperwork was straight. We had to see a dentist, we had to see a doctor, and there we were again standing in really long lines in order to turn the corner only to stand in an even longer line. It was similar to the experience at Ft. Snelling and, in some cases, identical. The Army liked to be redundant and thorough. It was also during this time period that we started receiving our batches of shots. I can't remember how many shots we were given, but it was definitely a lot. The small pox shot was probably the most difficult one because it hurt your arm pretty badly for a few days and produced a very bad scab that you had to be careful didn't come off prematurely. There were health risks associated with all of these shots, of course, and one of our medics actually fell ill from the smallpox shot. SGT Milenkovic, one of our company's medics, was one in about a million that had an adverse reaction where the lining of his heart filled with fluid causing him to fall mysteriously ill. Thankfully for him and his training, he knew to get to the hospital right away to get things checked out. Had he not been so quick to get treatment, we may have lost him.

There were thousands and thousands of soldiers who entered Ft. McCoy at the same time. Everyone had the same story; none of us knew how long we were going to be there or where any of us were headed. The in-processing was difficult because this was new to all of those involved and lots of mistakes happened adding to the confusion. I give the staff at McCoy my utmost respect. The civilians and soldiers working these processing centers were doing the very best that they could; it was just the sheer volume of soldiers in-process that was overwhelming and caused a great deal of problems. As the years went on with these wars, things were refined and it all became an easy process. At this point, though, there were growing pains.

During our stay at Ft. McCoy our company stayed in two different sets of barracks at points in time. The first set of barracks we stayed in were closer to the gate of the post and were World War II-era barracks. The second set of barracks that we moved to months later was in a new section of the post and were very nice. By very nice I mean they had stalls for the toilets!

While we were still in the old barracks, our dining facility was right across the street. When we would finish PT in the morning, we'd usually have about an hour and a half until the first formation would take place. Everyone would shower and get cleaned up and then you would go over to the chow hall for breakfast. If you were smart, you would eat very quickly and then catch that twenty-minute nap before the call for formation!

Now as you can imagine, it was a very rough time for a lot of people at the beginning of this mobilization. A lot of people had young children at home or had left their spouses. It was very hard on a lot of these soldiers and it took them a long time to adjust. Not knowing when we would leave or how long we'd be activated for was the hardest on everyone. Despite these circumstances, I want to point out something very positive that took place every day in this chow hall. There was a civilian man who worked the sign-in station who always had a big grin on his face. He was a tall black man about six feet three inches tall, middle-aged, and he looked like he kept in pretty good shape. His hair was grown out a bit and he had a mustache that sat on top of his wide, happy smile. Every time you saw this man when you went to sign-in for meals, he had the most positive attitude and would greet you like you were his long, lost best friend. I remember one particular morning Bob and I got to the front of the line and this man asked me how my day was going as I was signing my name. I told him it was going pretty well and I thanked him for asking. He gave me this huge smile and said, "That's right – you don't never let them take your joy!" I've always kept that with me and I always appreciated how nice that man was. He really made a difference to soldiers in those initially dark times. Over the years, Bob and I would repeat the phrase to each other and think back fondly of that man. That civilian cook was a very positive contribution every day and brought a ray of sunshine into people's lives when they most needed it.

After breakfast and after our first formation, we would then head off to training. There were a certain amount of ranges and qualification courses all companies had to go through in order to "certify" to deploy. I honestly think they were completely making up the certification program since all this was brand new and thousands of units had been activated at the same time. Sure, there were training units in the Army that had plans in place, but I think the total volume of units activated at once changed these plans. Each day we would go to a range or a course to "certify." The first ranges we hit were the rifle, pistol, and machine gun courses.

Before we qualified on the rifle, we were sent to a shooting training course that was being held in an empty barracks building. I was never a naturally good shot with the rifle. In fact, I barely qualified in basic training. I've talked about how embarrassed I was and how I practiced with a .22 rifle to build up my mechanics. Due to this training, I qualified sharpshooter at our annual qualifications. If I didn't take it upon myself to practice, I don't think my skill-set would have ever improved. Our platoons all had to rotate through this rifle training course that was being held in one of the old parts of McCoy. I remember that Bob Allen and I were partnered up for this training session. Bob was just like me, he qualified as a sharpshooter and his basic mechanics were solid, but neither of us were elite by any means. The man running the training for this course was probably in his mid-thirties. He was a First Lieutenant and was too old to be a First Lieutenant. He had a 10th Mountain patch on his right shoulder, (the combat side) and he also wore a Ranger tab in addition to his air assault tab, his airborne tab, and his combat infantryman's badge. My best bet was that this man had been prior enlisted and had become an officer later on. Judging by the patch on his right shoulder and it being 2003, I could only assume that he had been in Somalia. Either way, this man's training changed the way Bob and I shot firearms forever.

In basic training back then, they would teach you that you had to be "comfortable" to shoot, that your gear had to be "comfortable", and everything should just be this wonderful cushion pocket that made it so easy to fire your rifle. This lieutenant taught us otherwise. He worked hand in hand with Bob and I and totally changed the way we held, gripped, and fired our rifle. He also taught us how to adjust our gear so that our body was prepared right. He taught us that you should be tight, uncomfortable, and to the point of being in pain. He encouraged us to use our sling as a strap around our forearm and to bury the stock hard into our shoulders. He taught us how to close our elbows and where to properly put our hands around the pistol grip and magazine insert. There was no joking around or kidding between Bob and I on this training. We absorbed everything this lieutenant told us. We practiced positioning over and over again. This was a totally new way to fire a rifle for me and by the end of this training, I felt totally in control of the rifle and fully confident in this new skill set. The training we received that day was, single-handedly, the greatest training I ever received in the Army.

Later that week, range day for the rifle was held. It was brutally cold and snow fronts were coming in and out throughout the day. The range itself was frozen solid and it was in single digits outside. It was very rough conditions to do something you don't get the chance to do every day. When I walked out to the range that day and took up my assigned position, my hands quickly started to freeze up when I removed my gloves to grip my rifle. When shooting commenced and I rotated between the two firing positions, I did exactly as I had been taught by the lieutenant just a few days before. I tightened my body to my rifle as much as possible, making my body and rifle as one. I wrapped the sling around my arm, I focused on my mechanics, and I made sure my gear was in the proper place. I focused down range with one eye as the pop-up targets came up. One by one, I saw the targets come up and I used the meat of my finger to pull the trigger. One by one, I saw the targets fall back down as my rounds pierced them. When the qualification ended, I heard my lane number called off with those that had qualified. As we came off the range, I was curious so I checked in with the range NCO about my score. He told me that I had only missed two targets. For the first time in my career I had qualified as an expert on the rifle. I was very happy and felt totally dialed in. Later on, when I caught up with Bob, who had been in a different shooting group, he told me that he had the same success. I can only imagine how many other men and women that lieutenant helped. I'm sure his training saved lives over the years.

For the rest of that frozen day we rotated between a warm-up tent and going back on the range to help others qualify. No matter what, there will always be soldiers that have difficulty qualifying when shooting. Sometimes it is out of the soldier's hands as their weapon could be damaged, but most of the time it is due to mechanics and lack of practice. I always found it odd that in the Reserves we would qualify once a year and not do any type of live fire practice beforehand. I strongly recommended to fellow Reservists back then to buy a rifle and practice on their own.

On top of qualifying on the rifle, we MPs also had to qualify on the pistol. We used a Beretta 9 milli-meter pistol back then as our service side arm. The advantage of the Beretta 9 millli-meter pistol, known in the military as the M-9, was that it was a thin, light pistol. Qualification with that pistol either on paper targets or on pop-up targets was not difficult so long as you understood basic shooting mechanics. When I was in MP school, I had already qualified with the pistol once; but that lieutenant's training changed my firing process and to this today, I shoot a perfect score on the pistol. The mechanics are the same: get tight, focus, and squeeze the trigger with the meaty part of the finger. I don't recall any of the MPs having difficulty qualifying that day.

The last ranges we MPs had to hit was the machine gun range, the Mark-19 range, and the .50 caliber heavy machine gun range. MPs were trained to guard convoys for short distance or long-distance travel. At that period of time, we would mount a mix of heavy weapons on the Humvees. We would either mount an M-249 SAW, a Mark-19, or a .50 Caliber heavy machine gun. I was fortunate to have had experience with all three weapons because we were trained on these when I was in advanced training for chemical. If you remember, they were training us to go to infantry units, so we had to take a heavy weapons course. They tried to train us on these weapons while I was in MP school in Ft. McClellan, but the instructors kept contradicting each other, arguing, they couldn't find the weapons, and eventually they just gave up.

An M-249 SAW is an automatic rifle that fires a 5.56 round. This is the same sized round that an M-16 or an M-4 fires. This was a replacement weapon for the old M-60. Although the M-249 fired a smaller round, the barrel would not melt down like that of the old M-60 if hundreds or thousands of rounds needed to be expelled. It was also lighter and easier to carry. These automatic rifles were meant to be suppression machine guns, which means when firing them they were intended to put pressure on an enemy downrange. Pressure from a machine gun would change plans quickly for an enemy's attack or make them scrap their plans altogether.

Soldiers were trained to fire the SAW by pressing the trigger and walking rounds to your target in a backwards L motion. I always felt this weapon was underpowered for convoys, and in theater you very rarely saw it mounted for that purpose. On the other hand, the M-249 was a great squad weapon to be carried on foot. SAW stood for "squad automatic weapon" after all.

A Mark-19 is a weapon that fires grenades. Depending on what situation your convoy is going to be in, the type of grenade used would be determined by the mission. A Mark-19 is very effective and will inflict a great deal of damage to the enemy. It will disable vehicles, smash through buildings, and pretty much annihilate whatever gets in its path.

The .50 caliber heavy machine gun is one of the meanest weapons ever created by the U. S. military. Obviously, it fires a .50 caliber round. This size round is meant to penetrate light armor. It will rip apart cars, trucks, brick, mortar, and will cut a human being in half. A .50 cal is very heavy and is mounted on legs when in the field or on a heavy stand on a vehicle. The .50 is a belt felt weapon and you fire it with your thumbs while holding onto the grips. When in the field, you fire a .50 cal with a spotter and you work together to walk the rounds to the target. A .50 cal is a ferocious weapon and learning how to fire one properly makes you a dangerous human being.

We spent two days at these ranges qualifying. The first day was spent qualifying on the Mark-19 and the M-249 SAW. The Mark-19 was an easy qualification; you just pretty much had to land a grenade in a designated area. The M-249 SAW qualification was done on an odd paper target. They were satisfied to qualify you so long as they saw an arc of rounds make their way to the paper target.

The second day on the range was spent on the .50 caliber qualification. The first thing they made you do with this heavy machine gun was to 'zero' with it. Zeroing means that your weapon is properly calibrated to its sights. Different definitions of zero apply to different weapons and different eyes of those firing them. A zero can be subjective.

I found this to be total bullshit and I had a very hard time trying to zero the weapon. As a matter of fact, I was the last one to zero and I never even officially did it. The OIC (Officer in Charge), who was a young second lieutenant, was getting fed up with me. I finally said to him, "Sir, I have no issues qualifying with any other weapons. I don't know what the problem is here, but I know what I'm doing and if you'll just let me move on to the range, you'll see that I'll be a first time go." Out of frustration, he relented to my request.

When I climbed up to the qualification lane, Bob Allen came with me as my spotter. It was a cold, snowy, brutal day to be outside all day. As the tower called off the targets, Bob guided me to their location and I annihilated them. After only a few minutes into the live fire and the targets being successfully hit, I heard the tower announce my lane and I was instructed to stand down. I did as I was told. After the lane was closed, we cleared our weapons and walked off the range. Bob and I were confused as to why I was shut down. The NCOIC of the range informed me as I came off the range that I had quickly qualified and there was no reason to expend any more rounds. At the conclusion of this range I went 5 for 5 overall and scored expert for the first time on every weapon. It was very exciting for me.

Although I had qualified expert on the M-249 SAW, I was not named a

SAW gunner for our platoon. I was perfectly happy with that as I didn't want to lug around that son of a bitch. Jessie Antia and Bob Allen would be named as our gunners and Bob took this very seriously. That was the beginning of his love affair with his M-249.

CHAPTER 8

LOADING UP RAIL CARS

After in-processing was done and we had qualified on our ranges, word came down from our command that those of us who built the crates back at the unit were needed again for a special detail. This detail involved us being taken to a huge warehouse at the far end of the post. This massive warehouse was set over the top of a rail line and it had huge doors that would open up with hydraulics. With the doors open, flat-bed railroad cars would be brought into the work area three at a time. It was our responsibility to load up the container boxes that sat on the floor of the warehouse. Once the container box was full, a giant overhead crane would then pick up the container and load it onto the flatbed rail cars. That work was handled by Army engineers, but it was our responsibility to find our equipment and get it into these container boxes.

I had never been a part of an operation like this before and this was all new to me. Some of the soldiers with us had been in the first Gulf War and had an idea of what we were doing. This process was one of the ways that the Army moved equipment to the east coast to be shipped overseas.

The tractor trailers that we had loaded up in Arlington Heights had brought their loads to this giant warehouse. All the crates in the back of the trailers had been unloaded and then stored in this rail warehouse. I had never seen so many crates stacked up as I saw here. There had to have been over five thousand crates sitting in that building. Our equipment, naturally, was packed up with the equipment of all the other hundreds of other units on post. It was simply our turn to load up. Our task was to find our crates, bring them down with forklifts, organize them, and then place them into our assigned container boxes.

In the beginning, some of our crates were stacked well over the height limits of the forklifts we were given to use. In this case, our NCOs would coordinate with the engineers or the civilians working this warehouse and they would use a specialized forklift to make the picks for us. Once we got the swing of how things had been packed and stacked, it became business as usual and just one more thing that had to be done.

In working this detail, I got to know one of our new platoon staff sergeants well. He had volunteered to help supervise our crew on this detail. I had first met SSG Scofield about a month before the 327th was activated. He had replaced John Wiley in December as our platoon sergeant after he had first transferred in. Scofield himself was replaced in February by SFC Fielding, who transferred in just before the deployment.

SSG Scofield and I had never really talked a whole lot and I didn't know too much about him at this point. What I did know was that he was a big, very powerfully built man, and he had a very intimidating presence. Also, the chest of his uniform was stacked. That's old-Army slang for having airborne and air assault tabs. He also, which again was a rarity in those days, had a combat patch on his right shoulder. I never learned too many details of how he earned that combat patch besides the fact that he had served in Desert Storm. SSG Scofield was the type of guy that if he wanted you to know something, he'd let you know. If he didn't, you knew better than to ask. With the way he carried himself there was no need to ask: the man was the real deal.

All of the young testosterone-filled soldiers like me immediately took to him. He was a rarity in those days, a man with real combat experience who had been there and done that. If you were halfway worth your salt as a young soldier, you glued yourself to senior soldiers like that to learn as much as possible. With the hours we spent together on this detail, it didn't take very long for SSG Scofield to take to us too. I'm not sure how old he was then, but he was probably in his late thirties or maybe even his early forties. He was married with a step-daughter and a young son, and he hailed from Freeport, Illinois.

As we got to know him better while working this detail, Scofield shared with us about his family life and he told us fun stories about his partying days. He was over those party days at that point and I never once saw him take a sip of alcohol or go out to the clubs with us, once we were permitted passes. He certainly never went out on the town with us during passes either. He was a very committed family man and a dedicated husband. It didn't stop him from laughing at all of us and giving us that "I've been there" look, however.

More than once he helped put us to bed after having too much to drink or made sure that we got up and were okay for the first formation. He was an E-6 and he didn't have to do that. That kind of babysitting was the responsibility of E-5 sergeants one rank lower than him. SSG Scofield looked out for us still and was a good man that I had the utmost respect for.

One thing I always truly appreciated about the man is that he was always at the same level. I never saw him upset, I never saw him excited, I never saw him angry, and I never once saw him lose his cool. Keeping your composure while facing the unknown and dealing with tons of bullshit day in and day out is difficult. It's damn near impossible to keep your composure while shepherding a bunch of kids in their early twenties that want to do nothing more than party, fight, and complain. And not necessarily in that order. He did it. That man kept us on the right path repeatedly and really looked out for us.

Papa Sco always got a kick out of our party stories too. We'd come back from a pass and he'd say, "Well boys, what kind of hell did we raise this weekend?" He'd remind us to have all the fun we could, because someday we were going to find "the one" and those days would be over. He always called us "boys" and then he started calling us "his boys." Within a year he referred to us as his "sons."

With SSG Scofield and a few other NCOs working with the civilians and engineers, we took those hundreds of crates out of their ridiculous stacks and brought them to manageable levels. From there we dropped the crates to floor level where we verified their paperwork, cut them up by company, and then slowly started loading them onto the railcar containers. This was quite the process at first because only two of us had real forklift experience. The rest of our detail was using electric hand trucks and motorized skid machines to move the pallets. Warner and I were doing the best we could loading the containers, but we were getting overwhelmed and our progress was getting choked because we needed more people operating forklifts. Eventually, others stepped up and our loading speed increased fivefold.

The process of loading cars took a good seven days with twelve to sixteen-hour work days to accomplish. Again, I never heard anyone bitch or complain and this composite crew from all three companies of the battalion came together and made it happen.

CHAPTER 9

I'LL NEVER DRINK WITH

JOHN WILEY AGAIN

After a few weeks of being at Ft. McCoy, our company was given our first weekend pass. Unlike others that would come later down the road, this pass restricted us to a fifty-mile radius and we had to be signed back in each night. They released us at noon on a Friday and the pass concluded at six in the evening on Sunday. This means you could go out and go wherever you'd like within a fifty-mile radius, but you had to sign back in by 11:59pm on Friday night and Saturday night at the company office. This was what they would call a restricted pass.

John Wiley took Bob, Ivan Beal, and me out to the local town known as Sparta. John had made the arrangements for a driver to take a large group of us out there in the company van and come back later on to pick us up. Ryan Suthard, Nicole Ward, and Dennis Rolke all went to see the new X-Men movie and promised to meet up with us later. This Friday afternoon was a beautiful March day with the sun high in the sky and tolerable weather. John had the van drop the three of us off at the Sparta American Legion Hall on the edge of town. Now I want you all to realize that I was freshly twenty-one and had only been drinking with these guys for a few weeks. Boy, was I about to learn a thing or two!

I had known John Wiley for two years at this point and he was a charming SOB with a silver tongue. As I said before, we went through MP school together and he had also been our acting platoon sergeant. John was a tall man, over six feet tall, and he spent years on active duty in the Navy. He was recently divorced and looking to have fun. He was good at it too; John could make friends with anyone, anywhere. When you went out with him, he also wouldn't let you pay, but you had better keep up. So here we are in this American Legion at one o'clock in the afternoon on this Friday and John is sending beer after beer after beer our way and the three of us were keeping up pretty well at this point. Ivan Beal always got kind of quiet when he drank, whereas John became even more of a social butterfly. Bob and I just became the way Bob and I always were: we'd talk about movies, music, and we'd make fun of people. Bob would call a lot of people assholes too. It was truly his favorite word.

Sitting to Bob's left at this bar was an older man who looked like he was in his early sixties. He was wearing a Vietnam Veteran hat and the four of us introduced ourselves to him. The man told us his name was Woody and that he was an American Indian of the Winnebago tribe. His tribe had ownership in the casinos throughout that part of Wisconsin. He said he hadn't worked in over ten years because the casino money was so good from his tribe. He even showed us his official tribal identification card! Woody had a big smile on his face and it seemed he was very happy to be able to talk with us young GIs. He was a very friendly, very nice man to have an afternoon drink with.

Bob absolutely loved war history and knew more about it than anyone I had ever met. Bob got to talking with Woody while the three of us just listened. Woody was a Marine in Vietnam and he had served three tours in the infantry. He was the real deal; a real life badass Marine infantry veteran. Bob and Woody discussed battles that Woody had been in and the old Marine went on to tell us some great stories. They were the type of stories that made your jaw drop and made you sit on the edge of your seat. The type of hell that he had seen and lived through was mind blowing to us. Woody really took a liking to us and he mentioned more than once how polite and respectful we were and how he appreciated it so much.

It was about four in the afternoon at this point and John had kept us at a furious pace with beers and here is where the trouble started. Woody started buying shots for us, his new friends. Shots are intended to be plural. Woody kept buying shot after shot after shot and John kept telling me it'd be rude to turn him down. What Woody kept sending our way in these short glasses was Dr. McGillicutty. I had never had Dr. McGillicutty before that night and I have never had it since. From my right kept coming more beers from John and from my left kept coming more shots from Woody. Now Bob, John, and Ivan were experienced professionals at this point, but I had just been called up from Triple A not too long before. I was struggling with this power drinking. The next thing I knew, due to this ridiculous pace, was that I was seeing about three of Woody, three of Bob, three of Ivan, and three of John. Apparently, I wasn't showing it or maybe the three of them just didn't care. If I had told Bob he probably would have told me to shut up and stop being such an asshole anyway. Woody continued with his stories telling us all about his time in Vietnam and we just sat there listening and taking in this valued history. We were all having a really good time. The most interesting part, by far, was that when I looked at Woody I could see three of him talking at once. This made for one hell of a conversation!

Finally, at about six o'clock or so, John decided it was time to move on. We had promised that we'd meet our friends when they got out of the movie back in the main part of Sparta. We shook hands with Woody, said our goodbyes, and John picked up the tab. If you've ever been to Sparta you would know that the Legion is a good couple of miles away from downtown Sparta. The four of us walked drunkenly all the way back into town. I honestly have no idea how I did it because I couldn't see straight. Somehow, we managed to make it into town safely.

When we got to town, John took us into another bar which was called The Theater. Do you want to know why it was called The Theater? That's because a month before it was an abandoned theater and now with the boom of GIs at Ft. McCoy, it had been reopened as a bar. I kid you not there were still ramps leading down to where the seating used to be! The sign on the building was also plywood with spray paint. We got inside, caught our bearings, and sat down at the bar. John ordered another round of beers while we waited for Rolke, Suthard, and Ward to arrive from their movie. I was drinking my beer when the next thing I knew Bob ordered a round of shots. Guess what he ordered? More damn Dr. McGillicutty! I put down the shooter and that was it. I took off in a running sprint for the bathroom with Bob laughing hysterically at me. I couldn't get in the stall quick enough when six hours of beer and Doc's came out of my mouth and into the toilet. Something magical happened in that stall, though. After I finished heaving, I felt absolutely fine.

I washed my face off in the bathroom and I headed back into the theater, or bar. I was no longer seeing three of everyone and I felt great! It paid to be twenty-one and in great shape – you could recover quickly! I rejoined my friends and they were all laughing loudly at me. They knew exactly what had happened. John asked me if I was alright and I said, "You know what? I feel fine. It was like a pressure relief valve went off." Being a pipefitter apprentice, I had already seen my share of these kinds of valves. They are a safety on a steam system. If the line is overloaded, the valve opens and blows off steam. My body had acted the same way as one of the valves would to the beer and Dr. McGillicutty. It had too much and it had opened the relief. I saw a glimmer in Bob's eyes when I said that and he and I quickly patented the phrase, "Pressure Relief Puke" when drinking. The pressure relief puke became a common thing for the rest of my drinking career.

I can't remember if we got food or not at this theater slash bar but we continued to drink at John's ridiculous pace. We were now at the goofy stage of being drunk and we were having a lot of fun. We were there for only an hour and in-walked Suthard, Ward, and Rolke. Now Suthard and Ward were both underage and the bartender checked. We quickly learned the Sparta policy at that time: if you were under twenty-one but in the military and had someone that would take responsibility for you, then you could drink in the bar. The party continued!

Somewhere during the course of this night, Bob and I went outside. I have no idea why we went outside, but we did. We were in no condition to go exploring and it's probably one of the dumbest ideas we could have had. I'm sure it was my idea. Downtown Sparta is an old town setup with little alleys between the buildings. When Bob and I went out into the alley next to The Theater, we heard music coming from somewhere and not just any music, but really good hard rock 'n' roll stuff. I decided to urinate against the building while Bob stumbled around aimlessly in this alley. When I finished, I turned around and Bob was gone. I had no idea where he had gone and I was yelling out for him with no response.

As I looked around I saw a little stairwell that went down to the basement of the building next door and I figured that had to have been where Bob went. As I went down the stairs, I realized that's where the music was coming from too. I walked into the entryway at the bottom of the stairs and there was Bob standing there, right behind the band on stage. This was where the music was coming from and we were standing right in the middle of it. There were a lot of people staring at Bob and I with confused expressions on their faces that read, "Why the hell are these two on stage?" I grabbed Bob, apologized to the band, and we walked back up the stairs and back into the alley. With us missing for so long, the others went on a search for us. We came in contact with them in the alley and we told them about what had just taken place. All together we walked further down the alley and found the real entrance to this bar.

Just through the entrance there was a guy at the door checking IDs. The same Sparta policy applied, of course, to this place which we came to find out was called The Breakaway. There were bathrooms off to the right and then the bar was split into two large rooms, each room about fifty feet long by fifty feet wide. One side had a long bar with a few tables and a few pool tables and then in the other room was an area where they had a stage and bands were playing one after the other in a contest of some sort. All of us felt right at home, right away in this place. We caught one band on stage, which we later learned was called Skullfuckers, Inc., playing the song "Snap Your Fingers Snap Your Neck" by *Prong*. Bob went nuts! I knew the song too because it had been a pro wrestler's theme song. Ryan Suthard was also familiar with Prong and knew it. We rocked out and I can't begin to tell you how much fun that night became!

After this night we unofficially made The Breakaway our unofficial "home bar" and we found out that every Friday night the bar hosted Battle of the Bands. If we weren't heading to Lacrosse on pass, we would definitely be at The Breakaway. Bob really liked the style of music they played, we all did, and it was just a fantastic time. I also never drank Dr. McGillicutty again and swore that I would never go out drinking with John Wiley again. That plan lasted about two weeks when his shit eating grin suckered Bob and I into following him to some bar in Sparta where he got us so drunk that we lost the ability to speak. Bob and I liked to call that phase of drunkenness "Hyperspace Rocketfaced."

When we returned to the unit later that night after the pass, we told all the others in our platoon about our discovery. For future passes, we started taking them all with us to the bar. We had a guy in our company with us who was named Josh Baldwin. Josh was only in his mid-twenties at the time but had the look of an older man. I can't really say in what way or why, but he just looked older. We used to call him "Old Man Baldwin." He became a regular with the rest of us at The Breakaway and enjoyed the place just as much as we did. On top of being a fun place to watch bands play, this bar was also a haven for beautiful young women. Well, Josh had some kind of way with women where they would be magnetized to him. I can't explain it. Every time we went out, he would have some beautiful girl on his arm. On this particular night Josh was sitting down talking with this beautiful ten out of ten girl. A lot of us were up there that night including Bob, Nicole Ward, Ryan Suthard, Ivan Beal, Matt Bender, Dennis Rolke and several others. We were all watching Josh work his magic when I looked over at Bob, Bob looked at me, and we knew just what to do. We walked up to Josh and started screaming at the tops of our lungs, "YEEEEEAH! JOSH JUST GOT OUT OF JAIL! WOOOO!" The rest of our group didn't miss a beat and joined us. Ivan Beal even ordered a round of tequila for half the bar in celebration of Baldwin's release from the penitentiary.

This beautiful girl stood straight up and walked right away from Josh. The look on Old Man Baldwin's face was the saddest look I'd ever seen and all of us were waiting to get punched in the face. After he finished cursing us out, we took our shots of tequila. Old Man Baldwin then puked the tequila right out on the bar and Ryan, Bob, and I laughed so hard that we almost puked ourselves. The bartender didn't find it funny, unfortunately, and angrily threw a rag at Josh and told him to clean it up.

Rest assured, about twenty minutes later a new woman was drawn into Josh's magnetic field and the whole process started again. This one happened to think it was cool he had just gotten out of prison. It was a win for all!

CHAPTER 10

LOVE & LEATHERFISH

The best way I can describe the mindset of us at Ft. McCoy in those days is that you had to think of every day as your last chance to party. We had no idea when our unit would get the call or when we'd be sent overseas. No unit did, and there were hundreds of units and thousands of soldiers there on post at the time. Every night could be the last night. Everybody acted accordingly and partied just like it was their last chance to do so. Now multiply that times thousands and thousands of young GIs on a military installation. Imagine thousands of young men and women in their early twenties packing a club and partying like it's the last time they'll ever party. It was as wild as you'd imagine, and how it was every night. It was exciting, it was fun, and it created great memories and lifelong stories.

When we were finally allowed to start going out after training which was about three weeks into our Ft. McCoy stay, Bob and I went out together every night. We weren't alone. Most of our company and battalion went out every night too. Beer and liquor were so cheap at the club on post that everybody frequented the legendary McCoy's. McCoy's was a huge facility that had a full bar with seating, a bowling alley, a large dance floor, a full-service kitchen, and a pizza stand. It was packed every single night to fire capacity and they would have to turn people away at the door so as not to violate fire code.

It was not uncommon to meet a female acquaintance while out at McCoy's. It was not only soldiers partying like it was their last party ever at this place every night, there was also a contingent of civilian nurses who were attending a training school on post. I'm not sure what the arrangement was, but these nurses would stay in housing on post and attend school for a few weeks at a time. At night, they'd head out to the club and party just like us. That's how I met Annie.

One night I was at McCoy's and drinking at the bar with some other GIs that I didn't know all that well. They were from one of our sister companies and I recognized them from the mobilization, but that was about it. Bob was sick at this time and stuck back at the barracks. He had a bad throat infection that caused him to cough stuff up every five minutes and he had difficulty swallowing. It didn't stop him from slamming beers or smoking cigarettes, however. He was crafty like that! Sadly, he just had to do his partying back at the barracks and not at McCoy's with the rest of us.

While sitting at the bar with these guys I didn't know too well, I turned my head and saw a group of young ladies come walking into the bar. I could tell they were not female GIs with the way they carried themselves. There was one girl in the group who was absolutely beautiful and she immediately caught my eye. She was about five feet four inches tall and had an athletic build like a gymnast or a cheerleader. I remember she was wearing a white top with darker denim jeans and she had just taken off her black coat. She and her friends were looking around for somewhere to sit. She had darker skin, long black hair, and beautiful brown eyes. I'd learn later that Annie was of Polish descent and she had acquired her skin tone and complexion from that eastern European heritage. I noticed the two guys sitting next to me were also staring at these young ladies that had just walked in, particularly Annie.

I said to one of the guys next to me, "I'm going to go ask the girl in the white top to dance."

The two guys couldn't believe I was going to make a move. I bet them the next two rounds of drinks that I'd get her out on the dance floor. They accepted my bet. Luckily for them, I never came back that night to collect.

Before I made my way to Annie, I walked up to the DJ and slipped him a ten spot. I asked him to play a slow song next. I kept my eyes on Annie as she and her friends finally found a table and sat down. I knew I had to move quickly, there were way too many men that saw this beautiful girl come walking in. The DJ agreed to play the slow song next and I made my way over to Annie.

I walked up, introduced myself, she introduced herself, and then I asked her if I could buy her a drink. She smiled, a very pretty smile at that, as she said "sure." As I was trying to flag down the waitress, my slow song started playing. I asked Annie if I could get her the drink after a dance? She chuckled and smiled as she took my hand and I led her out to the dance floor. I remember a lot of details from that night and I remember that the song that was played was "Picture" by *Kid Rock and Sheryl Crow.* It was a very popular, hybrid slow rock / country song at the time.

Annie and I joined dozens of other couples on the dance floor and we got to talking while we danced. I learned what I had figured; she was a student at the nursing school and would be on post for a few weeks. Annie was a good dancer, she had a soft voice, and she had a very gentle demeanor. I liked her immediately and judging by her smiles, she liked me too. After that dance, I found a small table for us to sit at. We spent the rest of the night talking, completely ignoring our friends.

Annie and I got to know each other well that night and all the nights that followed over the next few weeks. I learned that she grew up on a dairy farm in a small town in southern Wisconsin and she had hopes and dreams of moving out of that town when she finished her nursing school. She was the same age as me, she came from a second-generation Polish family, she had six brothers and sisters, and she liked bottled beer. We clicked that first night, Annie and I, and we tried to get together every night for the rest of the time she was there. I didn't have a cell phone at that time and neither did she, so I would call the office at the nursing school from our barracks phone and leave messages for her to meet up.

On top of bottled beer, Annie also really liked to dance. I was never a bad dancer, but most of the songs that were played were not ones that we could dance to. Outside of "Picture" and a couple of others, the only songs that couples could dance to were salsa-style music. Several Puerto Rican Reserve companies had been activated at the same time as us and they were always in the ear of the DJ to get this style of music played. I had nothing against it, only Annie and I had no idea how to dance that style. Fortunately for us, Jessie Antia and Anna Martinez, a non-MP who was in our company, taught us. Annie could move well, we moved well together, and we got pretty good at this style of dance together. We had a lot of fun for those few weeks and, as crazy as this may sound because we didn't know each other long, I felt we had a deep connection that I never again felt with another woman. Without saying it, because she didn't have to, I could tell that Annie felt the exact same way.

After a few weeks, Annie's training had come to its conclusion and she was headed back to her hometown. When I walked Annie back to her housing that last night, she was crying and saying how we'd probably never see each other again. I told her that wasn't true, we could keep in touch, and we could meet up when I had passes and when this mobilization was over. I really believed what I said, and I really hoped this wasn't the last time we would be together. We had had so much fun, I wanted it to go on forever.

I took off one of my dog tags that night and gave it to Annie. She had tears in her eyes as I wrapped her up in my arms and held her tight. We exchanged addresses and she gave me her home phone number. We wrote back and forth for a few months and we had a few phone calls, but then we lost touch. I can't remember anymore who stopped writing or why we never connected when I had passes, but Annie was right. In the end we never saw each other again.

Annie crosses my mind from time to time and I wonder how life turned out for her. I still have a picture of us together. For years I had it in the drawer of a display case I own, but two moves later I don't know where it ended up. The picture was taken while we were at McCoy's. One of Annie's nurse friends snapped a shot of Annie sitting on my lap while I was seated on a bar stool. I had my arms wrapped around her and we were both smiling. We were two young kids in the initial feelings of what may have been love. Annie sent me that beautiful picture a few weeks after she returned home, and I made sure I never lost it.

I wonder if Annie's dreams came true and if she ever got out of her small town. She had a heart of gold and I hope she made it far. I'll never forget her.

We had a curfew back then that was ten o'clock at night during weekdays. I didn't follow it all when I was seeing Annie those few weeks. Each night for those few weeks I would walk Annie back to her housing area and then make the long trek back to our barracks. On one of those frigid April nights I returned back to our barracks at about two o'clock in the morning. To avoid detection from the NCO rooms, I made sure that I went in through the back entrance. The back entrance was a metal fire escape that could be very loud when you walked on it. You had to take your time, climb slowly, and hope that the back-door's lock was still open. When I got back this night, or morning if you prefer, standing outside the back entrance was Bob and he was smoking a cigarette. He shook his head, laughed at me, and called me a derogatory name. Bob never slept much. He would sleep two to four hours a night and then, once a month, he'd crash for about sixteen hours straight. The poor guy had that problem for as long as I knew him. Bob and I, both intoxicated, were laughing and joking around outside the barracks and then we headed quietly back up the stairs and into the barracks. As we stepped into our open bay room, I saw the light in SSG Rivas' room go on.

SSG Rivas was likely in his early fifties at the time. He was a tall, slim man who was freakishly intelligent. He also sounded like Kermit the Frog when he spoke and always seemed to be in a different place and time in his head. It was almost like he was permanently distracted or confused. He was our NBC NCO, finally filling the vacancy that had existed in that position for years.

SSG Rivas came out of his room in his white, brief underwear with no other clothes on and motioned for Bob and I to come to his room. I'm thinking, "We're in deep shit now." When we entered SSG Rivas' room we stood at parade rest and prepared for the ass chewing for violating the company curfew. Bob hadn't violated the curfew, but there was no way that Rivas knew that. He probably heard us come in together and now we were both in for it. Instead of an ass chewing, he pulled out a box from under his bed and offered us cookies that his mother had made. Bob and I had a few cookies and then made our way to bed. We laughed for the next fifteen years about this!

The weekend after Annie left to go home, I met a new girl when we were on pass in Lacrosse. Her name was Jenny. If Annie was a classy Cadillac, then Jenny was a high-speed Corvette. Jenny was about five feet two inches tall with a very impressive build. She had all the right bumps in all the right places. She was very pretty, very friendly, and had blonde hair and blue eyes. The clothing style for women back then was low rise jeans and belly shirts. Jenny had that look down very well and would turn heads wherever she went. Jenny was not from the area and would travel up to that part of Wisconsin from Wonder Lake, Illinois with her friend, whose name I cannot recall, just about every weekend. This friend of hers was dating a guy who was permanent party at Ft. McCoy. That means he was active army and was assigned to a unit on post. This soldier would be off on weekends and would hit the town with his girlfriend and her friends.

Jenny's favorite place to go when traveling up in Wisconsin was Lacrosse. She and her friend, and the boyfriend, would get a hotel room in town and then hit the bars and clubs. Oftentimes, other girls would travel with Jenny and her friend. I happened to meet Jenny at the bar of this nice dance club in downtown Lacrosse one night. A lot of us from the unit had booked hotel rooms and were staying the weekend in this college town. This was a classy looking club and I recall it had swanky red booths in the lounge area. Remember Scarface with the sunset art in the boss's office? That's the style in which the walls were painted in this place. It was a really exotic and unique look.

Bob Allen was there with us and, knowing Bob as long as I did, I thought it was strange that Bob didn't seem to have much interest in getting together with Annie's friends, now Jenny's friends, or any girl for that matter. He just wasn't interested one bit. I never asked him about it, I just let it be. Something was going on, though, and I couldn't put my finger on it. Well, we were all out at this club and we're all just having the time of our lives and I can remember everybody having these huge smiles on their faces and enjoying the freedom of the pass (and the alcohol that was flowing freely.)

It was a special weekend for one young female MP in our platoon named Bridget Keane. I didn't know much about Bridget at this point, but she was a tiny girl that was the most Irish-looking Irish girl I'd ever met. I knew she had a college degree, she was very nice, and she had some funny stories of her Dad beating up her ex-boyfriends! On this specific evening, Bridget was excited that a group of her friends had made the trip up all the way from Peotone, Illinois. After they had checked in at the hotel, these ladies came and met up with us at this club. Upon Bridget introducing these friends to all of us, Bob nicknamed them, undeservingly for the most part, the Omega Mus, a reference to the female sorority in the movie *Revenge of the Nerds*. What a jerk!

I had already met Jenny at this point of the night, and we were talking and spending time together. Jenny wasn't a dancer and I couldn't get her to go out on the dance floor no matter what music played. She was no Annie, that was for sure! I had been drinking, obviously, and felt like hitting the floor. The song "Ready Steady Go" by *Paul Oakenfold* was still hot at that time and they were playing it. Just for the heck of it I walked over and asked Jamie Hasenfang if she wanted to dance.

Jamie had been new to our unit and was a very nice lady. She was a tall woman, about five feet nine inches, was slim, and had blonde hair and blue eyes. She was older than us and was way past our sophomoric humor and collegiate-style ways of partying. Looking back on it, I don't know how she tolerated it! Jamie had previously been on active duty and had served for a while in Germany. She joined our reserve unit as a cook and she conducted herself as a professional, a lady, and her demeanor commanded respect. She certainly had mine. I had no love interest in her at all and that was never even a thought when I asked her to dance. Jamie and I went out on the dance floor and began dancing. About a minute into our dance I glanced back at our group of friends and I saw this look on Bob's face. Anyone who knew Bob knew "the look." His eyes would set back, he'd clench his jaw, and he'd start to turn red. In the two years plus of our close friendship we had never argued, fought, or crossed words. Never once. This seemed to be getting the closest to it, though. I felt something was funny, so I stopped the dance with Jamie.

When I walked off the floor, Bob's "look" went away. It now all came together in my mind, the reason Bob never wanted to get together with these other women was because he had a thing for Jamie! I confirmed a few minutes later when I was chatting with Matt Bender.

Matt, in his cigarette inspired, deep voice said, "Yeah, man. You didn't know that? He's obsessed with her!"

I never said a word to Bob about this and it would be a few months until he and I talked about it. It finally came up one morning, months later, while drinking coffee and smoking cigarettes on the cot outside of our tent in Afghanistan. He was really smitten with Jamie. Good for him – I just hoped she felt the same way and it would work out and he wasn't setting himself up for heartache.

My fling with Jenny went on for several weekends. She was a nice girl with a touch of wild and she really liked to party. Our relationship concluded when one night after partying we went back to a hotel room. Jenny had been acting funny at the bar, hyped up and on edge even though we had been drinking the whole night. Looking back on it, I'm pretty sure she was indulging in other party favors that I was ignorant to. I didn't see her take anything, but that doesn't mean much when it comes to drugs.

When we got back to the hotel, Jenny said that she was going to take a shower. When she went into the bathroom, I laid down on the hotel bed and turned the TV on. There was an NHL hockey game on, and I remember hearing the water turn on in the shower. I had been drinking all night and now was in this nice, warm hotel room, I inadvertently drifted off to sleep. I snapped awake about forty-five minutes later and Jenny was not in the room.

I called out her name and knocked on the bathroom door as I heard the water still running. I sobered up quickly out of fear as I saw water collecting underneath the door jamb along with shower steam finding its way through the cracks of the door. I knocked, and knocked, but there was no answer. I feared the worst and I took my belt off and forced the metal latch into the door lock to pop it. When the lock freed and I opened the door, the floor was soaked wet and there was so much steam I couldn't see. I don't know how the room's smoke detectors didn't go off when the steam rushed from the bathroom into the rest of the room.

When I looked in the tub Jenny was naked, on her belly with her head cocked to the side, and water was coming from the shower head and hitting her back. Most of this water was bouncing off her back and making its way over the tub, but some of it was pooling underneath her and her nose and mouth were barely above the water line. I yelled out her name and shook her, but she was not responding. I was terrified that something awful had happened. I quickly turned the water off, stepped into the tub, and then picked her up from under her armpits. When I lifted her up, I was yelling her name and shaking her. Finally, she woke up. Jenny pushed me away, got furious, and then started cursing me out saying that she "does this all the time" and it was "no big deal."

The truth of the matter is, Jenny was on some kind of drug, if not a multitude of drugs. I don't know what it was, but I fear that had I not woken up she may have ended up drowning in that tub that night. After Jenny got dressed and we cleaned up all the water, I started to collect my things to get out of there. This really shook me up. I couldn't wrap my mind around how through the evening she had gone from normal, to totally amped up, to now in a lethargic state.

Jenny was begging me to stay, but I walked right past her and got out of that room and the hotel. I spent $90 that night taking a cab from Lacrosse all the way back to Ft. McCoy. Jenny called the barracks the next day and attempted to apologize, but I told her it was over.

When we started getting full, unrestricted weekend passes in late April, most of us would travel home for the weekend and then come back to Ft. McCoy. A lot of us even brought our own personal vehicles back up, which was permitted at the time. After a couple weekends of driving back and forth, a lot of us stopped going home or at least we didn't go home as often. It was nothing against our families, we just had such a good time together that we wanted to spend our weekends partying together.

After one night of heavy partying, Bob and I woke up mid-morning at the barracks on a Saturday morning. For whatever reason, nobody else was in the upper part of the barracks that day. They were either out already or just hadn't slept there the night before. When Bob and I got up, we did what we always did: we cracked beers and went right back to it. After we sat around bullshitting and recalling the events of the night before, we decided to get cleaned up. We took our showers, drank some more, and then decided to head to the weekend chow hall. It was a good mile walk away. By the time we got there, it was around eleven-thirty in the morning and we were the first ones in the dining facility, or at least we thought. As soon as we stepped in, I smelled it. Bob smelled it. We both cringed.

Ft. McCoy cooks had a habit of overcooking fish. It may have been re-cooked for all I know. Bob and I had named this dish "leatherfish" due to the leathery surface of the fish from the re-cooking or whatever the cause was. It was all they were serving that day and we had no choice but to take it. The cooks slapped the leatherfish on our trays and we found seats. Now Bob's back was to the rest of the dining hall and he couldn't see that some senior NCOs were sitting at tables in the back of the dining facility. I saw them right away, but I couldn't stop what was already in motion. All at once Bob erupted, "This damned leatherfish again! I'm sick of this shit! These lazy assholes cooking this asshole fish and serving it to us assholes three times a week! I'm sick of this bullshit! Fuck these people!"

Bob was on a rant so loudly that the senior NCOs in the back and the civilian cooks had their eyes glued onto him. I did everything I could to calm him down and try to warn him that we were being watched, but he ignored me and continued to go off. He was really pissed! He got himself so worked up that he even punched the leatherfish on his plate! Despite being pissed and outright aggressive, he ate it anyway and so did I. Bob bitched the entire time he ate, he bitched the entire time it took us to clean our trays and turn them in, and he bitched the entire walk back to the barracks. Bob was still condemning the leatherfish as we were sitting on the back porch of our barracks an hour later. I was laughing so hard that I think it just fueled him to keep going. I have never in my life, to this day, seen someone so angry about food.

Apparently, I wasn't the only one that had never witnessed an outrage over food like that. Two days later on Monday, after our first formation of the day, I saw MSG Holder pull Bob aside, lock him up at parade rest, and have a very stern conversation with him. I saw Holder's hand pointing at Bob, pointing toward the chow hall, and then pointing toward me a couple of times.

When this ass-chewing was finally over and Bob was released from the talons of this senior NCO, he walked back over to me. Bob told me that due to his protest over the leatherfish two days before, he was now BANNED from eating in the weekend chow hall. Bob also said he couldn't talk to me long because he had to catch the company van to be escorted to a psych exam!

I don't know what the results of that psych exam were, but it never stopped Bob from cussing out leatherfish again.

CHAPTER 11

BIRFDAYS AND BACARDI

Alan Garretson was from just outside of South Bend, Indiana. He had gone to basic training with Bob, Ryan Suthard, Matt Bender, and a multitude of others in our unit who all went together at the same time. He was a quiet guy with a gentle demeanor. He was married with one child and his wife was expecting their second when we were mobilized and sent up to Ft. McCoy. I don't know how in the hell he ever became friends with the rest of us since his personality was the very opposite of the rest of us. I never once saw him get mad or upset and he was the most likable and most laid-back guy you'd ever meet. He and I struck up a friendship right away over our love of Notre Dame football. Everybody liked Garretson and to this day, I've never heard anyone say anything negative about him.

Bob and I liked Garretson so much that we gave him the nickname "Garretjerk" and we even wrote a nice little sing-along song about him. It went a little something like this, "Garretson's a hillbilly fuck, a hillbilly fuck, a hillbilly fuck. Garretson's a hillbilly fuck, a hillbilly fuck is he." Garretson wasn't a hillbilly at all and hardly even had an Indiana drawl. Bob and I were jerks, though, and that was all that was to it.

When we were allowed to start going out at night and we were no longer confined to the company area, our whole company, practically, would head up to McCoy's and party with thousands of others in wild escapades. Remember, it could always be the last chance to party since we could be sent overseas at any moment. One of these nights happened to be Alan Garretson's 21st birthday. Alan was doing pretty good for a while just drinking a few beers with the rest of us. That was until I saw Bob get ahold of him. Next thing I knew, Bob had Garretson at the bar and was calling over Shorty. Bob called this one bartender Shorty because she had a deformed arm that was shorter than the other. The first time I heard him refer to her as Shorty, I thought it was one of the meanest things I had ever heard. I thought that way for about 2.5 seconds and then I busted out laughing. Within no time, Bob's nickname for this disabled bartender caught on and the rest of us started calling her Shorty too. It was not a nice thing to do, but at least it was an easy way to quickly identify her.

Shorty responded to Bob's call and he started buying shots. I tried to warn Alan not to drink with Bob because he'd regret it later, but he didn't listen. Bob and Garretson began slugging them down one right after another. It wasn't quite at the pace of John Wiley, but it was a respectable second. Next thing I knew, everybody was buying Garretson shots and he was drinking everything being offered to him. I knew right then and there that it was over for Alan that night. After about an hour of this, he started having trouble getting around. Do you remember how boxers used to put their arms on their trainers on the way into the ring? Garretson had to do that with at least one of us, at all times, in order to keep himself walking upright.

This kind of heavy drinking damage went on for a good couple more hours and Alan Garretson was now annihilated and totally drunk. There was a very popular song at the time called "In Da Club" by *50 Cent*. McCoy's played it quite often. Alan really enjoyed that song and, that night, when it came on at that specific moment, he suddenly had a physical revival and was able to move around again independently! A couple of girls from the unit saw him in his groove and pulled him out on the floor. His moves that night resembled a dog chasing its tail, but hey, he was having a blast!

Upon leaving the dancefloor, Bob roped him in and once again poured into him more shots. Alan started to yell out randomly, "It's my birfday! I'm going to drink Bacardi like it's my birfday!" Now you would think this would have caused a scene and that they might have cut him off or thrown him out, but at that time period at McCoy's, that was the norm. All the other GIs, whether in our unit or not, were cheering him on and joining in on the party! It was a mess.

We all finally left McCoy's late that evening and we had to keep Garretson supported to get him back to the barracks. I think Ryan Suthard had his left shoulder as I was supporting his right. It wasn't too long of a walk back to our barracks, but it was long enough when supporting a drunk human being in that obliterated condition. Drunk human beings tend to increase their body weight twofold because their limbs stop functioning correctly. With difficulty, we got Garretson back to the barracks and it took about four of us to get him up the stairs to the second level of the barracks. Suddenly Garretson had a second revival and he went crazy again! He was running around the barracks screaming "It's my birfday! I'm going to drink Bacardi!" I can remember Bob egging him on and providing zero help to get him under control. In fact, Bob was snapping pictures away with his camera and laughing the whole time.

Garretson started threatening to call his poor, pregnant wife at 12 o'clock in the morning in this condition and we had to wrestle the phone out of his hand several times. Bender was the only one who had a phone at that time and Garretson had snagged it from him. All of us were in stitches; we were laughing so hard trying to chase down and tackle him. The usually quiet, mild mannered Garretson was so loud and animated that he even woke up some of the NCOs who had private rooms. Some of them, laughing like crazy, helped us get Garretson into bed. We had to hold him down until he half passed out. That night, Matt Bender did one of the most courageous things I'd ever seen - he stayed by Garretson's bedside equipped with a garbage can. I know this because I heard the vomit hitting the garbage can. With every wretch and heave, Bender was there to catch that night's alcohol offerings. You couldn't sleep with this going on, so Bob and I just sat up in bed and laughed. Bob kept yelling out, "I'm going to party like it's my birfday!"

Alan moved a little slowly the next morning when we woke up for PT. He may have vomited a little on that morning's run too. After breakfast, however, he was a new man!

CHAPTER 12

I WILL NOT BE CAGED

LIKE AN ANIMAL

One of Bob's favorite people to make fun of during our mobilization, and mine too, was a man by the name of Pete Orlowski. Orlowski had gone through basic training with Bob, Suthard, Garretson, Bender, and the other five or so corrections MPs that went through all their training together. Orlowski was in his mid-30s (at least), was recently divorced, and had more college degrees and education than most two or three people combined, but in absolutely useless fields. Before the mobilization, Pete had been working as an over-the-road truck driver.

After this tour, and for years to follow, Orlowski was a returning topic of conversation whenever Bob and I spoke. In the short four months we spent with him, so many ridiculous things that he did were forever ingrained in our brains. Orlowski didn't end up deploying with us either. At the last minute, he apparently had severe back issues and was held back. Rumor has it that he was left to rot at Ft. McCoy for another six months before finally receiving a medical discharge.

Orlowski had some bad luck when the unit had dental exams too. He ended up having one of his front teeth pulled along with a few others. Bob was quick to point out that Pete now smiled like a jack-o-lantern. He was also one of the cheapest, most frugal people that you'd ever meet. If Orlowski didn't have to part ways with a dime, he certainly wouldn't. He refused to buy soap or any other hygiene products. Ft. McCoy had an area set up where civilians would donate hygiene products for the troops. Most troops would not take this stuff, we were getting paychecks after all, and the Army would then donate these unclaimed products to the local homeless shelters and churches with charity programs. Not Pete Orlowski, though. Without either shame, or dignity he would go straight there and load up on supplies. The MWR (Morale, Welfare, Relief) Center was Orlowski's favorite place on earth and he was like a kid on Christmas morning when he returned. He would take and use anything they had. We once caught him shaving his face with pink, plastic disposable razors that ladies use to shave their legs with.

"Well...free meals" was one of Pete's favorite sayings. He'd say it with this smile on his face that indicated he was perfectly content with whatever obstacles the Army threw his way, so long as he could still draw free meals. This quote became inspirational to us and for the rest of that tour we would use it. We could be in a really shit situation and all of us would be pissed off. Then one of us would invoke Orlowski and say, "Well...free meals!"

Pete Orlowski was very into his religion. I'm not going to name his religion because I'm not going to disrespect it, but I have to say that there were some weird things about it. First and foremost, Orlowski wouldn't spend $2 on soap, but he would pay $50 for a pair of special underwear that he had to wear for his religion. It was one of the oddest practices I'd ever heard of and the underwear looked like brown, cut off long john bottoms. It was very strange.

Another strange thing that Orlowski would do was some kind of weird martial arts stretches and poses. He would do this in his underwear when he first got up in the morning. We kind of got used to it and ignored it until one day he fell on the floor writhing in pain because he pulled a muscle. For the next year every time any of us would do PT, one of us would throw ourselves on the floor and mock Orlowski.

Orlowski didn't drink, he didn't smoke, he didn't consort with women, and he certainly detested any kind of pornography. He didn't have a single vice that we were aware of except for being just too educated for his own good.

One of the freakiest things Orlowski ever did was when we were getting ready to ride to a training site for the day. I hope you're paying attention to what I just wrote: RIDE. We weren't going to have to march 10 miles to a training site that day. We were going to load up on vehicles and RIDE to the site! All of us were happier than pigs in shit to load up on the back of a covered two-and-a-half-ton truck. There were a lot of us that had to get on the vehicle, so we packed this truck tightly. This was nothing new to us; this was how we traveled on trucks in the Army in those days.

This two-and-a-half-ton truck had a fixed cover on the bed and it also had padding and insulation inside of it because it was a specialized food truck used for transporting hot food around the post. I have no idea how our company had commandeered it, but all of us gleefully loaded right up in there in full equipment with our weapons. We were shoulder to shoulder, but we were so excited to be getting a ride that nobody cared. Orlowski was one of the last people to load on. I remember watching him as he got this really weird look on his face. He started shifting around and then I saw a crazy panic flash in his eyes. He screamed out, "I WILL NOT BE CAGED LIKE AN ANIMAL!" and he jumped off the back of the truck! We made fun of and impersonated Orlowski a lot before this, but after this incident we amped it up one hundred-fold. Bob Allen had the best Orlowski impression of all of us and it came out often and on demand. This was just more fuel to that burning fire!

As part of our training certification process, our company had a two-week field exercise where we ran a mock EPW (Enemy Prisoner of War) camp. We did this exercise in conjunction with our two other line companies. Under normal circumstances, we would all have had to stay out in the field at the training site. Unfortunately, the weather was too damn cold, and the command decided that the battalion would return from the field and return to the barracks each night. With this said, two enlisted soldiers had to stay on site overnight and guard our equipment each night. The two required soldiers were an NCO and a junior enlisted soldier. This duty was on top of the other mandatory daily duty of a CQ (Charge of Quarters) NCO and runner. It was really shit duty and none of us wanted to stay out in the middle of nowhere and freeze our asses off overnight. Every one of us MPs, when it was our turn for duty, got Orlowski to cover our shift by buying him a two liter of Red Mountain Dew. The man stayed overnight in the middle of nowhere freezing his ass off for Red Mountain Dew. He was really something else!

When the weather started to break, Orlowski somehow acquired a bicycle while we were at McCoy. He also picked up a helmet and a headlight for the bike.

We don't know what kid he stole the bike from or who he beat up for the helmet, but he suddenly had one of each. We knew that there was no way he actually paid for that stuff. From the barracks to the heart of the town of Sparta was probably a good 7 miles away. While on weekend pass, Orlowski would ride his bike to the outskirts of Sparta where there was a temple for his religion. The temple was probably 10 to 12 miles from the barracks, one way. Rain, shine, or storms, Orlowski was off on that bicycle and heading to the temple.

This will all come into play now with one of the craziest stories from that time period. At this point, all of the junior enlisted MPs on weekend pass were frequenting the bar in downtown Sparta talked about earlier called The Breakaway. This particular day, however, we didn't go. It was closed down due to a wedding reception. John Wiley and a few others had found this pool hall / sports bar across the street from The Breakaway that they would frequent while on weekend pass. That day John invited us over to join him. I was hesitant. I had sworn to myself that I'd never drink with John again, but I liked the crazy SOB and acquiesced. There was a bad rainstorm this day, I mean a really, really, bad thunderstorm that lasted all day and all night. It was the type where the power would flicker every half hour or so. Ryan Suthard, Nicole Ward, John Wiley, Bob Allen, Ivan Beal, Matt Bender, Josh Baldwin, myself, and a few others were in John's sports bar all day having a pretty good time. Ryan Suthard was quite the pool player and he liked the tables in this place.

This was also the beginning of baseball season and this bar had a couple of games going on the TVs. While sitting at the bar and watching a ball game, I made another grievous mistake. I was sitting with John, Bob Allen, Ivan Beal,

Matt Bender, and Josh Baldwin. What do you think happened next? John started buying rounds again and the next thing I knew, I was seeing two of everything. Luckily, I wasn't seeing three yet, but John was pushing to make it happen all over again.

Bob and I did our usual drunken pastime. We talked to the bartender, had gotten the jukebox cranked all the way up, and we were pumping money into it playing Creedence Clearwater Revival. We were having a ridiculously drunken good time. I remember the local people in this bar really got a kick out of all of us and we were all buying each other drinks back and forth. Correction: John was buying them drinks and they were sending drinks our way. Some younger locals that normally partied at The Breakaway also ended up coming into this bar. We recognized them, they recognized us, and the good time we were having just kept getting better. The girl I was seeing at this time, Jenny, was unable to come up to Sparta that weekend and that was a good thing: John would have killed her liver.

For those of you that have never served in the military, there is a duty called CQ. CQ stands for Charge of Quarters and it means just that. I know I've explained that before, but what exactly does Charge of Quarters mean? Somewhere the company will have an established office and one NCO and one junior enlisted will serve 24 hours on this special duty. In our full time at Ft. McCoy, I believe all of us ended up having to work CQ two to three times each. The junior enlisted on CQ usually is responsible for building checks and driver duties while the NCO stays in the office and answers the phones. If the NCO is a quality sergeant, he or she will usually allow the junior enlisted to sleep for a few hours while he or she keeps going for 24 hours straight on coffee and nicotine.

I bring up CQ because the 327th had a great policy back then. The CQ driver was allowed to drop soldiers off in Sparta and pick them back up. This was great for all of us that were going out drinking because nobody had to worry about driving or paying for cabs. I'm not sure who in the company's leadership approved this, but it was a really nice thing to do. Then again, if I was the company commander and had a bunch of knuckleheads like us under my command, I would probably do the same thing to keep people out of the hospitals and jails!

During the whole time we spent out at this bar in Sparta, it had continued to rain very hard. I can remember these huge puddles in the street and people walking into the bar soaked from head to toe. John had used the bar's telephone and had called the CQ back on post to come pick us up at about 10 that night. This had been a 10-hour drinking binge and all of us needed to go back to the barracks and sleep. We were waiting patiently in the bar when we saw the company CQ van come ripping down the street at about 50mph. It disappeared from our view, we heard screeching tires, and next thing we knew, the van came flying back towards the bar again. The driver jammed on the brakes, stopped directly in front, and sent water flying everywhere. I remember all of us looking at each other like, "What in the hell is going on?" Yet again, John had successfully brought us to a point where our motor skills weren't functioning up to par having been overserved; however, we could tell something wasn't right in this situation.

The junior enlisted CQ driver that night was a guy by the name of Ruiz. When we climbed into the van, we could immediately tell that Ruiz was hammered drunk and that there was a slight possibility other party favors may have been included. Now, I liked Ruiz a lot. He was a nice guy, but what the hell? How on earth he pulled off getting drunk on CQ duty is beyond me, but he managed to do it.

Immediately, we put an end to him driving the van any longer. Ruiz got very mouthy and was borderline violent with John Wiley in the front passenger seat. That was his first mistake. His second mistake was when he slammed the door of the van and walked into the bar. John looked over at us young MPs in the van and said, "Boys, let's go get him." I don't think all of us walked into the bar, but most of us did. I remember that Bob and I grabbed his arms and yanked him off the stool and onto the floor. Beal and Bender grabbed his legs and we stretched him out. Ruiz refused to relax or submit and continued to fight us. We rolled him onto his stomach, folded up his limbs, and carried him back to the van. With the way we had him folded up, he could not move. We threw him on one of the seats and our guys sat on him and restrained him until he calmed down or passed out, whichever came first. I remember sitting in the van trying to figure out what the hell was going to happen next or how we were going to get back to the barracks. John Wiley had walked back into the bar to use the phone while the rest of us waited patiently in the van. All at once Bender yelled out, "Is that Orlowski????"

Sure enough, Pete Orlowski was riding his bicycle down the sidewalk in the pouring rain. I remember him looking at us and waving "Hi guys!" Bob hopped out of the van to get John Wiley and Ryan Suthard got out and stopped Orlowski. Into the back of the van went Orlowski's bicycle and into the driver's seat went Pete. Disaster was avoided and Orlowski saved the day. Orlowski drove us back to Ft. McCoy that night whether he wanted to or not.

When we got back to the barracks, Orlowski parked the duty van and John Wiley escorted Ruiz to the CQ office. Ruiz was cooperating at that point, but he had no choice really. I'm not sure what discipline took place after that, but this was just the beginning of Ruiz's issues.

What on earth were the odds, though, that Orlowski would be riding his bike at ten o'clock on that sidewalk? It was a pretty funny situation. This was a very nice gesture by Orlowski and you would think that all of us would have been nicer to him afterward and gracious for what he did for us, but we weren't. In fact, I think as beers opened in the barracks moments after we got back, we went right back to ripping on him!

CHAPTER 13

MANDATORY FUN AND

THE LOAD OUT

In late May of 2003, the HHC 327th had a big blowout barbecue. It wasn't the first get together we had, but this one was the biggest. Somewhere at McCoy there was a giant park with softball fields and the 327th really did it up right. I remember a lot of the female soldiers really put a great deal of effort into it and this was the best Army barbecue I had ever been to. We had ribs, sausages, burgers, and one hell of a spread. They really outdid themselves!

Here lies the only problem that I had with the barbecue: I had CQ the previous 24 hours before this mega event. There was an E-7 that I had CQ with whose name was SFC Linden. He had been an MP trainer at the military police school previously and he had been involuntarily transferred into our unit for the deployment. SFC Linden never ended up deploying with us. He seemed to be a bit of a strange bird and in the civilian world he was a prison guard somewhere in Tennessee. He questioned me several times about a shamrock tattoo I have on my arm and he kept telling me it was a racist symbol. No matter how many times I told him it was just a stupid thing I did when I was 19 to show off my Irish heritage, he would bring it up again each time he saw me in short sleeves. It got old quickly and I tried to avoid him at all costs.

Unluckily for me, I got stuck with SFC Linden on the 24-hour CQ duty the night prior to this big barbecue. He did not allow me to get any sleep during the 24 hours. In fact, he had me do a bunch of manual labor like scrub down the whole office and much more. I think, at one point, we even started organizing files. I can't recall one minute of sitting back and watching a movie or anything like that. Linden was all business.

Outside of the work part of CQ it had been a quiet 24 hours. Overnight, I remember I didn't have to drive anywhere or go anywhere, he just had me doing menial tasks. I remember when I was released from duty that morning I was really worn out. I climbed up the fire escape, went into the barracks, and crawled into bed. About two hours later, I was awoken by a bunch of returning maniacs in uniform screaming and being juvenile in the barracks. Despite my pleadings to let me sleep, they just weren't going to allow it. I thought my closest friends might intercede for me and get everyone to be quiet, but neither Garretson nor Bender were of any help in my need for sleep. Bob actually came over and yelled at me, "Get up! We're going to mandatory fun!" Bob was the first person I had heard use that term: "mandatory fun." It's a pretty good oxymoron if you think about it.

I could see trying to sleep was futile, so I walked downstairs, took a shower, dressed in my civilian clothes, and joined everyone on the waiting bus. The man driving the bus was one of my favorite people of all time. His name was Richard Collier and he was one of the happiest, nicest men I ever met. He and I were close friends in the unit and we always greeted each other with a big hug.

Collier was a mechanic in our company and he had been really nice to me when I first came into the unit. We were assigned to the same platoon and he was an experienced soldier who eventually got promoted to sergeant. He looked after me like a little brother that first year or so that I was in the unit and I never forgot his kindness towards me. I would always do anything I could for him. I really liked that man and I thought the world of him. SGT Collier, while driving the bus, had this boombox going. He was playing classic MC Hammer songs and the whole mood on the bus was upbeat and happy.

When we arrived at the park area, the food was hot and ready to go. The atmosphere was one of a lot of friends having a good time. Something at this function was different from times of the past: this time we were allowed to drink. I remember Bob taking up a collection and he went off to the Class Six (military liquor store) with a few others. When they came back to the park, they brought foam coolers stocked with beer and assorted liquor. Bob was nice enough to bring me back my favorite beverage, which was ice cold Budweiser. I was on zero sleep and started putting back Budweisers. It probably wasn't the smartest idea in the world, but we started eating such great food and that seemed to neutralize things out. I remember a bunch of enlisted soldiers playing against the officers in a softball game. Bob and I sat in the bleachers and watched the game while ragging on the officers. I can't remember who won the game, but that ball game was no joke. There were some really serious players on both sides, and they were hustling and playing hard. It was an impressive athletic contest!

Our whole unit must have stayed out at this party for over 5 hours. Both of our sister companies had already deployed to Iraq at this point, so it was just our company and the battalion staff left. At this point in the mobilization, everyone got along very well and you could tell that this group of people really cared about each other. I had been on sports teams all of my life at that point, but I had never felt as connected to another group as I felt to these people. It was a good thing we were all so tight, because the big word was just about to come down.

One of my favorite memories of McCoy was coming back from that party. My man Richard Collier was driving the bus again and he had his boombox cranked up as loudly as it could go. He had the whole bus jamming out to MC Hammer's "Pumps and a Bump." He wasn't just jamming, he was full-out dancing and driving at the same time! It was great! I remember all of us going wild with him. Even Bob's pale ass threatened to bust a move!

It wasn't too much longer after that big party that our unit got "The Call." At this time at Ft. McCoy most units that hadn't been deployed yet were being deactivated and sent home. We were four months in at Ft. McCoy and most of us felt that being deactivated was in our very near futures. We were wrong. I can't recall the exact day the call came, but I remember the formation we were in when told. It was only a day or two later that we were issued our DCUs (Desert Camouflage Uniform) and we knew our deployment was here and real. We were told Afghanistan, but nothing more. Our last weekend pass was revoked. I remember many soldiers' parents and loved ones had to drive up in order to take back the vehicles that soldiers had brought to the post. My parents didn't have to make the trip because I had taken my truck home the weekend before, but I remember Bob's mom and step-dad came up.

The day we were to leave, Bob came up with the idea for us all to shave our heads into mohawks just like members of the 82nd did before jumping into France in June, 1944. About six of us went ahead and did it with Bob, including SSG Scofield. These haircuts were a complete violation of uniform policy, but we got away with it for about 12 hours.

We had lunch with Bob's mom and step-dad at McCoy's, and then we said our goodbyes. I really liked Bob's mom and step-dad Dave. They were really good people and I always enjoyed talking with them. Bob's mom was a smaller blonde-haired lady who had remarried and had two children after Bob and his brother. Bob's step-dad, Dave, was a union electrician that also owned his business. We used to kid around and call him "Chuck Norris" because he was in such good shape and had a mustache like Norris had at the beginning of the movie Delta Force. Sadly, I could see that this goodbye was really tough on Jean and Dave. Hell, it was tough on all of us. Again, we didn't know anything. We didn't know for how long we would be gone, where exactly we were going, or what our mission would be.

Later that day, we began the final load up and load out. We packed up all of our gear, loaded it on trucks, and then the trucks took the gear out to the plane. This was actually a very organized process, but it was one that required a lot of manpower and a lot of physical work. I remember how we were all running around like madmen, busting our asses, and hauling our gear. I also remember the contrast of watching the cooks and other non-MPs sitting around in lawn chairs drinking beer and smoking cigarettes. Remember the CQ driver Ruiz? I watched as he sat there drinking a forty ounce beer and smoking a cigar while the rest of us were hauling gear. To this day, I never understood how that was permitted, but it was.

Another thing I remember from that evening was a very humorous story. We had a non-MP who was sitting on his ass in the lower part of the barracks playing on his computer and doing nothing to help in the loading of gear and materials. Bob and I got really pissed at this guy and Bob screamed at him to get his ass up and give us a hand. The guy looked at Bob and I and said, "I on quarter!"

This soldier, Wang, was originally from China and had a strong accent. He was not going to lift a finger to help us because he was allegedly on doctor's orders of quarters – which means bedrest. His claim may have been legitimate, but it was still BS. Bob and I let him have it and for the next year whenever anyone wanted us to do work, Bob and I would yell out, "I on quarter!" This was yet again another phrase to be added to our readily growing list of phrases to be used when together and at opportune times in life.

I remember us MPs humping gear and working our asses off that whole night. We then had a final formation and loaded up onto busses in our full gear. This was another silent bus ride. You could have heard a pin drop on the whole trek out to Volk Field.

The adventure of a lifetime was about to begin.

CHAPTER 14

ENTER THE GHAN

Afghanistan is a country that has been embroiled in one war or another since its inception. It is a collection of tribes and states that collectively combine to create a loosely governed nation. The tribes and states tend to not like the other tribes and states. There is almost always some form of civil war taking place. Afghanis will create alliances with each other, break the alliances and fight, then reunite, and then they will fight once again. There are Tajiks, Hazaras, Uzbeks, Pashtuns, Noors, Turkmen, and many other types of tribes and states all thrown together into this country. Unlike the United States and other advanced nations where we've formed a melting pot, these tribes and states tend to never mix outside of their own and keep to their own homelands within Afghanistan. It is a complicated mess made much worse by the meddling of outside countries into the individual tribes and states' politics.

I own fourteen different books on Afghanistan, and I have probably read at least thirty more. I have watched tens of hours of documentaries, interviews, and specials on the subject. In addition, I have listened to countless hours of podcasts, PBS radio series, BBC radio specials, and personal stories of friends who did multiple tours to that country. I've even had personal friendships with

Pashtuns living near my hometown in which we spoke deeply about the root problems of the nation. With all of this research, countless hours of additional study, and first-person experiences, I have never understood what it will ever take for there to be permanent peace in Afghanistan. Outside of splitting the country up into several smaller countries and re-taking the Durrand Line from Pakistan, I don't think Afghanistan will ever cease having war or civil war.

In short, Afghanistan is an extremely complicated mess with no sure solution in sight. The U. S. involvement in Afghanistan since 2001 is just another war in that nation's long and bloody history. For those of you who may not know much about Afghanistan, I highly suggest looking into the history of Afghanistan from the 1960s through the present day. You will see a king deposed and one ruling party or dictator after another put into power. That ruling party or dictator will then be removed followed by the rise of another. Just since 1960 alone, Afghanistan has been engaged in three major wars and hundreds of smaller ethnic and regional wars. It is a brutal country with a bloody history and there is no peace in sight even after two decades of international peacekeeping presence.

I knew none of this as our company rode on the busses to Volk Field outside of Ft. McCoy, Wisconsin. Once at the airfield, we were quarantined into an area where there was food and water available for us. It was here that the other MPs and I who had shaved our heads into mohawks had them removed by the command. As a company, we waited in this holding area along with the battalion staff for several hours until we were told that our plane had arrived. Once our plane was there, we walked one-by-one onto the tarmac and into the plane.

Upon being loaded onto the plane, some high-ranking officers from Ft.

McCoy came aboard to give speeches. Most of them were the typical "do your best, we're proud of you" type speeches, but there was one speech that forever stuck in my mind. There was a major who was a trainer back while we were going through the certification process at McCoy. He was probably in his late 40s and wore his hair very short on the sides with the top combed forward. He had a good deal of gray coming in on the sides, but the top of his head still showed jet black hair. He was a tall man with an athletic build and his presence was the type where you knew he was a man to be respected. On his chest was an air assault tab, an airborne tab, and on his right shoulder he had a combat patch. He was an even-keeled, quiet man, but you could tell that he really cared about what he was doing while evaluating the training. This major wasn't just there to tell you what you were doing wrong; he made a point to help you correct it.

His name was Major Massala and after the senior officers spoke and exited the plane, he grabbed the microphone next. MAJ Massala told us that he knew how we were feeling at that very second. He told us how he knew exactly how we were going to feel until the tour ended. He told us how he had begged to come with us, he begged to be transferred to our unit, but that his command would not release him from his training duties. Massala then started to tell us to look out for each other, and to trust our guts at all times. In the midst of this speech, his voice broke, he paused, and he then became overcome with emotion. The only other words he could get out were, "I wish I was going with you. God bless you." And with that he climbed off the plane, weeping.

At the time I couldn't understand what it was inside of this strong of a man that could have overtaken him like that. It was a shocking thing to see at my young age. As I sit here two decades later, I know exactly what was inside of him that day. MAJ Massala wanted to be a soldier again and he wanted to relive the camaraderie, triumphs, and tribulations that come with it. He was stuck in a boring training company, but he wanted to feel alive again in his boots. Not a day has gone by since I got out in 2007 that I also don't long for that feeling again.

On June 18, 2003, our civilian airliner took off from Volk Field and we flew towards Shannon, Ireland for a long eight hours. We got off the plane and went into a holding area that quarantined us off from the rest of the airport. This layover was only a few hours and it gave us time to line up at the bar and have a few drinks. I know I took part in the drinking. I had a couple pints of some very dark beer that was as thick as a milkshake. It wasn't Guinness, but it was that style of beer. I asked the bartender about the Lollis name, my mother's maiden name. My mother's family had come from County Clare, Ireland and I wasn't exactly sure if that was close to where we were now in Shannon. It couldn't hurt to ask, right? The bartender's face lit up with excitement as he told me that the Lollis Clan was not far from where we presently were in Shannon.

I wouldn't be surprised in the least if that bartender offered the same response to the 75 other soldiers who asked the very same question about their Irish last names. He sold it well. I'm sure it helped the tips!

From Ireland, we loaded back on the plane and flew another several hours to Turkey. We landed at an air base in Incirlik where the same drill was repeated. It was very hot in Turkey, but it was also one of the most beautiful places I'd ever seen. Incirlik was not your usual, bland air base with rows and rows of white buildings. Incirlik had color and character to it. There were housing units all over of different sizes and different colors. We counted several swimming pools and palm trees lined the streets. There were perfectly manicured lawns, and airmen and airwomen everywhere with great tans and smiles on their faces. By the weather and what we were seeing, it was like we were in California!

Our stay in Incirlik only lasted a few hours and then it was back on the busses and onto the plane. From Incirlik, we began our in-air trek to Manas, Krzygistan. This country was a former Soviet Republic and still showed the effects of it; the Krzygi soldiers still wore Soviet style uniforms; the runway was still plagued with old hammers and sickles that hadn't completely faded out yet; and the transport busses and Krzgyi airplanes still had the blue hammer and sickle on them from the Soviet state airline Aeroflot. Bob and I, both passionate about history, got a real kick out of this antiquated place and couldn't help but think we had taken a time machine back to 1985.

In Manas, things became serious. Our command had us meet in a formation and then all soldiers were divided into serials, or groups, for the flight out to Afghanistan by C-130 early the next morning. There were three serials in total. I was assigned to serial number two and Bob was right there with me.

I remember that night was the first time they issued us a full combat load. What this means is that you are issued your full supply of magazines (or ammunition). This was ten thirty-round magazines of 5.56 ammunition for our M-16s and additional magazines for our M-9 pistols. The games were over, and this was the real thing. We slept on metal bunks in tents that night. I remember it was very quiet and most of us didn't sleep all that much. Again, nobody knew where we were going in Afghanistan, what we were going to do when we got there, or how long we were going to be gone for. The unknown was the hardest part.

The next morning, we were woken up long before sunrise. We were given a short amount of time to get cleaned up, put on our gear, and then load onto Aeroflot busses by serials. We didn't even have breakfast. When we rode out to the flight line, I remember seeing a C-130 for the first time. A C-130 is a very common propeller-driven cargo plane used by the Air Force. It is a work horse for the military and has been for several decades. C-130s are fairly large and this one seated about 40 of us. When the engines crank up on this style of bird, it becomes very loud and it is difficult to hear. When the plane finally levels off at flying altitude, it doesn't get any quieter. This is not a civilian jet, either. You will feel every air pocket, roll, and shimmy on a C-130.

I can't remember anyone trying to speak as the silence continued on this flight. Everyone was fully loaded down with sixty pounds of gear of brand-new combat loads and we were all strapped into our seats. C-130 seats are nothing more than cargo nets with seatbelts, just so you know. For most of us, we had spent our entire military careers in training, and this was our first experience at doing any of this Army stuff for real. As I looked around I saw a lot of nervous faces, but I remember clearly seeing SSG Scofield's face. He was as calm as could be and was spitting Copenhagen into an empty water bottle. He wasn't phased in the least.

Our plane touched down after about an hour-and-a-half. When the Air Force crew dropped the back door of the cargo plane, we all felt an extreme rush of heat and dust. It hit us. It hit us hard. The heat and dust greeted us inside the plane with the rudest of greetings. We all stood up quickly and filed off the plane in a hurry. At that time, it was roughly seven in the morning in Afghanistan, but it was already in the upper 90s and it was a choking, dry heat. When I looked around the tarmac, outside of the plane, I saw that we were on top of a mountain ridge, around 10,000 feet into the Hindu Kush mountains to be exact. I'd never seen such a view like this one before and it was really something special seeing mountains all around for the first time. As we shuffled down the loading ramp from the C-130 and down the tarmac, the heat, the dust, and the smell of burning garbage blasted me in the face for the first time. A voice in my head said, "Oh man, what have you gotten yourself into?"

The first serial was waiting for us in a holding area. They had already dropped their gear, were sweating, and were drinking from bottles of water with labels written in Arabic and Russian on them. We joined them, neatly stacking our gear, and grabbing our own bottles of water from the boxes on a pallet nearby the holding area. Everyone was full of excitement and the silence was broken as we all realized that we were at Bagram Air Base.

We weren't there for more than a half hour when the third serial arrived on the tarmac. At this early stage in the tour, we heard everything on the flight line. Our brains had not yet adapted to silencing out the noise of propellers and jet engines humming twenty-four hours per day and seven days a week. The flight line at Bagram in those days was as busy as any major airport in the States. Over time, we'd learn how to drown out the sounds of fixed-wing-aircrafts and of helicopters. In the beginning, though, it was very exciting and inundating to see all this equipment for the first time!

After we assisted with the third serial drop's gear, our First Sergeant put the company into a formation and we marched off to breakfast. Yes, we were doing formations and marching because we didn't know better yet. As we marched down the road, I couldn't believe my eyes at the high number of international troops on this air base! During just the walk to the chow hall, I saw soldiers from France, New Zealand, the United Kingdom, and Egypt. It was the same way when we entered the dining facility. When we were sitting at the table, we heard several different languages spoken all at once. Bob Allen loudly exclaimed at our table, "Do you know where we're at? This isn't Bagram. This is the Mos Eisley Cantina on Tatooine in Star Wars!" He wasn't too far off.

Most of us ate very little that morning and played it safe. It can be dangerous to your system when you're in transit for a long period of time to then eat too much. It can make you really sick and put you and your intestines in a miserably bad way. After breakfast we had to arrange into another formation and we marched back to the in-processing area. As we marched, all of the other soldiers on the sides of the road were giving us strange looks like, "What the hell are they doing?"

While back at the in-processing area and while waiting to receive our briefing, several troops started becoming ill. Their bodies were working hard to adjust to the elevation amongst balancing other factors such as heat, travel, and the food most recently consumed. I was one of the lucky ones where it didn't get to me.

The in-processing briefing was held in a large wooden hut with a concrete pad as a floor. A senior Air Force NCO was the one that conducted the briefing. He was of average height, a touch overweight, and had thick glasses on. His hair was a graying spiked up flat top and I was certain that he had landed this good of a job because of his seniority in service. His briefing mostly dealt with rules of engagement, snake and animal concerns, and all around what to do and what not to do while being in the country. We were all pouring sweat in this wooden room as none of us were used to the high temps. The Air Force NCO conducting the briefing looked as fresh as a daisy. We would get there too, eventually, but not the first day!

At the conclusion of the in-processing briefing, we broke out into platoons. Our platoon sergeants received information on where we were going to stay while on post. By this time, the Air Force had brought over the pallets containing our duffel bags and gear from the C-130s. They also provided some of the two-ton trucks that we had loaded with our duffel bags. This was all done per each platoon and each platoon sergeant had already been given information as to where the trucks were to be going while on post.

By this point, our command had been informed by the Air Force that formations and large group movements out in the open were forbidden on Bagram. They put it simply when they said, "The enemy is always watching and likes to hit us with mortars from time to time. Don't give them a good target." Our command took heed and our formations ceased.

We MPs split up into small groups and headed toward the temporary housing. Our platoon sergeant, SFC Fielding, had relayed to us this information and from there it was our job to figure out how we were going to get there. We did our best to follow the trucks, but it wasn't easy, especially while trying to navigate through the large rocks that made up the ground of the airbase. Many ankles were rolled on those giant rocks! As that first day went on, it just kept getting hotter and hotter. I would learn, later on, that northern Afghanistan was in the midst of a seven-year drought. There was very little vegetation anywhere and it would climb to about 120 degrees during the day that summer.

When we finally arrived at our new transit tents, we all pretty much maintained the same layout as we did back at McCoy. We arranged our cots in the same fashion, Bob was right next to me and Garretson was on the other side. The Army Command on the base gave our company and battalion staff two weeks to "acclimate" to the heat, but I think the post command was really trying to figure out what they were going to do, exactly, with a headquarters company and its battalion staff.

Over those two weeks we did our best to get used to our new living situation. We acclimated ourselves to the heat, the food (which was very good), and learned the nuances of our dwellings such as the location of important places like the chow halls, the post office, and the post exchange (PX). We hadn't spent too long in the transit tents, though. We moved to our permanent tents that sent us all the way across the airfield and closer to the in-processing building.

During the first few days in country, there was another very funny SSG Rivas incident that took place. Bob, Ryan Suthard, and I decided one afternoon that we were going to walk to the PX. The PX wasn't far from where we were staying in the transit tents, but the layout of the tent cities could get you lost very quickly if you didn't pay close attention. We didn't quite know where we were going, but we were determined to figure it out. As we were walking toward the PX, we happened to bump into SSG Rivas. He asked us in his Kermit the Frog style voice if we knew where the PX was. We told him we thought so, and that was the same place where we were headed. We told him he was more than welcome to come with us, but he declined our invitation. We then parted ways and moved along. Bob, Ryan, and I did some exploring and then ended up at the PX where we found the barbershop, a coffee shop, and the larger PX building.

While walking around we saw German troops, Italian troops, British troops, UAE troops, Egyptian troops, Thai troops, South Korean troops, Canadian troops, French troops, and many others. It was mind blowing! About two hours later, we made our trek back to our transit tent. The three of us ran into SSG Rivas again who had obviously gotten lost. His skin was burned red and he looked like hell. He asked us, like we'd never talked before, "Excuse me soldiers, could you tell me how to get to the PX?"

I answered respectfully, "Yes, Sergeant. We just came back from there. If you stay on this road and turn left, you will run into a bunch of buildings. The large one is the PX."

He looked confused, so I gave him the instructions again and then, in desperation, he responded with, "Excuse me, but would you happen to have any water?" We shared what water we had with him and we were worried about him. It didn't stop us from immediately laughing at him when he walked away.

In those first two weeks, we did get acclimated to our environment. We learned where important places were, we learned where not to go, we learned where the phones were, and we were getting used to our surroundings. We were quickly adapting to this new place and starting to fit in. One of the first things we learned was that not everybody wore floppy hats and the people that did certainly did not wear the drawstring under their chin. This was another thing that was earning us strange stares while on the street. Most of the soldiers in our company dropped the floppy hats and went to a standard patrol cap. I dug the floppy hat and continued wearing it for the rest of the tour.

These first two weeks did not go without unusual incidents, however. The first full morning we were in Bagram, Bob and I headed to the shower tent. There were a couple of options as to where you could shower, but this was the only one we knew of at the time. When we stepped in, there was a changing area with hooks and shelves where you left your gear. Then there was another area where there were makeshift sinks and mirrors. The showers themselves were off to the back. Bob and I stripped down to our towels and shower shoes and started heading toward the showers. There was a line and in that line were fat, hairy, foreign soldiers. To this day I have no idea what language they were speaking, but these guys were all huge, fat, and had hair over every centimeter of their bodies. If the Wolfman was real, these men were Wolfmen.

They were also talking as loudly and as obnoxiously as they could and were taking ridiculously long showers. After about a 15-minute wait, we were finally able to score stalls. I'll never forget when Bob and I went to the sinks afterwards to shave and brush our teeth. These guys were standing around naked in the changing area conversing in whatever language they were speaking. They glanced over at us a few times as we were brushing our teeth and shaving. As soon as I finished the last swipe with the razor with the naked men still standing there, Bob said to me, "Let's get the hell out of here. I think they're taking a liking to us." I agreed and we quickly dressed and got the hell out of there. The fat, super tall, hairy men were still standing there naked as we walked out. Neither one of us ever went to that shower tent again!

It was around this time that I started smoking. I had been chewing snuff and long leaf tobacco already for a few months and I wanted to quit. I remembered a few years before this, I had tried to smoke a cigarette and I got sick to my stomach from it. I figured I'd get sick again if I smoked a cigarette and maybe that would make me not want to touch tobacco anymore. I know, I know. It was a weird thought process and stems from a very weird place. I bummed a Marlboro Menthol Light from one of our MPs. That one cigarette started a love affair with smoking that lasted, on and off, for the next 12 years! What was I thinking?

Another issue we had to deal with during this time were mortar and rocket attacks. Just about every night after we had landed in Bagram, there were rockets fired at the airbase. Sometimes there was contact and other times there was not. At first it was a scary experience, but after a while we were used to it and it just became a regular thing.

Throughout the whole airbase there were large concrete bunkers with sandbags placed on them sporadically placed. You could easily find a spot in one of these bunkers during the rocket attacks and take cover. During one of these attacks, it just so happened to be Bob's 22nd birthday. While crammed for a few hours into one of these bunkers along with a bunch of other soldiers, rockets flew overhead and landed in various places on the base, we managed to take some time to recognize Bob's birthday.

Someone had a cupcake and passed it down. I then took the cigarette out of my mouth and stuck it in the cupcake with the lit end up. I passed it over to Bob and we sang him happy birthday. He had a goofy grin on his face that night as he blew out the lit cigarette and then ate the cupcake. Every year after this when I'd contact him for his birthday, I'd ask him if he'd feel more at home if I caused some loud explosions!

CHAPTER 15

WELCOME TO THE BEAST

This was a strange period of time in that tour because we were in country, we were a part of what was going on, but we had yet to have been assigned jobs. That ended very quickly as the functions of our company and our battalion got put to work. The cooks got put to work at the aviation chow hall, our finance people got sent to headquarters finance, our admin people landed jobs all over the post, our computer specialists landed jobs, our construction workers got tasked out, and our mechanics found work at the motor pool. Slowly but surely each military MOS found themselves doing their jobs. For us MPs, we would get the experience of a lifetime as we made our way to The Beast for the first time. The Beast was the nickname Bob Allen and I gave to the Bagram Theater Internment Facility (BTIF.) This nickname came from a combination of the two things. The first was a movie by the same name that had come out about a Soviet tank in Afghanistan and the other was from a detainee, who spoke perfect English, who told us once that he had, "been in The Beast for over 3 months." We're certain he intended to say BTIF instead of beast, but the name stuck.

This was the big house jail that held all enemy detainees in the country. When detainees came to The Beast from other Regional Internment Facilities

(RIFs), they would either be released eventually or they would be condemned to Guantanamo Bay, Cuba better known as GITMO. This facility would go on to collect other nicknames such as the "Hotel California", "The Facility", or "The Shithole."

The Beast was a giant former Soviet MIG aircraft repair shop. Old machinery was still on the floor and there were shot up aircraft wings lying about and leaning up against walls. This building was never intended to be used as a jail. I did not even remotely resemble one. Part of that was on purpose, I'm sure. When you walked inside The Beast, there were some offices in the front area and a stairway that led to the upper area. Wooden doors had been fashioned and this was turned into a sally port area to control those who came in and out of the building. Once you made it through the sally port, you walked through an open area where there were some old machine rooms to the right, old machine rooms to the left, and a wall that had been chiseled out with a large storage closet exposed. This storage closet now had a refrigerator with some wooden bench seats and was used as a break room for the soldiers working there. As you continued down the hall there was a green wool Army blanket that served as the last barrier between you and the floor of the jail.

Once inside, the jail floor was just a large machine shop with plywood floors and concertina wire used as cells. There was a catwalk that had been built behind these cells where soldiers with shotguns would patrol. While on the catwalk, the soldier had a full view of the toilets and the cells. The toilets themselves were half porta-john toilets that would have to be removed and changed out twice per day. That detail was referred to as the "Brown Mile" and was by far the worst duty you could draw while working in The Beast. You were guaranteed to be splashed by human waste.

Behind the catwalk remained the last 25% of the jail's floor. There was heavy machinery bolted to the floor in great need of being cut out or removed. The catwalk contained large, heavy duty fencing that ran to the edge of the walls and isolated this part of The Beast off from the rest of the facility. A paint booth remained on one end of this isolated section of the building. It had a door that locked, and this area served as the Quick Reaction Force (QRF) area. This was where we stored all the riot gear.

Further down from the catwalk to the end of the building were giant metal doors that swung open. These were obviously in place so that aircraft could taxi their way into the building. The Army had installed heavy duty bars to keep these doors secure, but there was still space overhead where birds flew freely in and out.

Above the facility was a giant crane that had long been disassembled and deactivated. The rails for the crane still remained and the roof of the building contained its original steel beams and structure.

The materials used to build this large facility were of a traditional Soviet style. The floor was a polished terrazzo-finish over concrete. This was a Soviet trait in shops and factories built in the 1950s and 1960s so that the floor could be easily cleaned of oil and chemicals. The walls of the building were solidly poured concrete that had been painted over. I never asked, but I'm sure the paint was lead.

The upstairs I was referring to was a section taking up about 1/8th the width of the facility and two floors. The rooms upstairs were originally designed to have additional machines and offices. The machines had been removed by this point and the offices were stripped. In its place were isolation cells for detainees, offices and interrogation rooms for Military Intelligence (MI), and a room with couches and some telephones. The couch and telephone room became known as the MWR Room where both on and off duty workers of The Beast could kick back for a little while to relax. On the first floor level of the building, underneath this second floor design, were some rooms that still had machines in them and would later be made into additional isolation cells.

The Beast had an eternal smell of body odor, urine, and feces. It was repulsive and the odor was so strong that it would work its way into your clothing and the material of backpacks and briefcases. A few million cans of aerosol air freshener were used in the ten months we were there, but nothing could ever overcome that awful stench.

The building itself was not in good shape. There were holes in the roof where water would come in when it rained, there were birds that would fly in through smashed-out windows, and there were mice everywhere. One room toward the front of the jail, that was used for showers, had a hole about ten feet deep where unexploded ordinance had once landed. The live bomb had long been removed, but the hole it left in the floor remained and the hole in the roof was terribly patched.

The Beast had character. A nasty, punch in the face style of character, but nonetheless, character. We all felt at home right away.

CHAPTER 16

RED BLOODED AMERICANS

When we first reported to The Beast, there was an active duty component still running the day-to-day operations of the jail. We were there to relieve this component and take over control of the operation. When we reported the first day, the active component placed us into a makeshift classroom of peeling paint that was located towards the front of the building. The active duty company's first sergeant came in to address us. We thought our presence was going to be acknowledged and our relief about to be offered a nice welcome. Instead, we were berated and given a condescending lecture. We were just a Reserve unit. This first sergeant let us know that he and his command had put in for an extension because they didn't think a Reserve component could handle an operation like this. He let us know that he thought we were second rate and incapable of handling this duty. The first sergeant words were very inappropriate and disrespectful, especially to many of our soldiers that had experienced combat zones and detainee operations before.

The first sergeant ended his rant by saying, "Well, if you're here then that means you're red-blooded Americans, I guess. At least you have that going for you."

After these kind words from the top enlisted man of the company we were replacing, we really felt welcomed. We never saw that First Sergeant anywhere near the jail again and I'm not all too sure that he remained a First Sergeant. It wasn't until over a decade later, I learned that when our Battalion Command Sergeant Major heard about the attitude and remarks of this First Sergeant, he personally paid the man a visit at his tent. It didn't go well for that First Sergeant.

When work started, our platoon of MPs was split into two and we were put on opposite 12-hour shifts. If you were smart, you begged to get on the second shift to beat the heat. At first, I remember we used to rotate monthly and then eventually they let us pick a permanent shift. Bob, Garretson, Beal, Balderas, Rolke, and all of us that were in the same tent volunteered for the second shift. If you were an NCO, a 12-hour work shift really meant that you worked 14 to16 hours. If by chance you were to get stuck on an off-base pickup, another six to eight hours were tacked onto that shift. It wasn't uncommon for some teams to go two to three days without sleep due to the obligations of these missions. Although this job was steady and very easy compared to the hell a lot of others in the Army were going through, The Beast could take its toll on you over time. It's mission intensity alone hardened the hearts of the softest of soldiers.

Bob used to refer to Afghanistan as The Ghan. The first time I heard him say it, it stuck. For the next 15 years, that is what we called it. In the coming months, the greatest friendships of my life would be forged and some of my life's best experiences would be had. The Beast was where young men became men and sweet, young women would become tough and hardened. You had no choice but to do your job and put your emotions and thoughts aside. If you didn't do your job well, you would let others around you down. We couldn't afford to let each other down.

CHAPTER 17

HELICOPTERS

Our company formally took over command of The Beast in late June, 2003. During this tour and as time went on, we quickly fell into a routine or as close to a routine as possible. When the active duty component left, there was a contingent of MPs from the Disciplinary Barracks that stayed back another few months to work with us. They were not friendly to us and they held elitist attitudes until they were put in check by our own NCOs. Eventually, they learned to work with us and realized that the majority of us were quite capable of handling the day-to-day operations of a jail.

The day-to-day operations of The Beast were simple. When new detainees came in, we performed something called an "in process" where we quickly allocated them into the population of the jail. When detainees went out, we would "out process" them which meant they either got released to their home area or they would be condemned to GITMO. Everything in a jail is a routine. There were established meal times, established prayer times, established sleeping times, established recreation times, and there were established rules. In those days, detainees were not allowed to talk, look around, or touch anyone or anything. It was that simple. Violations of those rules could lead to punishment like being taken out of the general population and put into isolation.

Detainees were fed boxed food for two meals a day and they were given one hot meal at lunch time. The food that they were given was very similar to the meals we ate in MREs. These meals were "Halal", however, which means they met Muslim standards. One of the odd things the detainees would do is that they would take their water bottles and smash all the food up and then eat it in smaller pieces. When I asked about this, the more experienced soldiers claimed they did this because the detainees' teeth were so poor that they couldn't chew large chunks of food.

Showers were given twice a week per cell, haircuts were given once a week, doctor visits were mandatory, and sometimes interrogations could take place overnight instead of just during the day. Interrogations were not what you see on TV and not what you read in newspapers or magazines. I know because I was present for hundreds of them.

When it was time for an interrogation, a detainee was brought from his cell. Placed on his head were blacked-out safety glasses. His legs would be shackled with leg irons. His hands would be cuffed and shackled. Two of us would take the detainee to the designated interrogation area and at least one of us would have to stay in the room while the interrogation took place. In the hundreds of interrogation sessions that I was present for while in those rooms, never once did I see a detainee physically harmed, verbally abused, or even touched by an interrogator.

Countless times, we would bring the detainee in, remove the blinders, sit him down in a chair across a table from where the interrogator and interpreter already sat, and then the interrogator would ask us to take the short cuffs off of the detainee. The interrogator would then give us a nod and we would sit in a chair in the corner as security.

Almost every interrogation was the same. The interrogator, the interpreter, and the detainee would smoke cigarettes and talk about what needed to be talked about. Sometimes interrogations would go on for hours and we'd have to swap out guards, other times they could be ended in as quickly as five minutes. When the interrogator announced the session was over, we'd call our partner back, and then we'd hook the cuffs back on the detainee and return him to his cell.

What I heard in those interrogations will never leave my mouth. I was sworn to secrecy by an oath I took, and I will never violate that oath. What I will tell you, however, was that in our jail were murderers, rapists, serial killers, foreign-trained terrorists, homegrown terrorists, jihadists, opportunists, gangsters, pedophiles, butcherers of aid workers, and men who had personally been responsible for or took part in the killing of Americans. The detainees in our care were dangerous people on the outside. They also had all the time in the world to figure out how to be dangerous on the inside. The only way we could make sure they didn't hurt us was to always stay alert and to keep everything controlled.

When the MPs from the Disciplinary Barracks rotated out in mid-September, there was a time gap before a new group came in. We were shorthanded staff at this point. I remember everybody being a bit strung out in handling the increased workload. We were working longer hours, our company had required training during the day, and we also had to conduct transportation missions. It was a bit rough and was the toughest stretch of the tour.

Transportation missions were a thorn in our side while being on the night shift. Most missions took place during the daytime and all were done by helicopter. Blackhawk and Chinook helicopters were what we flew in. These helicopters already had daily assigned routes, or "ring routes" as they were known. We would piggy-back on these helicopters and either take in detainees or drop them off at certain points on this already established route. Sometimes there were designated helicopter missions or fixed-wing aircraft missions, but those were very rare.

These ring-route missions were a certain six to eight hours of our time, at the very least. Our company did not have the qualified manpower to conduct these missions without bringing in off-shift MPs. I was a night-shift MP and we would often be sent out on the missions during the times when we should have been sleeping. By the time the mission was over, we'd be lucky if we could catch one hour of sleep before we had to be back at The Beast again for work. It really beat you up. Sometimes, we could end up on these missions two or three days in a row.

I remember clearly my very first helicopter mission. Our staff had only taken over the duties of The Beast days before. Bob Allen and I were both assigned to the first shift for the month of July. I had not been promoted to sergeant yet, so Bob and I were working on the same team under the supervision of Sergeant John Wiley. During our shift that hot July day, SGT Wiley let us know that we were going to be going on a helicopter mission that evening and that we should use what breaks we got during our shift to gather our gear and make sure that we were ready.

Bob and I did just that. We went back to our tent, grabbed our body armor, kevlar helmets, web gear, full combat loads, day packs, and; most importantly, we grabbed our weapon cleaning kits. During our break periods that evening, we cleaned our weapons in the arms room, double checked all our gear, and got ourselves ready for our very first mission later that night.

When our shift ended at 7pm local time, SGT Wiley went with us to the chow hall where we ate lightly and then reported back to The Beast to assemble for our assignment. We never ate heavily before a mission, it could prove disastrous on a rough ride. Bob, John, and I put all of our gear on and then we went to the QRF room in the back of the jail where we met up with another team consisting of Eddie Balderas, Jake Warner, and Staff Sergeant Pace. SSG Pace was a total badass female soldier who was a Chicago Police officer in the civilian world. I respected and admired her a great deal. She was a good NCO and we always got along very well.

The six of us waited in the QRF room for a few hours that night until we were finally told that we would be boarding a Chinook helicopter for a direct mission for a pickup. This was rare, for direct missions did not happen often. Looking back on it, we must have been picking up some high-value targets who had recently been captured. Because we were new, we didn't understand how rare this was. Usually helicopter missions took place during the day and meant that we would be stuck on an entire ring route for several hours. This was a special deal, but we were too green to realize it at the time.

Our two teams walked, in full gear, down to the flight line where we boarded a waiting CH-47 or Chinook helicopter. It was a hot night. As we approached the helicopter, the smell of fuel blasted our nostrils and the deafening sound of rotors at full speed swept away any chance at conversation. I was scared.

I'd never done anything like this and this was for real. I can remember tapping the rosary I had in my left breast pocket, under my body armor, resting over my heart. As we climbed aboard the Chinook, we took seats on the benches off to the sides and strapped ourselves in. Both teams made sure our rifles stayed pointed to the floor, a requirement for aircraft flight in theater. I recall there was a great deal of gear strapped down in the middle of the helicopter, but it was dark and I couldn't see exactly what it was.

I knew nothing of this mission. I didn't know where we were going, what we were going to do, or how long it would take. I didn't know a thing. Someone knew, maybe one of the NCOs, but not any of the rest of us who were junior enlisted. As the Chinook lifted off of the flight line, we were tossed and rolled a bit as it moved into elevation. This was our first helicopter flight and it was rough and it was a learning experience for us. The crew chief, who was free to move around but strapped to a line on the ceiling of the helicopter, cracked open the back door halfway and we suddenly had fresh air flowing throughout helicopter. This simple act of bringing fresh air into the helicopter helped calm my nerves a great deal.

Bob and I never said a word to each other on this trip. Nobody did. In the air was the dead silence of fear, seriousness, adrenaline, and excitement mixed in. Anyone who has ever experienced it knows the feeling. If you're not careful, you can long for that feeling, and then if you're really not careful, you can get addicted to that feeling.

While cruising on our way to our LZ, I nudged Bob as we saw Apache helicopters ripping in and out of the sky behind us. Our open door gave a perfect view of the graceful killing machines bouncing around in the night sky stalking down any potential threats. In what seemed like days, but was really hours, we felt our helicopter begin to drop. Eventually we felt the wheels touch down and the back gate open up all the way. The crew chief and another soldier aboard the helicopter began pushing off the gear previously strapped to the floor of the Chinook. As this was going on, SGT Wiley had given Bob and I a nod. We removed our safety belts and we shuffled, quickly, to the rear of the helicopter. SSG Pace's team did the same.

As we came out of the rear of the CH-47, we saw a couple of pickup trucks with their head lights turned off, but their engines still running. Bob and I, instinctively, spread out a few meters and took up fighting positions, pulling security to the sides of the helicopter. Two members of our other team did the same thing on the other side of the helicopter. As Bob and I scanned the perimeter, we saw nothing but darkness and Afghan dust everywhere from our propeller blades. We were on a mountain, somewhere, and it was a beautiful night, but we didn't have time to enjoy it. We had a job to do. Our job was to kill anything that would threaten our mission. Our Apache escorts were swooping in and out, making it known to anyone or anything that they would rain hell upon them if any harm came our way. It was an impressive sight watching them as they cut through the air and defied gravity.

SGT Wiley and SSG Pace met the bearded men in woodland uniforms at the pickup trucks. These men were American Special Forces soldiers and they unloaded six captured enemy combatants off the backs of the trucks. With a nod and a hand motion from SGT Wiley, Bob and I peeled off security along with the two others from the other team. There was no sense using verbal commands, the engines of the helicopter were so loud we wouldn't have been able to hear anyway.

Bob and I quickly grabbed our share of the detainees and brought them on the Chinook. We changed out the zip ties on the detainees' wrists with handcuffs, slapped shackles around their ankles, and then strapped the detainees into their seats. Our other team did the same with their detainees. As SGT Wiley and SSG Pace came trotting back onto the helicopter, the gate returned slowly back to its half-closed position. We watched as the Special Forces soldiers grabbed their unloaded supplies as our Chinook elevated itself back into the dark Afghan night.

Once in the air, SGT Wiley and SSG Pace took their seats back and we began the journey back to The Beast. After a few hours of further silence, our helicopter touched down back on Bagram's airfield. Once the wheels were secured back on the tarmac, the back gate lowered all the way down. Waiting on the flight line already were trucks to bring our detainees back to The Beast for processing.

Our two teams hopped on the trucks and escorted our charge back to the jail. Once the detainees were inside, the night shift took over and Bob and I were relieved of our duties. We stepped outside The Beast, jacked up with adrenaline and relief. We lit cigarettes and talked about what had happened. This was our first mission, but it was only one of dozens more to come. This one was easy, although we didn't know it at the time. Much more difficult missions, and the stress they came with, were in our futures.

John Wiley, Eddie Balderas, and I once were on missions for three days in a row. Over the course of 72 hours, we only got about two-and-a-half hours of sleep each. Sometimes, these missions were complex. They weren't a simple land then hand-off either. Sometimes, you had to wait or travel to the destination. Sometimes, the detainees weren't detainees yet either and didn't willingly want to go.

John Wiley used to always say that these missions would put "hair on your face."

I was puzzled by this and once asked, "SGT Wiley isn't it supposed to be hair on your chest, you know, like make you a man?"

He shook his head no and responded, "No. It's hair on your face because there's no damn time to shave!"

Bob Allen lived for these missions and he would volunteer for as many of them as he could. In turn, that meant I had to volunteer too because Bob and I stuck together. I don't know how many of these in total we did together in that first tour, but it was well over two dozen. That number doesn't include the missions we did away from each other while on other teams.

Months into our tour, our company smartened up. SSG Scofield was placed in charge of these missions. This helped us out greatly because this meant that our NCOs were no longer getting burned out by these missions. An NCO had to go on each one of these three-man teams and the NCO would be responsible to sit in on the flight briefing and security briefing pre-flight. There were only so many NCOs and they were overwhelmed with these missions. Once SSG Scofield took over, it really made things a lot easier. He was made for that job, too. He handled it like a true professional.

CHAPTER 18

THE FIRE

By September, 2003, our company was making a lot of changes to The Beast. We had an R&U (Repair and Utilities) platoon in our company with skilled men and women in the trades. Our command put them to work along with Army engineers and other elements from around the post in order to upgrade, repair, and build things in the jail.

One of the first things they did was cut out all the old machinery from off the floor. Then they cut out what was left in the vacant rooms. This was hard, tedious work, and SSG Garcia and his staff made it look easy. I had known Ron Garcia since I had first come into the unit. He was in his late 30s at this point, he was about 5 feet 8 inches with a naturally muscular build, and he was a go-to man for anything. SSG Garcia was very nice to me since the first day and we always got along well. When I became an NCO, I tried to model myself after him as someone that really cared about and took care of his soldiers.

The second thing that R&U started doing was building new cells. Not only were they building wooden isolation cells, but they were pouring concrete pads with plumbing for additional large, general population cells on the floor of The Beast. This was not easy work, but they were doing it, and they were doing it very well.

R&U also focused on improving the security situation of The Beast. They built new doors, new door frames to go with the doors, and they built a whole new arms room. They also built several new offices in the old, corroded Soviet rooms. It was very impressive what they were able to accomplish in those ten months.

On a Sunday afternoon, an Army engineer platoon was in The Beast working with our R&U. They were using oxygen-acetylene torches to cut out old duct work in an abandoned room in the jail. I'm not exactly sure what went wrong, but within a few minutes the floor of The Beast had turned black with smoke.

It was difficult to see, it was difficult to breathe, but we had a job to do. We had to evacuate the general population and isolation cells and bring all the detainees out into the recreation yard. There was no panic, but there was definitely a sense of urgency. We cuffed and shackled up detainees as quickly as we could and began moving them to the outdoor rec area.

An operations E-7 at this time named SFC O'Neill was not a man many of us liked. He was a massive, intimidating man who had a powerlifter build. O'Neill was about 6 feet 2 inches tall and probably weighed 240lbs. HE was an active duty 95C and had come from Ft. Leavenworth to be a subject matter expert at the jail. O'Neill spent most of his time inspecting our logbooks, checking our cell blocks, and making constant corrections. He was a quiet man and was not friendly in the least. He was the boss, he knew it, and he liked to show his authority when given the opportunity. We dreaded his presence and we avoided him like the plague. You knew that if he stopped you, it was not going to be anything positive.

When this fire started, SFC O'Neill was the first one out of the admin offices to rush out onto the floor. Not only did he help us cuff and shackle detainees, he also started carrying detainees out of the building on his shoulders two at a time. If they were small enough, he'd carry three or four at a time. It was quite an impressive sight and also a reassuring one. Despite him being a total jerk, when it came down to it, he was not afraid to climb into the trenches with us and get to work.

While the fire continued and the smoke thickened, I was surprised to see flight crews and random soldiers running into our jail to see if they could help. We had no idea how they had gotten into The Beast and this was confusing, but there was no time to figure that out. I later learned that our MP who had been working the sally port of the jail had abandoned her post when the fire started. She left the front door to The Beast wide-open and ran back to her tent.

Signaled by smoke billowing out the front of the jail, the flight crews and other soldiers will always be admired for their willingness and courage to run in to help. Despite this, they should have never been able to set foot into the jail. It was a secured facility and their eyes should not have seen what went on in there.

All the detainees were out of The Beast and we took a head count. The First Sergeant had taken over the scene. First Sergeant Cooper was probably in his early 50s at the time and he had spent over 30 years in the Army on active duty and as a reservist. He had been an MP his entire career and, on his chest, he wore airborne and air assault tabs and a drill sergeant's patch. First Sergeant Cooper was no-nonsense, all business, and he had whipped our company into shape in a hurry to prepare for the deployment. All of us had a great deal of respect for him and he set the example for all to strive and be like him.

First Sergeant Cooper had alerted the rest of our company, armed them, and had total control over the recreation yard. When Cooper asked for volunteers to go back into the facility to do a final clearing; Bob Allen, Ivan Beal, Eddie Balderas, and I volunteered to head back in.

When we re-entered the building, the smoke was so thick that we could barely see in front of our eyes. At a hurried pace, we checked all the cells on the first floor and then cleared the second floor. When we were coming down the stairwell back to the first floor, Eddie Balderas passed out. Ivan Beal picked Eddie up and threw him over his shoulder. We then stacked ourselves into a straight line, held onto each other's shoulders, and moved out into the rec yard where there was fresh air. There Eddie received aid from our medical staff and right away he came to.

Fire trucks and teams arrived from the post and snuffed out the fire. Within an hour, we began the process of moving all the detainees back into the jail and returned to our work positions. I will never forget the actions of SFC O'Neill or 1SG Cooper that day. They both really took over and made things happen.

Also, I'll never forget the bravery of my friends to head back into that smoke-filled building to clear it. My hat goes off to Bob, Eddie, and Ivan.

CHAPTER 19

A PUNCH BELOW THE BELT

In the fall of 2003, military police platoons from the 805th MP Company out of North Carolina began rotating in and out of The Beast. There were just not enough MP's needed to handle the daily duties of our jail between my company and our battalion staff. Since we had relieved the former component that was previously in place, the number of detainees had tripled. Several large operations had taken place throughout the country and into our custody were their captured enemy combatants. We needed more MPs in the facility, and the 805th started rotating platoons in and out to assist us.

The 805th was a line company and they had been assigned to gate duty and tower / perimeter duty on the air base. This company had been in Bagram for just about as long as we had, maybe arriving only a month or so later, and we welcomed them into The Beast with open arms. Even though we had only been in country for a few months, our MPs working the jail were tired and worn down already.

I first met SSG Mowris from this other company, and his two squads of soldiers, when they showed up on our second shift one evening to be trained. He was about 5 feet 10 inches tall, but he was a powerfully built man that looked like he could have played center at the collegiate or pro level for football. He wore his hair in a tight flap-top and he had a close-cropped mustache. Mowris looked to be in his mid-to-late 30s and I'll always remember his massive shoulders. I've seen very few men command respect by just stepping into a room as he did. There was an aura about him that he "meant business." What also helped this aura was a chest full of tabs and a 10th Mountain combat patch. He had obviously done time in Somalia. Doing time in Somalia with 10th Mountain had immediate respect from everyone who wore the uniform.

As the days went on, all of us on the overnight shift formed a bond with these soldiers from the 805th platoons. They were likeable men and women and they quickly learned the job. They merged right in with us and we became a well-oiled machine. Something positive happened during this time period too, some of the holding cells started to get a bit thinner and all of us NCOs were called into a meeting with our operations staff. We were told that we still wouldn't be able to give days off to our people, but we could put a certain number of soldiers on a Quick Reaction Force. This duty would be 24 hours duty, but it would be the closest thing to giving our people time off to get some much-needed rest.

This job would consist of the selected team being in the old paint room with the riot gear. The duties for this team would consist of vehicle transfers if needed and we were also responsible to haul the toilets out twice each day, better known as the Brown Mile. Outside of that, the team could lie around on cots and sleep if they wanted to. We all enthusiastically agreed and got to work quickly in creating a schedule to rotate soldiers on QRF and to assign NCOs to be with them.

It just so happened that when my QRF turn came up, Bob Allen and

Eddie Balderas were scheduled with me. Can you imagine the odds of something like that? It's almost as if I intentionally pulled my two favorite soldiers to be with me on this duty! It didn't end there either because Bob, Eddie, and I ended up becoming a permanent team.

For this particular 24-hour duty, it just so happened that SSG Mowris and two of his team members were assigned to the duty with us. All six of us sat in this walled off room for 24 hours talking and getting to know each other. Soldiers really get to bond with each other well when they haul out toilets that are filled to the brim. There's nothing like a splash of fecal matter to bring soldiers together!

I remember getting to better know SSG Morris during this 24-hour duty. He talked about his wife and children and how he had been in every single combat zone since Panama in the late 1980s. It all came together here why this man walked the way he walked, talked the way he talked, and why his mere presence made you want to fall in line behind him and follow him. He never bragged or gloated, he just told us his story. He was an impressive man who had had an impressive career. My respect level for him was as high as could be. This was reinforced when he, as an E-6, was pushing toilets with the rest of us who were beneath him in rank. He could have sat by and watched us work, as many would do, but he never shied away from these menial tasks.

When I think about that 24-hour shift, I remember Bob Allen and SSG Mowris talking the most. I remember them raving about the movie Hamburger Hill and, somehow, someone came up with the DVD and the two of them watched it together. They talked at length for hours and hours and developed a respectful bond with each other.

After that 24-hour shift together, SSG Mowris and his squads started having breakfast with us every day after work. They'd also meet up with us at the chow hall for dinner before shift. We really liked them, and they really liked us, and we all worked well together.

This carried on for about three months. SSG Mowris and his squads were sent back to doing their previous duties and were replaced by other squads in the jail. We would still run into them around the air base, on the flight line a couple times, and while just being out and about. When we'd see each other it'd always be handshakes with smiles, movie quotes, and whatever rumors were going around at the time.

The last time Bob Allen and I saw SSG Mowris was in late January outside of the PX. It was a brutally cold morning and Bob and I were walking out of the store after loading up on cigarettes. We stopped and chatted with SSG Mowris and the guys from his squad. He told us that they were being moved out to another area to run some patrols. He wasn't sure as to how long they'd be gone, but he expected to be back in rotation at the jail at some point. We looked forward to it, we all shook hands, and then we went on our way.

Two days later, Eddie Balderas and I were dead asleep in the jail's MWR room. Along with Bob, we had just returned from a ring route mission on a Blackhawk with only about an hour before our next shift started. We hadn't slept at all in well over 24 hours and were desperate. Eddie and I decided to head straight to the jail, store our gear, and try to catch a few minutes of sleep before our next shift. Bob was hungry and headed to the chow hall, promising to bring us back some food. Only moments later, Eddie and I were roused awake by Bob who was very upset. I never saw Bob this upset before or like this ever again. Bob shared with us that SSG Mowris, along with several others, had been killed earlier that day in an explosion in Ghazni.

I felt as if someone had punched me below the belt. The three of us sat looking at each other in stunned silence. It was hard to believe that someone that had been through so much hell in previous combat zones, and for as long as SSG Mowris did, could fall this way.

SSG Mowris' death haunted Bob Allen for the rest of his life. He never got over it. One of his heroes in life was taken at the age of 37. Over the years and with the hundreds of beers we had together, SSG Mowris' name would always come up. That punch below the belt feeling would return. Every year on January 29, Bob would call me. We'd talk about that horrible day and we'd talk about SSG Mowris.

He was one of a kind and a horrible loss. To this day I can't watch the movie Hamburger Hill.

CHAPTER 20

ADDITIONAL HELP ARRIVES

Even though the 805th was rotating platoons in to help us, we were still hurting on total numbers to handle our operation. Operations picked back up again, we were receiving higher numbers of detainees, and we became overwhelmed. In October, a group of three volunteers from a Minnesota Reserve unit came into The Beast to supplement us. I can't remember their names, but their faces stand out in my mind. There was a tall, young kid fresh out of basic training that looked exactly like Squiggy from Laverne & Shirley (without the pompadour.) I appropriately nicknamed him Squiggy. Bob liked that nickname and that's all we ever called the kid until the day he rotated out. Squiggy was a happy, go lucky kind of guy that always had a massive wad of chew in his jaw. He didn't chew snuff, but old school Red Man. Squiggy was a cool kid and he became a member of our breakfast club too. Eating together was a very important thing for us and breakfast was like our dinner due to working the overnight shift.

We also really liked this group's staff sergeant. This staff sergeant was a police officer on the civilian side and he was a good, fair NCO. He wore a patch on his right shoulder because he had served in the First Gulf War. He was knowledgeable and experienced. It was smooth sailing when he split the role of sergeant of the guard on overnights with one of our own company's staff sergeants.

The third guy amongst these volunteers was a specialist who was also a civilian police officer. I remember specifically how he was a police officer in Minneapolis and that he had worked in a really bad area dealing with the Hmung and Somalis. He had some great stories. I remember that he too was a good, solid soldier and fit right in with us. I think he and Ivan Beal went on to become pretty good friends and they'd go to the gym together. Ivan kept in touch with him long after the tour ended.

Our company started running range qualifications during this time too. I remember on one of these range days we loaded up early in the morning right after our shift got off and drove the half hour or so to the secured German range outside of the post. We were seated in the back of covered two-and-a half ton trucks. I slept on the way there. When we got to the range we unloaded, qualified, and then many hours later we loaded back up and returned to Bagram.

There was a female soldier with us in the MPs back then that most of us absolutely despised. She did everything half assed, and she would screw over anyone to get her way. Fortunately, I didn't see her often while overseas because she was on another shift, but she was just a walking disaster and a WGM. WGM in those days stood for Waste of Government Money. It's okay to be a soldier and to not know what you're doing, but it's not okay in refusing to learn and to willingly screw others over. Schraeder did this at every opportunity. So anyway, we're loading up the trucks after the range, I climbed up onto the back of the vehicle, and handed off my rifle. Getting on the back of a two and a half ton truck takes effort if you're not 6 feet 8 inches tall. You have to put a foot on the gate and then lift yourself up. If the soldier before you has any class, they will hand off their weapon, hold your weapon for you, and then offer you a hand as you raise yourself up. After I got onto the truck, I turned around to help up the next soldier. It was Schraeder. Schraeder was unable to pull herself into the back of this truck. She tried at least 5 times with me holding her arm and pulling her. She would slide back off the gate and onto the ground. I finally leaned over and grabbed her by her body armor and pulled her onto the truck. When she got onto the truck, she was flushed red, breathing really hard, and she was completely exhausted. She was also sweating profusely. I said to her "Schraeder, here, you've got to drink some water. You don't look good." She looked at me with a deer in the headlights look and responded, "Bhejahskfib." I couldn't understand a single word that came out of her mouth. I handed her a water and just shook my head in disgust.

When we returned back to the base, it was already later afternoon and turning into early evening. I remember unloading off the truck, completely exhausted and looking forward to bed. If I figured right, if we got back to the barracks right away, we could score about an hour of sleep before we had to be back at The Beast for work. That was when Bob and I got taps on the shoulder. Our fireteam had gotten called out on a pickup. John Wiley (who worked first shift) had already received the flight brief and mission instructions. We met up with him and headed down to the flight line. We ended up on a ring route that had a delay and we did not get back to Bagram until early evening of the next day. Bob and I had been up for roughly 72 hours straight and we had just enough time to shower and head back in to work. I tell you, stretches like that could be rough!

Bob and I kept ourselves occupied that whole mission by making fun of Schraeder, of course, and repeating "Bhejahskfib" every chance we got. It was a shit situation, but we made the most of it. John Wiley to this day is still impressed with our creativity and our ability to make fun of anyone, anywhere, anytime. I believe it was a coping skill.

Time went on like this some more and something very funny took place around November of that year. Remember SSG Rivas? Well, SSG Rivas served as an operations NCO in The Beast. He didn't work the day-to-day systems with us, but he handled phones and such with a small team. One of SSG Rivas' duties was that he would drive and pick up hot breakfast every morning at the chow hall. Josh Burket and I happened to be outside smoking cigarettes this particular morning. For the record, Josh Burket is one of my favorite people of all time. He and I entered the 327th about the same time and we were immediately good friends. He carried the same ability to make fun of anyone, anytime, anywhere and was a lot of fun to be around. While we're puffing away, Josh and I saw SSG Rivas come walking out to The Beast's parking lot. He was talking to himself and looking around strangely and going through all of his pockets. Josh and I asked him if everything was okay and if we could help him out. He responded to us in his Kermit the Frog voice that he had, "I seem to have misplaced the keys to the Humvee." Yes, you read that right. SSG Rivas lost the keys to the Humvee and was unable to drive over and get breakfast.

Burket and I watched him go back inside. A few minutes later he came out with the keys but looked even more confused than before. We once again asked him if everything was okay and he turned to us, scratching his head, and stated, "I seem to have misplaced the Humvee!"

Burket and I lost it and we immediately went back into The Beast to tell everyone on shift. Needless to say, there was no hot breakfast when the first shift came in to work a couple of hours later!

CHAPTER 21

THE HOLIDAYS

The holidays are tough on people to be away from their families overseas. I remember Thanksgiving of 2003 like it was yesterday. I woke up a few hours earlier than I normally would to get cleaned up. I then came back to the tent and woke up all of my guys in the tent. They got cleaned up and we all headed down to the chow hall together to have Thanksgiving dinner. The line at the chow hall was incredibly long. We were standing outside in that line for about two hours and the start of our shift was approaching. Bob got pretty fired up and called many people "assholes" in frustration.

Eventually, we had to leave the line and we headed into The Beast for work. We figured there would be hot food left over since the first shift would most likely wait to eat until they could go to the chow hall. Boy, were we wrong! When we got to the break room we found that all that was left was some cold ham and some MREs. We were very pissed off, but we made the best of it. Bob and I talked and laughed about that Thanksgiving meal a lot over the years.

On Christmas and New Year's Eve, the battalion staff officers, senior NCOs, and all of us junior NCOs took over all the positions and responsibilities of the second shift in The Beast. We did this so that all of the enlisted soldiers could have the night off and call their families. The time difference meant that if you called late at night local time, it was normal time back home in the States. It was a great gesture by our leadership and something our soldiers appreciated. For Christmas Eve that year I bought my tentmates cigarettes or their favorite chewing tobacco. Alan Garretson and Eddie Balderas didn't use tobacco, so I bought them iced teas and beef jerky. They really enjoyed it. Steve Dinger told me it was the best Christmas gift he ever received and Bob, if memory serves me right, thanked me and then we spent the rest of the afternoon listening to Bruce Springsteen CDs until we had to report to work.

On Christmas Day, we woke up even earlier than we had on Thanksgiving and rushed down to the chow hall. We waited in line for the hours it took; though this time, we sat down together and had a meal. I can tell you this, as a young, single soldier back then; I missed my family a lot. It was hard to be away from them over those holidays, but it also felt really good to be with my other family, too. With us all seated and our plates full, Alan Garretson asked us to join hands and we said grace. He then said a little prayer of thanks for all of us being together. Yes, even Bob held hands with us. It was a special moment and something I'll always remember. Garretjerk, that hillbilly fuck, was a classy guy and a great friend. I remember for that Christmas dinner we were all laughing and joking at the table and I think all of us really realized how special of a time it was in our lives. We were very lucky to get along so well and to be together. That was a very memorable Christmas.

I would go back to that moment in a heartbeat to have a meal with all those great people again and to hear Bob laughing and joking like that again.

CHAPTER 22

THE MIDDLE TO THE END

I think it's important to establish to you, the readers, how things worked with deployments in that time period. Afghanistan was still a pretty fresh war and was only in year three of its campaign. Iraq was brand new and was what we were originally mobilized for. The Army really went full speed into these two campaigns without any true plans or methods to the madness. Even while in Afghanistan doing our tour, we never knew how long we were going to be there for. We went day to day without knowing a thing. If someone did know, they certainly didn't share it with us. We just continued the grind each day, making it happen one day at a time, and just doing our jobs the best we could.

I don't think that morale was ever low in our unit or among the MPs, specifically. The reason I say that is that we kept complaining, laughing, and joking. Had any of us stopped any of those three things I would have said that morale was low. There's an old saying that says, "If a soldier isn't bitching then that soldier isn't happy." That is a very true statement!

Morale may not have been low, but soldiers were starting to get tired and overall fatigue was starting to set in. This was not only from the work we were doing, but just the overall time that we had been activated by then. By February,

2004, our unit had already been activated for 12 months. That's a long time for a Reserve unit. Companies were being extended 6 months at a time in the Iraq theater. Some Reserve units ended up doing 18 months in country in addition to the time they had spent at the mobilization site. We read the Stars N' Stripes frequently and had an idea of what was going on with the extensions. I don't think any of us would have been surprised had we been extended out another 6 months.

When fatigue takes place, tempers get short. Some people, myself included, started snapping a bit at normal, every day razzing from others. I remember one time I gave Ivan Beal a hard time about something, as I usually did each day, and he came right at me. I didn't back down, but I sure as hell knew I didn't have a chance if it came to blows. Thankfully, Ivan cooled off and that was the end of it. We never had a disagreement again after that.

Ryan Suthard and I also had a screaming match one time and we came chest to chest. SSG Scofield got between us before anything could happen. To be honest, I don't even recall what it was over. I do remember about a half hour after it happened, though, I stepped out of my tent to apologize to Ryan as he was stepping out of his tent to come apologize to me. It was over that quickly and he and I never got heated with each other again. These mini confrontations happened and they always happened when people got fatigued.

Bob Allen and I were a different story, though. In what would become a 15-year friendship, Bob and I never once had a disagreement, we never once got mad at each other, and we never once crossed words. That says a lot to me about our friendship and about our respect for one another.

Our unit had a senior Operations NCO vacancy for a few months at this point. Around this time in February, our new senior Operations NCO was in place. His name was SFC Orland and he was from the Disciplinary Barracks. He stood about 6 feet 4 inches tall and was about 240lbs. He was a large, intimidating man, who turned out to have one hell of a sense of humor and was someone that I respected very much as an NCO. I'll tell you why later.

Some of our senior NCOs were taking SFC Orland tent to tent one afternoon introducing him to the enlisted soldiers. I was in my tent with a couple of the other MPs getting ready for dinner. Waiting for them to finish preparing, I stepped outside to have a cigarette. For some reason, Bob was awake earlier than usual, and he got into it with another one of our tentmates while I was outside smoking. The guy's name was Shram. Shram was about 19 years old, was a whiner, and was not well-liked by any of us. He had transferred into our tent because he had been chased out of his previous tent for pissing off the occupants there. I took him in hoping he could get along better with us. I was wrong.

As I stood there trying to figure out what I was going to have to fix once back inside, MSG Holder approached me with SFC Orland. As we were talking, I heard Bob's voice from inside the tent screaming at Shram, "I'm going to come over there and beat your ass!" Next, I heard stomping followed by the sound of bodies clashing. All of this takes place, of course, while I'm talking to our new Operations NCO. MSG Holder just stood there shaking his head and doing everything he could to keep from laughing.

SFC Orland stopped mid-conversation and said to me, "SGT Drake are you going to head in there to take care of this or do I have to?"

"I'll take care of it right now, Sergeant," was my response. When I walked into the tent, I saw SGT Dinger and Rolke holding back Bob while Garretson and Balderas were holding back this kid Shram. It was obvious that Bob landed a few shots in and Shram's lip was opened up with a trickle of blood coming down his mouth. I went in there and screamed at the top of my lungs for them to knock it off and get back to their bunk areas. I also told them that our new operations NCO was outside and if he came in there would be hell to pay. The fight was over instantaneously. Imagine that!

I'm going to tell you now the reason why all of us respected SFC Orland so much. At work one night there was a situation with an unruly detainee. I was escorting the detainee to the latrine. He attacked me by throwing an elbow to my face and attempting to bite me. This detainee was no daisy either. He was a big guy with some muscle to him. He'd obviously lifted weights at some point in his life. The worst part of it all was that we were on a ramp and the force of his body against mine knocked me off my balance.

While falling, I put a waist lock on the detainee and pulled him down with me. We both crashed to the floor – the detainee on his belly and me on his back. He didn't stop fighting here either. I stayed on top of him the best I could and I immediately called for help. Bob, Alan Garretson, Ivan Beal, and Eddie Balderas ran over right away to help control the situation.

One thing that always bothered me was I remembered Jake Warner yelling from the catwalk, "SGT Drake just fucked that guy up!" The fact is that I didn't. I did a standard thing to defend myself and to neutralize the situation. I was worried about where that statement that Warner had made would go. I worried it would get sucked up into the rumor mill and spread around.

There was an immediate level of discipline for attacking a guard and this detainee received his punishment. The Sergeant of the Guard that evening, Monica Grossman, made sure that we all wrote up incident reports and she noted it in the logbook of the facility. That was the end of the situation, at least I thought it was.

I was shaken awake in the middle of the day by SSG Scofield. He told me that he had been at The Beast and there was talk that I had abused a detainee. He was pretty certain that our command was going to come at me with an Article 15 (discipline charges) when I arrived at work that evening. SSG Scofield took me outside the tent where CPT Camarda was standing. I had known CPT Camarda for a few years at this point and I had once served as his driver and his personal radio operator when he was our company commander. I respected him a great deal and he had always treated me very fairly. There was mutual respect as a boss and as an employee would have with each other after being together a while.

CPT Camarda had tipped off SSG Scofield as to what was going on. Scofield told me to get dressed. I did as SSG Scofield instructed and he took me straight down to the first sergeant's office where he respectfully asked for a meeting. Our meeting was granted and SSG Scofield spoke on my behalf to our first sergeant and explained everything. The first sergeant asked me a few questions, I answered them, and then I was told not to worry about anything. SSG Scofield told me to go back to the tent, get some sleep, and he'd pick me up later for dinner.

True to his word, a few hours later he picked me up and we walked to dinner. He told me that he knew the accusations were false and he acted as quickly as he could so that things wouldn't get out of hand. He didn't want anything bad to happen to me for doing my job and he didn't want to see my career ruined by politics. Papa Sco also told me to remember this because someday I might have to do what he did for someone else. I took what he said to heart.

When I returned to our tent, the others were all awake and they were aware of the allegations. They were as concerned as I had been. I can remember really sensing a feeling of solidarity among us. We were simply doing our jobs and people with no knowledge of what took place were trying to punish us for that.

As I headed into the break room that night at The Beast to start my shift, SFC Orland intercepted me and walked me outside. At this point, I didn't know the man well at all. I stood at parade rest as he questioned me about what had taken place the night before. I explained to him exactly what had happened. I told him about the logbook. I also told him about the reports that were filed. Orland told me that he had seen the reports. He told me that he believed me. He then told me that he had ended this investigation along with the facility OIC. Orland said to me that I was doing a good job, that I had a good reputation, that I had a bright future in the Army, and then shook my hand. I was taken aback by his confidence in me and his words really made me feel good. A senior NCO had never spoken to me with such regard before and I could tell that he really cared about his people.

Now if that wasn't enough, SFC Orland showed up at our shift change meeting, which we called guard mount, before we went on shift. He addressed the guard force and told them flat-out that I had been wrongly accused of something and that he stuck up for me and that he would stick up for anyone else if they were doing the right thing. Orland called us all out by name that were involved in the situation and told us that we had done the right things and that we had done exactly what he or any other MP would have done. It was a classy move. Years later, Bob developed a pretty good SFC Orland impression, but he also remembered that incident and spoke about him with the highest levels of respect.

March rolled around and we heard rumors of a replacement unit heading our way. There was pure elation among us all since we knew that the end was finally near. As I said, fatigue was a factor at this point and soldiers were looking forward to putting a bow on the tour. Even Bob, the man who enjoyed being a soldier more than anyone else I'd ever known, was tired and excited at the possibility of returning to "the world." As our first sergeant would say, it was time to "get off this rock!"

Soon enough, our replacements landed in country and we were issued a fly-out date. It was now our responsibility to train the new unit. Unlike those that trained us, we treated these folks with respect and went out of our way to help them. Unfortunately for Bob, Eddie Balderas, and I, we had become very efficient at running detainee showers. This was never the most glamorous job because nobody wants to look at naked men any longer than they have to. Due to our efficiency, we were assigned to spend a full week training the new unit how to handle shower operations. They struggled at first, but then got the hang of it. By the end of the week they were pros.

Eventually, our enlisted soldiers were cut loose and we NCOs stayed on for another week to help. I remember the final month was the first time that SGT

Wiley and I had worked together in several months as he had now bounced back to the night shift. We NCOs didn't do much this final week and we pretty much sat in the MWR room on call and occasionally walked The Beast checking log books and conducting counts. After that week, the NCOs were cut loose. I remember as I walked out of the front door of The Beast in those last moments, that a certain feeling came over me. It wasn't goodbye; instead it was just so long for now.

In our final week in country, our First Sergeant did something very nice. He cut the MPs loose. It was a serious sign of respect for the work we had done all along throughout the mobilization. The MPs all stuck together those final two weeks and we played a lot of beach volleyball, we slept a lot, and we caught three hot meals a day for the first time in a long time. It was a great way to end an exhausting tour. I remember laughing a lot, smiling, and joking around. It was also the first time we started talking about life after The Ghan.

CHAPTER 23

GETTING OFF THE ROCK

In April of 2004, after we MPs spent a week relaxing as the rest of the company and battalion staff packed up, we finally made our way to "get off this rock." Bob and I packed up all of our extra gear and had it mailed home so that our travel duffels were as light as possible. We had accumulated so much over the last ten months, it was shocking.

On the night of our fly-out, our company headed to the flight line by platoon and loaded our duffel bags onto pallets. The pallets were loaded onto whichever plane would arrive to take us out of the country. Platoon by platoon we returned to our tents and waited for the final word. It was odd being in those tents. There was nothing left in there but our backpacks, our empty cots, and us. The pure joy and elation in that tent was really something special. Yet, it was scary at the same time. We were up all night just waiting to be called down to the flight line. I watched all three of the Lord of the Rings movies because I was too excited to sleep.

Finally, we got word and traveled to the flight line. They put us in a holding area again. The holding area was slightly off the flight line. It was a large, open area with a tent cover over the top and wasn't too far away from the in-processing building from where we had started over ten months before. While in this holding area, Navy sailors showed up with tables in order to conduct customs. Customs were simple here because we just had the clothes on our backs and small backpacks holding our computers and toiletries.

Once we cleared customs and returned to the benches, we waited several hours. After what seemed like an eternity, we received word that our plane had finally arrived. A loud cheer went up and we watched as our pallets of gear were hauled onto the flight line.

The Air Force put us into small serials of single file lines and we walked out onto the flight line. I took in the beauty of the mountains from that vantage point at the very same time I was taking in the beauty of that gorgeous C-17 Air Force plane that was taking us back home. We walked up the bird's massive back gate resting in an open and declined position. It welcomed us as we filed on. All our gear was stored in the center and we sat on the side seats of the cargo hold.

It took about an hour for our company and battalion staff to load. Our numbers were smaller than when we had arrived due to the fact that a landing party had left earlier in order to prepare things for us at Ft. McCoy. As the engines fired on the plane and we hit cruising altitude, a loud cheer erupted inside the cargo hold of that plane. A lot of us were slapping hands and shaking hands. It felt great to be on this freedom bird!

After eight or so hours, we landed in Germany and exited the plane. I remember the entire flight crew, including the pilots, stood at the gate and shook our hands. It was a sign of respect and it was a humbling feeling. After we filed past the flight crew, we loaded onto busses that took us to the airport. We were told right away that we were facing a 12-hour delay, and given permission to leave the airport to patronage the enlisted and officer clubs on post.

SSG Scofield called all the junior NCOs together and told us something very important. He said that now more than ever, we needed to watch our people because they might do something stupid when they drink. We all agreed and made a pact that there would be no alcohol for us this evening, and we would keep an eye on the junior enlisted soldiers.

It was evening in Frankfurt, Germany and a few of us went over to the enlisted club on Rein Mein. As promised, the NCOs did not drink, but we did eat some good American-style food and our soldiers totally behaved themselves.

As ordered, we made it back to the flight terminal. The Air Force provided for us an area to take showers and change our clothes. These were locker rooms, actually, and judging from what we saw, it must have been the locker rooms for the male and female Air Force personnel that worked the airport. Not too long after, we loaded onto busses that took us back onto the tarmac. Once again, we filed onto the C-17 and within a half-an-hour, the large gate closed up and the engines fired full. We hit the air again, this time for Bangor, Maine. Another loud cheer erupted among us.

After another eight-hour flight, we landed onto the tarmac of Bangor, Maine. This flight crew did the same thing as the last flight crew did. They shook every one of our hands. The pilot said to each of us, "Welcome home. America wasn't the same without you!"

We marched from the tarmac in a single file line and the Air Force led us directly into the flight terminal. It was one of the greatest things I'd ever seen and to this day makes me very emotional when I remember it. There were about a hundred people in that terminal from the local VFW and American Legion cheering and holding up signs for us. We walked through a gauntlet of happy people. They shook our hands, patted us on the backs, and gave us hugs. I felt pure joy and elation on this walk. God bless those fine folks for taking time out of their day to do that and to be so good to us. That was really something special.

We started to catch our bearings and realized that it was first thing in the morning east coast time. Our command announced that we would be ready to leave Bangor in two hours. The airport opened up the bar for us, but our command decided that there would be no alcohol consumption on this final leg of the journey. Apparently, on the previous leg of the journey, a few officers failed to make their flight in from Germany due to being overserved.

Eddie Balderas and I walked directly to the phone bank at the back of the terminal and called home. It was a weekday and my folks were supposed to be working. I called them at their jobs but there was no answer. I then called my home number and was frustrated to discover that nobody picked up there either. Lastly, I tried calling my mom's cell phone. She answered. She let me know that the unit Family Readiness Group had contacted them earlier and that they were already heading up with Jean Drenth, Bob's mom, to Ft. McCoy to meet us. I thought that was great news and ran over to tell Bob. He had already talked with his mom and was also excited.

When we landed in Volk Field, Wisconsin, I remember the pilots and crew of the aircraft coming down and shaking our hands as we walked off that plane. Again, this was a really touching experience that is impossible to translate into words. The vivid memory that serves as a shock as we were filing off the C-17 was seeing green grass everywhere! We had been in a dry, desolate area for so long that it was a beautiful, refreshing site to see that much greenery at once. It didn't take long before I found John Wiley. John had left us in Afghanistan a few weeks earlier and came back early with the landing party. John had a big smile on his face and gave me a big hug. There were a lot of handshakes and hugs taking place everywhere that day. It was a feeling of pure joy knowing that the deployment was behind us and we were now living on easy street.

As we were hugging and shaking hands with each other, a gauntlet of officers had formed and we were instructed to form a line and greet them. The commanding general of Ft. McCoy along with his staff was present in this gauntlet. One by one we passed by and saluted him. The general returned our salutes telling each of us "great job" and how "proud" he was of us. After the gauntlet, we filed into a holding area where they had food for all of us. I distinctly remember a feeling of euphoria and a sense of accomplishment like no other. I also remember SSG Scofield sitting in the grass with a big smile on his face and saying how happy he was to see grass.

We loaded onto busses and were brought back to the post. This bus ride was not silent as everyone was greatly excited and happy. We pulled up in front of our assigned barracks and unloaded our gear from trucks that the Air Force had loaded for us. After we brought our duffel bags into the barracks, we saw that there was COLD BEER ON ICE waiting for us! None of us drank yet because we had a formation a half hour later, but you wouldn't believe how great that beer looked!

When we fell in for formation, our first sergeant told us that this would be our final formation of the day and that we were relieved of duty until the next morning. We were also informed that families had been invited up, were already here, and there were vehicles waiting to take us to see them. Bob and I hopped in a van together.

The vans drove us to a reception area where I got to see my parents for the first time in several months. It was a wonderful, wonderful feeling. I also got a nice, big hug from Jean Drenth. We sat there and visited with family for about two hours. Smiles never left anyone's faces that whole time.

As we were saying our goodbyes so our folks could make the trip back to Darien, my Dad called us over to the back of his Dodge Durango. In the backseat he had a cooler stocked with a case of Budweiser on ice! He gave the cooler to Bob and me with a sly smile on his face – he knew the feeling of euphoria that we were feeling from his own experiences. My Dad had returned home from Vietnam 35 years before.

Bob and I brought the cooler back to the barracks where we immediately cracked cold ones with everyone else. This was the greatest party I had ever seen in my life! Music was blaring and everyone was so happy. We took beers into the showers and everybody was just hugging and having a great time. Nobody was hugging in the showers, don't worry, but we were drinking while showering. I very vividly remember SSG Rivas walking around shirtless with two drinks in his hands and the largest cigar I'd ever seen hanging out of his mouth.

I said to him, "SSG Rivas what are you going to do when you get home in a few days?"

He responded, "Well, SGT Drake, I'm going to smoke the largest Bob-Marley sized spliff I can roll!"

CHAPTER 24

GOING HOME

After we showered, a bunch of us headed over to McCoy's to get some dinner. McCoy's was absolutely packed that night and the atmosphere was ecstatic and everybody in our unit couldn't stop hugging each other, shaking hands, and giving high fives. I remember the food line was ridiculously long and there was no chance of getting food in under an hour. As Bob, Nicole Ward, Ryan Suthard, a few others, and I sat at a table we heard the name "Wang" called over the PA. They were announcing that his pizza was ready. Bob never forgot when Wang sat on his ass and refused to help us load up.

Bob and I walked up to the stand and took Wang's pizza. We brought it back to the table and ate it in about 5 minutes. It was pretty good revenge! Poor Wang stood by that food counter for over an hour never realizing what had happened.

Since everybody's alcohol tolerance was so low at that point, nobody stayed at McCoy's long. Add the jet lag and we were all pretty shot. Back at the barracks we drank some more and went to bed.

Sleeping wasn't easy because more and more soldiers kept coming back to the barracks drunk and loud. I finally got out of my bed and went downstairs to use the latrine. What I happened upon in that latrine haunts me to this day. One of our soldiers was in the midst of a breakdown, a PTSD situation. The details of who it was will remain a secret because it's a private matter, but this soldier was rattled up badly. 15 months of pressure finally got to him after a few too many cocktails, and it all came out at once.

While out at the bars, we had consumed way more alcohol and greasy food than our bodies were used to. This alone was a shock to our systems. This soldier and several others took it another step further and went out to Sparta and got tattoos. When I walked into the latrine, this poor soldier was hunched over a sink in an odd state. I'd never seen anyone like that before. His arm was bleeding from the new tattoo and it was beginning to dry out. As I began talking to this good friend of mine, I noticed he was in no condition to take care of his arm. I washed my hands, then washed his new tattoo, and then gently applied the proper treatment to it. Sadly, my friend lost it and exploded with a year plus of pent up frustrations, anger, rage, and terrible sadness over the loss of SSG Mowris.

It was not a good situation to be in and it was a heavy situation to be in at 22 years old. I woke up our medic, SSG Todd Helms, and had him check on the soldier, who was sobbing uncontrollably and couldn't catch his breath. SSG Helms was concerned that this soldier was hyperventilating and made a call to get him to the hospital. I went to the hospital with the soldier, who I considered one of my best friends and still do. I refused to leave his side. They ran a bunch of tests on him and we were there all night.

I called our duty desk on post from the hospital to relay the information that the soldier had been released and we needed to be picked up. It was roughly five o'clock in the morning and we had a formation scheduled for seven o'clock. SSG Scofield, along with our First Sergeant, showed up about 20 minutes later in the duty van. SSG Scofield didn't have to do this, but he had heard that something had happened with one of his "boys" and immediately came to help. Again, this was the quality of man he was.

Two hours later, after our first formation that morning, SSG Scofield called a formation of his own with the junior NCOs and enlisted. He spoke to us from the heart telling us that what occurred the night before with one of our soldiers was nothing to be ashamed of or to be embarrassed about. He told us that we could talk to him at any time and gave out his phone number. He said that we should expect things like this to happen. Scofield then told us a story about the day he returned back stateside from Desert Storm. He told us he had seen the exact same thing happen to one of his closest friends in the bathroom of the bar where they had been partying. Scofield told us how the man slipped away during the party and couldn't be found. SSG Scofield found him in the bathroom, hunched over a sink, and a wreck just like I had found my own friend. I can't even tell you how much that meant to all of us young soldiers to hear this from a man that we respected so much. Again, he'd been there and lived it and he really cared about each and every one of us.

After this briefing with Scofield, our official out-processing began. Out-processing was a simple thing back then. All you had to do was make sure that paperwork was straight, clear out with the doctor, and you were stamped off on and approved to be on your way.

The party started up again that afternoon and we all had a terrific time.

Near the night's end and while fully intoxicated, I realized that this would probably be the last time I'd see most of these people ever again. I was right. It was a bittersweet feeling. Someone had a boombox in the barracks and Bob pulled out a CD. He put it in and cranked up the volume as high as it would go. *The Animals'* "We Gotta Get Out of This Place" blasted throughout the barracks and most of us stood arm in arm singing every word at the top of our lungs.

Eventually we crashed, and the next morning we showered up, ate breakfast, and hit the road on tour busses headed back to Arlington Heights. I was hungover this whole trip, really hungover, and I think most of the bus felt the same way.

Something really special happened when our entourage of busses crossed the border into Illinois. We were intercepted by Illinois State Troopers and issued a formal escort all the way to Arlington Heights with their lights flashing.

I remember how cold it was outside the day we pulled in, exited the busses, and embraced our families. I was so happy to see them, but also so hungover at the same time! That was a special moment in my lifetime and something I'll always cherish. I remember the smiles on my mom's and grandma's faces, especially. After a short ceremony inside, we were released. I remember shaking hands with quite a few people, some I've never seen since, and then I took the 40-minute drive in my parents' SUV back to Darien. I spent that afternoon and evening talking with my family and eating the Rosati's pizza I had missed so much. I vividly remember feeling so happy and so exhausted at the same time. Later that night, Bob picked me up in his pickup truck. We went out to Q where we met all of our friends. It was a wild, great party, and multiple times that night Bob would put his arm around me and yell out, "They can never take it away from us! We did it!"

Bob was right. No matter what ever happened, nobody could ever take our shared experience away.

CHAPTER 25

A YEAR AND SOME CHANGE

IN THE WORLD

When Bob and I first got home from Afghanistan, we got together every day. We bought memberships to a shooting range. We were there so often that we got to know the staff by name, and became friends with them. After shooting, we'd clean our weapons at the range, get lunch together, and then we'd either go see a movie or just hang around together. In the evening, or sometimes the afternoons, Bob and I would head to the bar together. We almost always went to Q, but sometimes we'd head over to Joanie's Dry Dock on the other side of town where my brother and his friends would hang out.

Bob and I never really talked about feelings or emotions. Bob was a closed off person that way and, frankly, so was I back then. I can tell you, though, that I could read Bob pretty well and he could read me the same way. We were both thrilled to be back home in the "world", but I can tell you that neither one of us was happy. Despite having loving families and great friends, something was missing in our lives. There was an emptiness, a loneliness, and a feeling of guilt that riddled us both.

The feeling of guilt came from turning on the TV and seeing the coverage on the Iraq War and snips of Afghanistan. The guilt came from a strong feeling that we should be there with our people and we should be doing our duty. Bob and I would never talk about this with each other, of course, because our egos wouldn't allow us to. This is what was going on inside, however.

There's a line in the movie Apocalypse Now where Martin Sheen's character says, "All you want to do while you're over there is go home and when you're home all you want to do is get back over there." I remember watching that movie with Bob and drinking Budweisers at two in the afternoon in my parents' basement and Bob saying, "Yep!" I fully agreed with him.

I want all you young GIs out there to read this and I want you to pay attention. If you are home from a tour and you feel that something's not right and you feel mixed up about something, go talk to someone. Go to a VFW and ask to talk to a veteran. Take advantage of the VA and go talk to a counselor. If something doesn't feel right, then talk to someone and get it out. Do not sit on it and do nothing, because it will not go away. It will eat at you and eat at you and eat at you. Find ways to live with or fix the problem as soon as possible. If you don't, you are going to live in misery and torment.

While I'm on my soapbox I'd like to tell you young GIs another thing: alcohol fixes nothing. If you think that drinking and partying is a way to feel good and get you away from this thing that's eating at you, you're wrong. It will temporarily numb an issue, but eventually that issue is going to work its way out. As a matter of fact, your issues will be magnified one hundred times when you combine them with alcohol.

Then you're going to need more alcohol to numb and the battle is going to start. Do not get sucked into that pattern. It's a waste of life. Fix your issues, live your life, and be happy!

Now that I got that out of the way, I'd like to point out that Bob Allen and I did the exact opposite of what I just preached to you. Bob and I were both unhappy. We both drank heavily to compensate for these new-found, uncomfortable feelings. While Bob and I would sit together at the bar, Bob often talked about things that took place during the first tour. He had an impeccable memory for people and events, and we would talk about everything over and over again. We would go through this same cycle almost every night. Sadly, we felt out of touch with our own friends and people our age. We felt like we were living in our own little world, and we were.

Bob was also very good with the Pashto language and I could hold my own with him. We'd be in the bar, drunk, and Bob would slip in Pashto phrases. Before we knew it, a conversation in full Pashto would then take place in describing the things going on around us. We'd be so removed and in our own little world, that we wouldn't even realize what we were doing. There would usually be a group of people staring at us. I vividly remember back then that Bob and I would meet our friends up at the bar, big groups of people, and within a few hours it'd just be he and I sitting by ourselves at the end of the bar. It was really a strange time.

I can remember a girl I was seeing briefly at this time say to me, "Why do you have me meet you up at the bar when all you do is sit with Bob and talk in some stupid language?" Needless to say, she didn't last long!

There were also some very funny things that took place during these days. Bob was not much of a fashion guy, but online shopping was just coming around at this point.

Bob called me up one day and he said, "Hey I bought this leather motorcycle jacket but it doesn't fit right. It's too small. I think it will fit you, though. Do you want to buy it from me? I don't want to pay $30 to ship it back."

I replied, "Sure. Bring it over and let me take a look at it."

A few minutes later Bob stopped by my house with this really slick motorcycle jacket. It was dark blue with these white stripes down the shoulders and it fit like a glove. It was a really great jacket and I gladly handed the money over to him. Well, little did I know that Bob went and ordered the exact same jacket again in a size more suited for himself. Soon enough we'd meet up to go out for the night wearing matching jackets. We both happened to like the same style of jeans, too and didn't hesitate wearing them when in the other's presence. Now to take this one level further, but we also had matching flat top haircuts. Don't you think that after having to look the same for fifteen straight months that we would be sick of it? Well, apparently not.

Actually, I did tell Bob that we needed to do something about the jacket situation. We'd make schedules of who would wear the jacket and when. This schedule never came to fruition because we'd get drunk and forget the plans. Then we'd show up at the bar wearing the same jackets again and have the same conversation again. Nobody ever said anything to us, but people probably thought one of two things when they saw us: either these two guys are Eastern European idiots or these two guys are gay. Neither applied, of course!

Bob and I knew every bartender and every waitress in Q back then and they knew us right back. After a while I got friendly with a couple of the waitresses and they'd invite Bob and I out to the 4am bar with them after Q closed for the night. Unfortunately, Bob still wanted nothing to do with any woman but Jamie Hasenfang. I'm not sure what transpired between them overseas because Bob never talked about it. From what I understand he had made his move and was rejected.

Either Bob or I would drive, and we'd go down to the after hours bar that was known then as Sean Kaley's. A girl that Bob knew worked part time there and her boyfriend was the late-night DJ. We'd continue the party after hours in our matching motorcycle jackets and then we'd sit at the end of the bar and talk to each other in Pashto further alienating ourselves from everyone around us. This sounds like a great time, doesn't it? Well a break in this would come when I'd give the DJ a few dollars and I'd get him to play Frank Sinatra or the Bee Gees so I could dance with the waitresses from Q. Bob never danced. Ever. The thought never even crossed his mind despite the encouragement of good-looking young women. They weren't Hasenfang so Bob wasn't interested.

One of these nights at Kaley's while Bob and I were on yet another bender, I went to go use the bathroom. Kaley's wasn't exactly the greatest place to be after hours back then and the men's room could be the site of various transactions. You had to be careful while on the walk to the bathroom, while in the bathroom, and during the walk back from the bathroom. As I was walking back out of the bathroom this particular night, there was another guy walking in. Bob was sitting at the end of the bar facing toward the bathroom and he could see exactly what was going on. No matter where we went back then, Bob and I always knew where each other were at all times. It was a developed instinct and had become a habit over time.

The guy walking toward the bathroom was a big man. He was over 6 feet tall and weighed well over 230lbs. When my shoulder hit his chest, it sent me stumbling back a few feet. Instead of apologizing, this guy said some unpleasantries toward me. I had a bad temper back then and I could go from 0 to 100 at the flip of a switch. My temper was the worst it had ever been during this time period.

I was also smart enough to be aware of my size back then and knew that in situations like this I always had to attack first, or I could end up in a bad way. Without saying a word in reply, I lunged for this guy's legs and took him down to the floor. He was not in very good shape, he was drunk, and he was obviously out of his element. In fact, his response to my assault looked a lot like a turtle flipped over on its shell. I was in survival mode now and I unloaded with fists into his face. I heard the bar come alive as people were seeing what was going on. I spotted another guy running over, obviously a friend of the man I was pummeling.

As I was planning to bury my head in the chest of the guy under me to protect myself against the boot that would most likely be coming into my face, I heard "Hey asshole! Where do you think you're going?"

There was Bob in a dead sprint coming after this guy. Instead of Bob punching this guy or anything like that, Bob put him in the worst left-handed headlock I'd ever seen in my life. He barely even had this guy hooked, but he was most definitely preventing him from coming forward. I kept hitting the turtle and I was trying to figure out where in the hell Bob learned a headlock like that. Bob's legs kept coming off the ground and he looked like a rodeo cowboy flailing on a bull! What was next, was Bob going to put The Iron Claw on him?

Soon enough the Kaley's bouncers had us separated. Due to Bob's connections at the bar they threw the two other guys out and Bob and I were allowed to stay. I was handed a towel by the bartender and I wiped the blood off my swollen knuckles. I handed the towel back and Bob and I went right back to the end of the bar and continued drinking, talking in Pashto, and talking about Afghanistan. I, of course, made fun of Bob every chance I could about the worst headlock in the history of headlocks.

Things went on like this for about a full month after we got back. Bob and I were partying very hard, getting into skirmishes, and it wasn't healthy.

One night after dinner my Dad said to me, "I'm going to give you the same speech that my dad gave me. He said, 'It's good to be home and to have fun, but now it's time to go back to work.'"

The next day I drove down to my union hall and told them that I was ready to go back to work. I wasn't ready, but I did what my dad told me to do anyway. The apprenticeship coordinator was glad to see me, but he told me that things were a bit slow and he'd find me something as soon as he could. As an apprentice, I was not allowed to find my own work. The coordinator made the arrangements for me. He had told me right away that the last contractor I worked for had finished their gas pipeline projects and that work had dried up. I thanked him and left.

Coincidentally, and later that day, my friend Matt Goodwin called me with news that the Ace Hardware chain we had worked for in high school was opening a new store and they were looking for help for the remodel. Matt had just graduated college and wasn't sure of his next move yet, so it sounded like a great idea. He and I went to work rehabbing this new store and preparing it for opening.

We worked hard manual labor during the day and partied at night, every night, and when Bob and I would get together it meant that we would party all night.

Also, during this time, Ryan Suthard and I drove out to Van Wert, OH for the Wileys' wedding. John Wiley and Colleen Saam were getting married. Colleen was an E-6 that had been transferred into our unit for the deployment. She was a very nice woman, a good NCO, and someone you could always depend on and trust. I was very glad to hear that John and she had developed a relationship and found happiness with each other. John had asked me to stand up at the wedding and I was honored to do so.

It was a lot of fun seeing a lot of folks from the tour! That was one of the best weddings I've ever been to and was just done right top to bottom. It was a great time! Sadly, this was the last time I would see a lot of the others.

When I got back from the wedding I went back to working on the new store and Bob and I continued our nightly partying. Soon enough I got a call from the union that they had a job for me. I started working for a company that had a contract at Morraine Valley College where we were putting in a new boiler and the thousands and thousands of feet of associated piping.

On this job, I worked for a very nice older pipefitter named Gene who treated me great. I really liked working for him. In early June of that year, as I was walking off the job site at 2:30 in the afternoon, my phone rang and it was Dennis Rolke. He called to tell me that Jake Warner had committed suicide. I felt like someone punched me in the stomach. On the way home, I drove straight to Bob's house and told him. Bob's face told me that he felt like he had gotten punched straight in the stomach also. We did the only thing we knew how to do at that point, and we went straight to the bar. We raised several glasses to Warner's memory, we played the album Californication on the jukebox, and we each refused to talk about the little part of ourselves that died inside that day.

I will not get into details surrounding Jake's death, but his death bothered me and it bothered Bob. Again, Bob and I never talked about feelings or emotions, but I know that Warner's death weighed heavily on him. Bob and I went to the wake in Chicago and paid our respects and Bob went back downtown the next day for the funeral. I couldn't attend because I had to work. In hindsight, I should have taken the day off and went. It would have been the right thing to do. Bob and I would talk about Warner a lot over the years and it always remained a punch in the stomach-like feeling.

I was transferred to another jobsite, this time at Joliet Junior College, where we were installing a series of pumps, expansion tanks, and a weird heated water system that I never saw the likes of again. On this job I worked for the biggest jerk I ever worked for in my life. He treated me terribly, screamed at me, and gave me shit every single day I worked for him. He wouldn't let me do any work, he wouldn't teach me how to do anything, and he used me strictly as a mule.

I spent all day moving equipment and material and nothing else. He would have me do stupid stuff that could get me hurt like unloading trucks by myself and moving pipe machines and job boxes by myself. I really hated working for this guy, but since I was an apprentice, I had no choice but to take it. I absolutely hated going to work every day. This guy was such a dick that his own friends who were working on the job with us would tell him to lay off me. Then he'd turn around and scream at them!

I was in pipefitting long enough after this to know what this guy's problem was. He was insecure in what he was doing and he didn't know how to manage people. Because of this, his way of dealing with the stress was to give apprentices a hard time. He abused apprentices because he knew they couldn't fight back or they would risk getting a bad reputation and get kicked out of the program. I talked to some other apprentices that had worked for him before me and they said he treated them the same way too. I'll tell you this much, if I saw that guy on the street today, I probably wouldn't hesitate to blast him in the face.

Life was very miserable for me at this point and Bob and I would get together every night and talk about Afghanistan. At this point we started seriously talking about how we could get back over there. I was already miserable as it was, but working this job made me 10x more miserable, and I missed being a GI with a sense of purpose more than anything.

For 4th of July that year my parents went up to their property in Wisconsin. I stayed home and threw a party. 4th of July fell on a Thursday that year and the Joliet Junior College was closed that Friday so we had a four-day weekend. Bob came over for the party that year along with a bunch of my other friends. I was also seeing a very pretty girl named Jeanie at this time and she and her friends came over too.

My parents' house had this huge backyard with this beautiful deck. We also had a pool with a deck on it. It was the perfect place for a summer party and we grilled and partied all day. My parents had a beautiful 110lbs German Shepherd named Shane then too. He was very tall for a German Shepherd and he was a great looking dog. He was also the nicest, most gentle, and most docile dog you'd ever meet. He really liked people. For some reason my parents didn't take Shane with them on that trip that year and he stayed home with me. Shane liked everyone, but he REALLY liked Bob! Whenever Bob was around, Shane would be glued to his hip. We used to joke it was because they were both of German descent and that Germans stuck together!

Bob was in the pool all day for that party and I remember throwing him beers from the deck of the house. I also remember that whenever he came out of the pool, Shane had to be right there with him. This party was very controlled and very mellow. Nobody got out of line and we partied until very late at night.

The next morning when I woke up, I fed Shane and ate some breakfast myself. I went out onto the deck to start cleaning up from the night before. When I opened the deck's sliding glass door, Shane took off in a sprint and he jumped up on the side of the pool. I couldn't see exactly what he was doing until I stepped out further onto the deck. Bob was still in the pool on a floating lawn chair and was now petting and kissing Shane. Bob had slept the entire night in the pool and had never left! When he got out of the pool a few moments later, his skin was all shriveled up like a prune and his pale white skin was sunburned horribly. I offered him some aloe after he got dried off, but Bob told me that aloe was for "pussies and communists." He was neither.

Bob stuck around the rest of the morning and helped me clean up the party and then he took off back home. I think if Shane could have, he'd have gone with him. Bob was his favorite person in the world! Bob came back that night and he ended up staying at the house the rest of that weekend. Shane was thrilled!

CHAPTER 26

A YEAR AND SOME CHANGE

IN THE WORLD PART II

As the summer of 2004 went on, I remember working a lot of heavy overtime and being transferred between job sites in the Cottage Grove area of Chicago, Munster, Indiana, and Joliet Junior College. Again, it wasn't a happy time for me but I pushed through because I had to.

Bob's group of friends would do things like go camping and take trips out to Buffalo Rock. Buffalo Rock was a large outdoor shooting range about 60 miles from where we lived. He'd always want me to go with him and his friends, but I couldn't because they'd be leaving on a Thursday or Friday and I'd have to work. Being a union pipefitter meant that if I didn't work, then I didn't get paid. Another thing about being a pipefitter too was that if you took time off or missed days, you'd find yourself out of a job really fast. Unfortunately, I never attended these outings with Bob.

Highlights of these outings were 3 o'clock in the morning phone calls where Bob would greet me, screaming into the phone, with, "Hey, you asshole!" and then I'd hear automatic AK-47 fire for a minute straight. Those were always fun calls. I'm not exactly sure where Bob was camping that allowed automatic AK-47 fire at that time in the morning…but apparently, he knew the place!

One night that summer Bob picked me up to go out for the night in his pick-up truck. When I hopped in the truck, Bob told me to open the glove compartment. I'll tell you that I was a bit nervous when Bob told me that. Knowing him, there could have been anything in that glove compartment. With great hesitation I unlatched the box and put my hand inside. When I did, I found a newspaper clipping from a small town in Wisconsin where Bob's grandparents lived. Apparently one of the officers from our company lived in that same small town and had given an interview to the local newspaper all about our tour of Afghanistan. He broke operational security in every way imaginable and it was disgraceful. Bob was fully prepared to bring that article to the next drill weekend and turn it in to command. He would have been absolutely right in doing so, but it never came to be.

Bob went camping one of the weekends before drill and when he came back the following Tuesday, he no longer had a pick-up truck. When I called Bob up to go out for our usual evening beers that Tuesday, he asked me to pick him up. When I pulled into his driveway, his truck wasn't there. I asked him if his truck was in the shop or if his step-dad Dave had taken it.

Bob, staring straight ahead, said, "I lost the truck."

I looked at him dumbfounded. "Lost it? You mean you lost the keys or you can't remember where it's at? That kind of lost it?"

Bob kept looking straight ahead, cool as a cucumber, and replied, "No. Like it went into a ditch and got totaled. Lost it."

I didn't ask too much more about it. Bob then got pissed and said, "And that damn article was still in the glove compartment! I forgot to get it out of there! That son of a bitch is going to get away with what he did now because I can't prove it!"

Bob was not bothered at all that he totaled his pick-up truck, his only mode of transportation. He was instead super pissed off that an officer had violated operational security and now Bob couldn't turn him in. Bob was a damn good soldier like that!

I've painted a picture here about two young guys in their early 20s who were disgruntled veterans who partied like rock stars and did stupid stuff together. All that is very, very true. With that said, however, I'd also like you to know that Bob and I knew deep down that we were going back to Afghanistan at some point. There was no doubt in either of our minds that we were going to find the first opportunity to go back and jump on it. With this mindset that we had adopted, we were getting ourselves prepared.

The internet wasn't quite the information machine in 2004 that it is today. There was information out there, but the information available was not nearly as detailed nor the sheer volume of information that is available now. If you wanted to learn about a subject back then, you had to read books. Bob and I did just that, we read. In that year and some change that we were home, he and I both went through every book that our local library and surrounding libraries had on Afghanistan, the Soviet-Afghan War, the Afghan Civil War, and the rise of the Taliban. Bob and I also bought a lot of books on these subjects. We learned as much as we possibly could about Afghanistan and the history of that country.

I would spend my lunch breaks on my pipefitting jobs with a book on Afghanistan in one hand and a sandwich in the other. The other workers would look at me like I was nuts. I'd also spent at least an hour every night before I went to bed reading these books. Most of the time I would have to close one eye to read because Budweiser wasn't kind to reading, but I still read.

On weekends, if I wasn't working, I'd kill a full book on Afghanistan before Bob and I went out for the night. Bob was doing the exact same thing and we would discuss all the information we learned. It was no joke, we took it very seriously, and we learned a ton.

Another thing we both took very seriously was learning Pashto. Bob had a natural flair for languages. I don't know what it was, but he could pick up on them very easily. Bob wasn't half bad with Spanish and I worked guard shifts with him overnight as he taught himself German. He and I put our minds to learning Pashto on that first tour and then we put our minds to it very seriously when we were home. I bought a series of CDs by an American from California of Afghan-Pashtun heritage. Bob and I would exchange these CDs and listen to them all the time. I would listen to these CDs on the long drives to and from work and I'd constantly practice. Sometimes I'd be stuck in traffic with my windows down and I'd get dirty looks from the cars around me wondering what language I was spitting out.

I can't say that I ever progressed to the level that Bob did, but I will say that I got competent. Over the years I've lost 90% of what I learned, but sometimes when I see movies or documentaries about Afghanistan I can easily pick up on words and phrases that are spoken in Pashto. I don't think Bob ever lost the language. He would leave me voicemails at odd hours of the night in Pashto. Usually, these were humor based where he would be pretending to be a guy in orange calling from GITMO and asking me if I could get him a lawyer. Bob was very creative like that.

That wasn't it with the voicemails either. I would get voicemails at two in the morning of Bob yelling at me in Pashto to take him to the toilet! Bob had a book that was the Pashto-English dictionary that he studied so much the binding tore loose on it. I borrowed that book from him once, never gave it back, and it's still on my bookshelf to this day. We meant business when it came to learning Pashto and to learning as much as we could about Afghanistan.

Before Bob lost his truck (and after) he refused to get gasoline from anywhere but the local BP station. It didn't matter what time of the day it was, where we were at, or how far away we were; Bob would only get gas from this one BP. I soon learned why.

The owner of this station, who also worked the register, was a first generation American but his family were Pakistani Pashtuns. Bob always wanted to go to this gas station to practice his Pashto with this man. Bob introduced me to this man and I learned that his name was Kamal. Sometimes, Kamal's father would also be at the gas station. He dressed in traditional clothing and was far more conservative than Kamal. Bob and I would always call him Baba-jan out of respect and he really got a kick out of that. "Baba" is a term of endearment in the Arab world close to "Papa" in English. "Jan" is a term of respect given in the Pashtun culture attached to one's name. Baba-jan thought it was great that two Caucasian men in their early twenties showed such interest in his culture also referred to him with such respect. These two men seemed to like our visits and would insist that we had tea with them whenever we stopped in.

From these two men we learned a lot about Afghanistan; they were teaching us the real Afghanistan and what we couldn't read in books. Kamal and Baba-jan taught us a great deal about the refugee situation during the Soviet War and the years of unrest during the Civil War. They seemed to be very excited and happy that someone had interest in their culture. Sometimes Baba-jan would come from behind the counter and take us by the hand outside where he'd chain smoke cigarettes and tell us his experiences in his broken English. He'd also slip over to speaking Pashto to test our knowledge. Looking back on all this I can tell you that it was a very enlightening experience and something really unique. Bob respected both those men a great deal and so did I. They taught us a lot and treated us like we were their family.

Around late summer or early fall of that year I had a new girl in my life. Her name was Amy. Amy was a bank teller, she was a couple of years older than me, and quite the beauty. Amy was of Italian or Greek heritage and had beautiful black hair, olive skin, and dark eyes. I had really outdone myself this time! There was a problem with Amy that came up after about a month or so, though. You see Amy wanted to do normal dating things. She wanted to go out to dinner, she wanted to see movies, and she wanted to have regular dates. Unfortunately for Amy, she just didn't understand the priorities of my life back then. The priorities in the early fall of 2004 were Bob Allen, Marlboro Mediums, Budweiser, Afghanistan, and Pipefitting.

Being in that mindset, I couldn't understand why Amy would get mad when I'd tell her I'd pick her up at six in the evening on a Friday night and then she'd receive a call from me at midnight (with Bob crying-laughing in the background) asking her to meet me at Denny's. She'd get really pissed off over that!

Needless to say, Amy didn't tolerate this for too long and she was out the door. I'd blame Bob for stuff like this for forcing me to drink with him. He'd called me a "stupid asshole" and laugh in that goofy high-pitched laugh he had.

I ran into Amy a lot over the years and she'd always give me the coldest, dirtiest look she could muster. Believe it or not I saw Amy not too long ago at the local Target. She looked almost the exact same and she was still gorgeous. She took one look at me, gave me the coldest, dirtiest look she could muster, and I could only laugh: at least this girl was consistent in her hatred of me!

In the late fall of 2004, I got laid off from the company I was working for when we completed the junior college job. I was the last one to be laid off and the company shut its doors soon after that. I had to wait about two or three weeks before I landed another job. During this period, Bob and I fell into our same routine of the range, lunch, and then the bar.

I had a very good friend at this time that worked at an after-hours bar a few towns over from where Bob and I lived. It was probably a Tuesday or Wednesday night, and Bob and I had been up at our usual watering hole until close. We called my friend Danny, and he was working that night at the 4am bar, so we drove out to see him.

When we walked into the bar, the place had a lot of people in it for 2:30am on a weeknight. Danny came right up to us and told us we had to sit and watch this guy at the jukebox. There was a guy running the jukebox who was morbidly obese, he had bad fitting clothing on, and he looked like he had climbed straight out of 1983. This man was having the time of his life, however. He was dominating the jukebox, but the people at the bar were pleased that he was playing really good music. Everyone was jamming along. This guy was jamming the hardest, though, and he was singing every song that came on.

Have you ever heard the song "The Boys are Back in Town" by Thin Lizzy? I'm sure you have so I'll cut to the chase. There's a line in the song where the singer says, "...and if that chick don't want to know then forget her." Well, this fat guy at the juke, singing every word, without hesitation added the word "cunt" to the end of that phrase. Bob, Danny, and I were laughing so hard that we nearly fell off our stools. Something had happened to this man somewhere along the line. Some woman had hurt him deeply and he remembered it right at that moment. He felt it very important to express his feelings for her by adding the "C" word to that line.

There has not been a time that I've heard that song since where I haven't sung out loud "...and if that chick don't want to know then forget her...cunt!" Bob liked it so much that he added that song to his jukebox set. Whenever it would come on, we would always scream out that line.

Now if you didn't know Bob, then you didn't know his ability to handle his liquor. I never saw Bob throw up, I never saw Bob hungover, he was just a drinking machine. I did see him slow a few times, though, and I did hear him go off on the tirade about leatherfish, but I never saw him shut down the next day from the night before.

218

I, on the other hand, could be shut down for the next day after spending all night with Bob very easily. Bob and I used to close out the after-hours bar and then go visit his friend Scott that worked at a gas station overnight. We'd smoke cigarettes and BS with Scott before going home and calling it a night, or morning. No matter how many times I lied to myself, there was just no way that I could ever keep up with Bob while drinking. I would try, though. This particular night, I found myself doing shots with Bob at the after-hours bar. This was odd for me, I don't know what the occasion was, the only thing I can think of is that I was celebrating my layoff and not having to work for that asshole anymore. Bob and I were doing our thing at Kaley's and I remember I entered the zone where "Space Oddity" by David Bowie plays on loop in your brain and things start moving very slowly.

When we left the after-hours bar, Bob drove and we went up to the gas station. I attempted to get out of the vehicle to go see Scott with Bob, but I fell out and couldn't get up. I then vomited all over the pavement and I still couldn't get up. Bob and Scott were hysterically laughing at me and finally they came over and helped me get up. I remember they had to help me back in the vehicle when we left, and Bob kept laughing the entire time and the entire drive to my parents' house. When we got into the driveway Bob had to come around and help me walk to the door. He helped me get the door open and then Shane, our German Shepherd, had to run out of the house and visit Bob, his favorite person ever, on the patio.

When their reunion was finally over, I had to enlist the help of Shane to make it to bed. The next morning, about nine o'clock, my phone kept ringing and ringing. Apparently, I had agreed to go to the Cubs game that morning with some other friends. Needless to say, I didn't make it out of bed and I swore I'd never do shots with Bob Allen again.

Later that fall I landed a job with a small company that had a huge project going on about 70 miles from my house. It was a long drive, but I was used to it at that point as an apprentice. These pipefitters turned out to be some of the nicest guys I would ever work for in my career as a pipefitter.

I partnered up with a couple of welders that really took a liking to me and really helped me to learn. They taught me how to layout, they taught me how to fit, and they taught me how to weld. I was finally getting to experience what I should have been experiencing all along in my apprenticeship. I really liked these men and to this day I feel indebted to them for being so kind to me. This was a heavy overtime job, though, and we worked from six o'clock in the morning until four o'clock in the evening every day, at least, and we worked every Saturday. Bob and I would still get together every night, regardless, and this didn't stop us from keeping up our studies of Pashto and Afghanistan.

About this time, I started seeing a girl named Beth. Beth and I had on and off again flings for about the past three years before this. Beth was a very attractive young lady that seemed to enjoy the male attention she received. It always seemed that despite all this male attention, Beth would always come running back to me in some way, shape, or form. During this run, Beth and I started getting a serious thing going and we were spending a lot of time together. Beth never gave me a hard time about hanging out with Bob, Beth didn't care about going out on dates, and Beth really liked to party. It was a pretty good fit for the time and we were having fun. Bob happened to approve of this girl too because she liked our kind of music.

Christmas Eve in 2004 took place on a Friday, so the jobsite I was on shut down after Friday's work and we wouldn't be returning to work until Monday. It was nice to have a break, because we had been working at least six days a week for over two and a half months straight. Keep in mind that when you're working ten-hour plus days and driving that far, it's really a 13 to 14-hour day with the commute.

I remember getting off work that Friday and going over to the jewelry store where I bought Beth a very nice pair of earrings. I even stopped at the home of a female friend and had her inspect them to make sure they were a nice enough gift. Megan approved of the purchase and I was excited to give Beth this nice gift.

Beth and I had already made loose plans to get together on Christmas Eve, so I called her on my way home from the jewelry store. I told her that I'd pick her up at about eight o'clock that night and we could head up to Q after we finished with our families. Beth told me that sounded like a plan. So that night after I finished Christmas Eve with my family, I drove over and picked up Bob, and then we went over to pick up Beth.

When I went to Beth's front door, she wasn't home. Her sister told me that a friend had picked her up already and she thought that they were leaving to go meet me at Q. I thanked her, wished everyone a Merry Christmas, and then headed over to Q.

When Bob and I got to Q, we ran into a huge group of our friends. Q used to draw quite the crowd at night on holidays, so this was no surprise to us.

Everyone was drinking heavily, having a great time, and then time started moving quickly. The next thing I knew it was nine o'clock, then ten o'clock, then eleven o'clock, and now it was nearing midnight.

There was still no sign of Beth and she hadn't returned my calls. I was getting concerned that something may have happened. Just after midnight, Bob and I were sitting at a table with a bunch of other friends when Beth came walking into the bar on the arm of some guy I'd never seen before. I remember the female friend that I had met with earlier to approve the earrings, Megan, gasped out loud. I was in absolute, utter shock since I had been with Beth just the night before.

Bob said to me, "Boy, you really know how to pick 'em, you asshole!" and he laughed in his high-pitched laugh. Even though I knew he was just razzing me, this was adding more steam to my already boiling temper.

Beth saw me, her face turned white, and then she did her best to try and avoid me like the plague. I was absolutely furious! Despite her best attempts at ignoring me, Beth eventually walked up to the bar to get drinks. As she walked past our table, I called her over.

I said, "Beth. What in the hell is going on here? Who the hell is that guy you walked in with? I just talked to you earlier today and we made plans and you blew me off."

Beth responded with, "Oh, that guy's just a friend. You and I never made firm plans."

"Yes," I said. "We made exact plans, Beth. You blew me off and then showed up here four hours later with some guy?"

I wasn't buying her BS for a minute and I finally got it out of her. Beth had been dating this guy for a while and, apparently, I was Beth's side project. This guy had no idea who I was, just like I didn't know who he was. Beth was all class, I tell you, and I was absolutely disgusted with her. Bob, meanwhile, was sitting there flushed red and laughing so hard that tears were streaming down his cheeks. He just thought this was the funniest thing in the world!

Bob, while still laughing, decided that we weren't going anywhere that night. He insisted that we stayed to see how this shitshow played out.

Bob and I kept drinking with our friends as my blood pressure kept rising. As I've said, I had a horrible temper back then, and it was just about to blow off. Bob knew this, he knew what was going to happen, and he wanted to see it happen. Bob always encouraged aggressive and explosive behavior on my part.

Soon enough, Beth, her boyfriend, and his friends, moved over and sat down at a table near us. This guy had his back to me, but he kept turning around and looking at me. It was obvious that Beth must have said something to him about me. Who knows what she could have told him, but judging by the glances, it was not good things that could have been said.

Bob, of course, egged me on by saying things like, "There he goes again, looking you over!"

Finally, I'd had enough. I walked over to this guy and I said to him, "Look man, if you stare over at me one more time I'm going to walk over here and lay you out."

This guy didn't argue or get nasty back and just kind of nodded. He wasn't much bigger than me and he had a soft body. I don't think he was looking for a confrontation and he was probably as confused as I was about what had taken place.

He stopped his glances, but a half hour later he turned around and looked at me again.

Bob exploded in laughter and yelled out, "Here we go!"

As Bob was encouraging me, my other friends were trying to talk me out of it. I ignored them and stormed over in the direction of this guy. He was still staring at me as I walked up, obviously thinking that I was bluffing with my previous threat. Before he knew what was happening, I grabbed him by the shirt collar and smashed him square in the nose with a right hand. I could hear Bob cackling-laughing at the top of his lungs as this poor guy crumpled off his stool and fell onto the floor. Beth sat there with a pained look on her face, not saying a word, and then put her head in her hands.

There were other people sitting at the table with them, though, and they were this guy's friends. They were not small guys either, and I quickly found myself surrounded by three of them. They were talking at this point and I didn't like to talk. I figured a rumble was coming, so I started pushing them in an attempt to create space. While I was plotting my attack on these three guys, which I was sure to lose, all of my friends sat there on their stools not doing a single thing. Bob, however, came flying up and joined me in the pushing.

I had just made up my mind that win, lose, or draw I was going to start punching these guys one by one. I could see Bob had his hand balled up and was waiting for my lead. I reached out to grab the large man directly in front of me, but I was stopped when the bouncers of Q pulled at me from behind and separated us. The bouncers quickly stepped in between these three large men, Bob, and me.

They were doing their best to de-escalate the situation as Bob kept reaching over them and trying to get it started again.

Bob and I knew these bouncers because we spent so much time in the bar, and they were totally cool with us. Eventually, we separated from the three friends of Bloody Nose. That's the name I gave to Beth's boyfriend who was now standing with an ice pack on his face and his head back. Beth was consoling him and changing out napkins for him.

The bouncers had cordoned off Bob and I into the corner of the bar. They sheepishly said, "Bob, Brad, you know we hate to do this to you guys, but we're going to have to ask you to leave."

Bob responded, "Hey man, didn't you see what was going on? That guy started the whole thing" and he pointed at Bloody Nose.

Tom, the lead bouncer responded, "Bob what are you talking about? We watched Brad walk right over there and punch the guy in the face. The guy didn't do anything."

"Well he was warned, man, Brad told the guy not to look at him." I couldn't help but laugh as Bob and I were allowed to walk back over, collect up, and put on our coats. We were then escorted to the exit of the bar.

Bob didn't let it go at that, either. With one arm in his coat, he pointed with the other in Beth's direction. He screamed out, "See what you caused here? You caused all of this. You're no good!"

Someone started a standing ovation and we pumped our fists in victory as we left the bar.

CHAPTER 27

THE CALL

Bob and I were banned from Q for a week after the fight. We went back to the bar on Christmas night, but the bouncers said that they couldn't let us in. They were under strict orders that the two of us were not to be let into the establishment. Why Bob got banned I'm not sure, he didn't do anything, but we served our time together once again. I never heard Bob complain once about the banishment.

We left Q that night and hung out at Joanie's Dry Dock for the next week, occasionally hanging out with my brother and his friends. I remember mutual friends at the Dock would ask us why we were hanging out there instead of our regular establishment. Bob would get this wide grin on his face, he'd let loose his high-pitched goofy laugh, and then he'd proceed to tell the story of me socking the guy in the face. Bob was really proud of that punch. What he conveniently left out of the story, though, was him egging me on to do it in the first place! I made sure to let that be known as Bob told the story and it only resulted in more high-pitched laughter.

Bob and I hung out on New Year's Eve that year as the clock turned to 2005. Ironically, we were invited to the private party that Q held every year. Beth and her boyfriend were not. Luckily for us, our banishment had ended just in time. Back then, Q used to be closed on New Year's Eve and they would hold a private party for their workers and for a small number of regulars. Some of our friends were also invited since they were all very tight with the staff too. I remember it was a good time and we stayed out until the sun came up. The best part was that we didn't pay a dime that night, the owner paid for everything.

Not too long after this, Bob and I had left Q one night after putting in a good deal of work. We were cruising down the road that led to Bob's house when I started to hear a rhythmic bumping sound. I remember it was a beautiful night, a freakishly warm night for that time of year, and we had the windows down. We were both smoking cigarettes and the stereo was blasting. I turned the stereo down and I kept hearing the bumping sound, louder now without music interfering.

I turned to Bob and asked him to look out the window to see if there was a flat tire. I had a 2001 Chevy Silverado and there were no tire sensors back then. Bob never moved from his position in the passenger seat. He stared straight ahead, as calm as could be, and he took a drag off his cigarette.

Without turning to look at me, Bob responded to my request with, "No, you stupid asshole, you jumped the curb a block ago and you're clipping mailboxes."

Sure enough, that's exactly what had taken place! You figure Bob would have told me when I hopped the curb, but that just wasn't his style.

During this time period, Bob and I were still attending our monthly drills for the Army. We had about three months off after our tour, but since August we were back to reporting to Arlington Heights one weekend a month. One Friday night, the night before drill, Bob and I were out partying pretty late. I stayed out even later because I had met a young lady at the bar.

I had crawled into bed at about 2:30 in the morning and was up again at 4:30 to get cleaned up and head to pick up Bob for drill. When I pulled into Bob's driveway that morning, I told him he had to drive because I was in rough shape. Bob took one look at me, laughed, shook his head at me, and then moved into the driver's seat of my truck.

I slept like a rock on the drive to the unit and when we arrived, I was given dirty looks by several people. I was hungover to all hell and everyone could see it. Shortly after the formation, I was pulled into an office by MSG Maddon, our operations NCOIC, and a man that I respected a great deal. He told me that I was in charge of running a weapons instruction course at the Motor Pool for that weekend's drill. He said someone was supposed to have contacted me about it beforehand. Nobody had, otherwise I wouldn't have stayed out as late as I did. I was expecting an easy drill weekend.

I told MSG Maddon it would be my pleasure to teach the course, I just wish I had some notice so that I could have been better prepared. I asked for an hour to head down to the motor pool to get things ready. He agreed.

As I broke my parade rest and prepared to leave the office, MSG Maddon spoke again. "SGT Drake."

"Yes, MSG Maddon," was my response.

"You smell of alcohol. I highly suggest that you stop at the vending machine and get something to eat and something to drink to mask your breath."

"Yes, Master Sergeant, I had a rough night," came out of my mouth and I immediately did as I was told.

On my way to the motor pool, I grabbed Ryan Suthard and Bob Allen and made them my AIs (assistant instructors) for the course and we headed down to the motor pool where we set up sandbags and a proper class setting. For a guy that had slept two hours, I put on one hell of a class with my two friends.

We covered all the proper Army instructions for a class and then we broke down pistol, rifle, and shotgun instruction. We covered the breakdown, cleaning, re-assembly, and proper firing techniques of the weapons. Ryan, Bob, and I took turns holding a stopwatch as we disassembled M-9s and M-16s and challenged each other in front of the classes. Bob won the M-16 breakdown and reassembly while Ryan and I tied times on the M-9.

The three of us ended up training not only the company, but all of the battalion staff too. I remember throwing several people out of the class who I felt were wasting my time. One student, specifically, was a young girl who was a clerk. She was an E-3 private first class and when I was trying to train her on the M-9, she told me that she'd never carry a pistol, so there was no reason she should be trained.

I looked at her and said, "You do realize we're at war and you will be deployed? When you get deployed you will want to carry a pistol instead of lugging that heavy ass rifle everywhere. Let's get you qualified on the pistol so we can make life easier for you down range."

She gave me a funny look and said, "I'll never get deployed…." I stopped her right there and threw her out of the class.

I recall Bob and Ryan throwing a few people out of the class also due to being flashed by weapons and overall non-cooperation and potential mental retardation. We weren't screwing around with this class, and we meant business.

After the second day of training, which I was well rested for, MSG Maddon pulled me aside again. He told me that the battalion commander had personally seen him to tell him how professional and how well done our training class was. He shook my hand and gave me a slap on the shoulder. I told the news to Bob and Ryan and all three of us were pleased to hear that. Compliments did not come freely or often in the Army, so it was a special occurrence when it happened.

The next drill they banned all alcohol consumption on drill weekends!

I don't remember much significant happening for the next few months. I was still working the heavy overtime job up north, and Bob and I were still getting together as often as we could. Some girls came and went during this time and our jukebox set kept getting more and more refined to barroom musical perfection. We were normal young men in our early 20s, but we weren't like those around us or our friends. We were different. We felt it, we knew it, and we knew what we had to do. We were soldiers, there was a war going on, and we needed to get back to doing what we knew best.

In March, 2005, as I hopped into my truck to go home from work I got a phone call from one of the unit administrators from the 327th. He told me that he had some hot information for me and something that I would be interested in. This was rare and I'd never gotten a phone call like that before. He asked me if I could meet him at the unit and I told him I'd be there in a half hour.

I took off from the jobsite and drove to Arlington Heights where I met with Mr. Cotto in a locked, secure office. He told me a mission had come down from the wire and they were looking for some volunteers. It just so happened that the mission was to head back to The Beast and that the current NCOIC for the mission was MSG Holder, the same man who was my MP instructor years before. Holder was also with us on the first tour and everyone respected him. Bob respected him too, despite the ass chewing and psych evaluation!

I cannot tell you how happy and excited I was during that meeting. I could barely contain myself. I gave Cotto my verbal commitment right then and there. Mr. Cotto then told me to feel free to call some friends but to keep operational security. I shook hands with him, thanked him, and I left the unit.

All these years later when I look back on that moment, I realize something: Mr. Cotto had spent roughly 25 years in the Army at that point. He was a civilian unit administrator, but he was also a master sergeant in the Reserve. He could have called anyone for that mission, but he called me first because he believed in me as a soldier and he believed in my friends as good soldiers. Cotto knew we were good at what we did. That still means a lot to me all these years later.

I called Bob on the way home and I told him that I'd be at his house in 45 minutes and that I had very important information for him. Bob met me in his driveway, and I told him to hop in the truck and we went for a ride. I told him everything that had been told to me and I asked him if he wanted in. Bob screamed out in elation that of course he wanted in. Bob and I then went out to celebrate.

While driving to the bar, Bob called Ryan Suthard. They made plans to meet up the next day to discuss the opportunity. Bob was not an emotional or a touchy-feely person, but I remember him hugging me that day. I remember hugging him back and being happy that we were going to get the chance to get back to doing what we knew best.

Bob called and left a voicemail the next day while I was at work. I checked it on my lunch break and the message simply said, "Suthard is in."

The home front didn't go so well, however. When I got home from work the next day, I told my Dad that I had committed to another tour. I remember he was cooking food on the stove and he wouldn't even look at me. He didn't say a word to me for three days after that. When I told my mom later that evening she screamed, cried, and sobbed for probably an hour. Although I knew this was putting strain on my family all over again, I also knew that this was what I had to do.

The job I was working on way up north ended shortly after I gave my commitment to the Army and I was laid off again for a few weeks. The two were unrelated. During those few weeks Bob and I tightened up. We practiced our Pashto frequently and we went shooting every day. We also bought gear and equipment that we wanted to take on the next tour, and we went up to the unit and received some secret briefings on the upcoming mission.

I'm telling you that after feeling awkward, out of place, and a bit lost for the previous year, I finally felt whole again and felt that I had a real purpose again. Bob was even more excited than I was. The best part of this for Bob was that this was a guaranteed promotion to E-5 Sergeant, for him as the mission required it. I was thrilled for my friend!

Mr. Cotto also called me and asked me to fill out a packet for promotion to E-6. Once again, I really appreciated him looking out for me, but I declined feeling that at 23 years old I was too young for staff sergeant and that I wasn't experienced enough. All these years later I stand by my decision. I was not ready for staff sergeant.

In late March 2005, knowing all this was going on, I was hired by a company called Martin Petersen Company and I went to work out of their shop in Kenosha, WI. I was only there a few weeks when we received our orders to active duty. Although the official date on the orders didn't start until May, I decided to leave my job early and spend some time getting things in order and having some fun before mobilizing. It was a good, smart move, and Bob and I had a lot of good times during this time. I also had a fishing trip to Canada planned.

Things were in order and it was time to return to the Ghan.

Bob in the late summer of 2003. This was a ring route helicopter mission held during the day. This picture hangs in my home.

Josh Burket and I at The Beast after a mission.

I'm standing next
to two of our
medics;
Todd Helms and
Matt Milenkovic.
March, 2004

Bob with German
soldiers on a
shooting range
just outside of
Kabul.

Tent city in Bagram,
Afghanistan.

Ron Garcia and I.
March, 2003

Bob with the love
of his life,
Jamie Hasenfang.
Spring, 2004

Bob appreciating a young boy's artwork in Kabul. Spring, 2004.

The world-famous Bagram bazaar, a glorified flea market. 2003.

Bob's bed area in our permanent tent. July, 2003.

Our tent in Bagram. July, 2003.

Eddie Balderas, John Wiley, and me. November, 2003.

A collection of landmines and rounds used for a booby trap.

Ryan Suthard,
Dennis Rolke, Bob,
Eddie Balderas, and
Ivan Beal.
New Year's Eve,
2003.

Myself, Bridget
Keane, and Jamie
Hasenfang at a club
in Lacrosse.
April, 2003.

Myself, John Wiley, and Bob. This is the first day back to Ft.
McCoy. April, 2004.

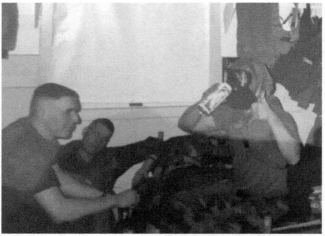

Bob, Matt Bender, and me drinking Budweiser through my
chemical mask. March, 2003.

Myself, Terry Scofield, and Bob with our unauthorized mohawk haircuts.

June, 2003.

PART TWO:

THE SECOND RUN

CHAPTER 28

DET 4 MOUNTS UP

In May, 2005 eleven volunteers of the U. S. Army Reserve entered active duty on orders. We knew exactly what our mission was going to be in country, it was just going to be an ongoing process until we got there. This particular group of volunteers were from a variety of units: six of us - including me - from the 327th MP Battalion, one from a unit out of Indiana, and three others from a unit out of Minnesota. All of us were from MP companies that fell under the 300th MP Command. Our official title was Detachment 4 (DET 4), 327th MP BN.

We first got together as a detachment when we had to report to Ft. Snelling, Minnesota to go through our deployment readiness program. This meant a few days getting medical checks, dental checks, and making sure our paperwork was in order. This was a lot easier than the last time we had gone through this as there wasn't nearly the amount of people on site. For most of us this also meant partying really hard at night at the hotel bar. Bob and I had a lot of fun in that hotel bar for the few nights we were there!

Among the group from Minnesota was a 25-year-old Staff Sergeant named Jim Roberts. Roberts was a tall, slim guy who at times, could be wired too tightly for his own good. I think he was in full blown culture shock when he got

, Ryan, and I. I don't think he was used to being around people like us

could party all night and still take care of business at an extremely high level

during the day. He didn't like it and it made him nervous for the first six weeks or

so. I think he finally realized we knew what we were doing, we were very good at

what we were doing, and we could turn it off or turn it on when we had to.

Overall, I liked and respected SSG Roberts a great deal.

Roberts said something once while we were in Afghanistan that's always

stuck with me. It was something I appreciated very much. I wasn't supposed to

hear it, but I happened to be within ear shot when he was talking to an operations

officer.

The officer was asking him about our detachment and Roberts said, "I've

got four guys on this detachment who have worked this jail before. Can you

believe that? These guys are fucking crazy. They volunteered to come back to

this shithole! Two of these guys read books on this country, they practice the

language, and I wouldn't be surprised if they apply for dual citizenship at some

point. I'm telling you, sir, these guys are crazy. And they're crazy good at what

they do. They're also the best of friends and they're inseparable. I walked into

the showers the other day and I overheard Pashto being spoken. I was about ready

to lock and load when I realized it was Allen and Drake. These guys are so into it

that they're practicing and studying in the showers! If we had a company full of

men like those two crazy sons of bitches, we'd have the best confinement

company in the Army!"

The second guy from the Minnesota crew was a huge, monstrous guy

named Doug Globke. I liked him immediately and I nicknamed him "Globs." In country he would get the extended nickname of Glob the Slob. I wasn't living with him yet, so at this point he was just Globs.

Globs was originally from Texas and he liked to drink beer as much as we did. He had a good sense of humor, a good personality, and he was no dummy. He had served in Iraq already with Roberts and Schlitz.

The third guy from the Minnesota crew was a clown by the name of Schlitz. Yes, you read that right, he was a clown. Schlitz had been in the Navy at some point and had already done a tour in Iraq with Roberts and Globke. He had an irritable way about him that could just piss you off, however, and he did stupid stuff like wear an MP badge on his belt. MPs in the Army don't wear badges. He also had this shifty eyed look where you couldn't tell if what he was telling you was the truth or not.

Something was off about this guy and none of us cared much for him right from the beginning. He was in his early 30s and was in pretty good shape, but he thought he was God's gift to women. He chased after every woman he could and many of those that he couldn't! When it came to smarts, he got the short end of the stick. He also almost got beaten up by at least four of us on the deployment. There will be plenty more to come on Schlitz.

Coming into DET 4 from Indiana was a guy by the name of Jason Cain. The first time I shook hands with Cain, I liked him. He had done a tour at The Beast before. As a matter of fact, he was there for the second rotation of that jail in '02. He had a lot of experience and on the civilian side he was either an EMT or a paramedic, something along those lines. I called him "Doc" and I still do to this day.

Doc had a calm demeanor about him and rarely got excited. He was down to earth, from a blue-collar family, and he had a friendship loyalty to him that clicked right away. He was also one of the world's greatest smartasses and wasn't afraid to tell you, or anyone else, exactly what was on his mind. Doc was another guy that for a year straight, and even in high stress situations, we never had a cross word. He was one of the four that almost beat Schlitz' ass.

Now, I can't remember if Lester Dodson came to us from the 822 or the 814 of the battalion, but he came from one of them. Lester was a former Marine, about my height, but he had about 30 pounds on me of pure muscle. He was built like a rugby player and was as hard as a coffin nail both physically and mentally. His intensity was rivaled by none. If Lester put his mind to something, he accomplished it.

Lester was in his mid-30s and had the body of a 20-year-old. His fitness was impeccable. Lester quickly fit in with Ryan, Bob, and I right away. He once gave me a haircut that caused me to put shoe polish on my head to try and invoke a look of stubble. Lester showed loyalty like no other and he became a great friend. I can't begin to tell you the respect that I have for him.

The next guy that volunteered with us was Andrew Blanco. I'm positive that he was from the 822. Blanco was about four years older than me and he was as tough as they come. He was a Cicero, Illinois kid, born and raised, and he had also been an active duty tanker. One day I saw Blanco walking stiffly after a PT session. I didn't say anything, but when we were changing, I saw him take his socks off. His feet were swollen and covered in scar tissue. Apparently out at NTC (National Training Center) many years before, Blanco was injured in an accident. He was working on the turret of his tank in the middle of the night when another tank drove by and clipped the gun. The impact sucked Blanco's legs into the turret, essentially destroying his legs from below the knees. That tough SOB spent two years learning how to walk again, refused any kind of a medical buyout, and honorably served the rest of his active duty time.

On the civilian side, Blanco was a prison guard. After being out of the military for a few years, he had joined the Reserves and became an MP. Bob, Suthard, and I liked Blanco right away. He was a smoker, he was a drinker, he was an insane partier, and he was one of the realest people you'd ever meet. He also held nothing back and would tell you exactly what was on his mind.

Blanco came to us with quite the reputation also. Apparently, on a training mission a few months before, Blanco got into it with another soldier. Later that night, after a few too many drinks, Blanco paid that soldier back by urinating in his boots. The other soldier didn't realize it until it was too late.

Blanco also came close to beating Schlitz' ass.

Next was our assistant commander of the detachment SSG Sanchez. SSG Sanchez was probably in his early 50s at this point and had been in the Army for decades and had done a few tours. He was a tough guy and he was a persistent guy. I respected him, but I later dreaded working for him. More on him later!

Lastly, was our detachment commander, SFC Anderson. He was a monster of a man who had been both active duty infantry and active duty as a corrections MP. He was AGR (Active Guard Reserve) for the 327th. You had no choice but to respect him because his experience and his rank commanded your respect. One thing I really liked about SFC Anderson is that he never lost his cool and he stayed professional. He was the same, day in and day out, no matter what. He was a fair man.

SFC Anderson never threatened to, or came close to, beating Schlitz' ass.

After Ft. Snelling, our detachment returned home to the mother ship in Arlington Heights. There we created classes and trained each other. It was kind of a nice routine, actually. We'd have PT every morning at 6, we'd get breakfast, we'd train, we'd get lunch, then we'd train a few more hours, and then we'd be released. The guys from out of state would go back to their hotel and have dinner, and the rest of us would go home. Bob and I would usually have dinner, get cleaned up, and head out for beers. It was a good routine.

It was during this mobilization period that I experienced a class that would stick with me the rest of my life. The unit had arranged with a local recreation center and a two-day class was scheduled. The first day of the class is where we did OC certification. That's pepper spray in civilian terms.

The second day of this two-day class was self-defense. An E-7 from Minnesota came down to train us. He taught us basic Hapkido, judo, hand grips, and defensive strikes. What that man taught us was the second greatest training I ever received in the Army. In one full day he taught us how to handle ourselves in bad spots. He was so good at what he did that if you had any kind of athletic background, and most of us did, you picked up on his training quickly. You knew how to handle yourself in a prison environment after his classes.

Bob and I talked about that training for years to come and he was right there in agreement with me on its importance. Just a few months later in Afghanistan, Bob and I would use what we were taught when we created an

Unarmed Self Defense training class for The Beast.

Life was good during this mobilization. The weather was beautiful out as it was May, and Bob and I were back doing what we wanted most to do. There was never a feeling of gloom or doom to return to the Ghan, it was a buzzing feeling of excitement in getting back over there. We really enjoyed the company of our new friends too. We started hanging out together during our little bit of free time away from the unit, getting to know each other and getting to know each other's humor. Blanco was one of the greatest guys in the world to drink with, he was a lot of fun. He really fell in with Bob and I and he would meet up with us almost every night at local bars.

CHAPTER 29

FT. DIX ARRIVAL

In early June of that year, the orders came down. Bob, Lester, and Andrew Blanco got their stripes. Being promoted to E-5 is a really big deal in the Army and it's something that you dream about from the time you first lace up your boots in basic training.

The Army has a lot of great time-honored traditions and one of them is that when you get promoted to sergeant. The soldier getting promoted gets to pick another NCO to pin them while in formation. When I got promoted to E-5 in September, 2003, I picked SSG Scofield. I admired and respected Scofield and it was an honor to have him pin me.

Bob picked me. Let me tell you, being picked to pin someone their E-5 is one of the greatest honors that you can receive as an NCO. Bob could have picked any other NCO, but he picked me, and I'll never forget it.

I was so proud of Bob and I took this honor seriously. I did it right too. I forgot to put the backings on the end of the pins, just like had been done to me! Bob, Lester, and Andrew all got to experience this time-honored tradition of having metal pins buried into the skin of their collars. It leaves red marks and some blood, but it's the greatest feeling in the world!

I remember hugging Bob after the ceremony and telling him how proud I was of him and how happy I was for him. I recall that after we were dismissed that afternoon, I drove us straight to Q and we proceeded to get shitfaced in celebration. I bought drinks for everyone at the bar that night because I was so happy for Bob. I think after the party was over that evening, we slept about 3 hours, and then headed right back up to the unit for training the next day.

One of the last things we did before we were sent off to Ft. Dix, our established mobilization station, was that we did a training exercise at the Navy Base in North Chicago. The Navy permitted us to use their brig and our senior NCOs in the unit created a series of mission scenarios for us. It was not difficult stuff, but at one point during the exercises one of our higher-ranking NCOs kept screwing it up. Bob, Ryan, and I simply took over the rest of the missions at that point and handled every scenario.

I remember MSG Maddon pulled us aside and said to us, "Just so you know, you three are going to have to take over down range. You have some incompetent leaders and you three know best what to do."

Fortunately, that didn't come to fruition. Our incompetent leadership learned quickly and did a great job in country.

In mid-June, 2005, DET 4 was sent to the Ft. Dix. On the day we were leaving, our families were invited to come and see us off. You see, despite the way things are now, back then things weren't yet totally refined when it came to deployments. In 2005, the wars were still relatively new, and you didn't know if you would get the chance to see your family again before heading off to the theater of war where you were assigned.

I recall the night before we left for Dix having a hard time saying goodbye to my four year-old nephew and my, almost, one year-old niece. That was tough because I spent a lot of time with them. It bothered me a bit knowing that since my niece was so young, she likely wouldn't know who I was when I got back.

Yes, of course it was tough leaving my parents and my brother Jeff again too. My brother Jeff was my best friend back then, I spent almost as much time with him as I did with Bob. Jeff would call me up on nights that he had off and ask me to meet him at Joanie's for a few drinks. And then he'd always ask me if Bob could come too! Jeff really liked Bob and they got along well. My brother Jeff loves 1980s action films and so did Bob. They would talk about them for hours on end.

It's always tough to leave your mother. I feel when you become an adult, a duty of yours becomes to take care of your mom. I felt bad about leaving my mom again. My mom could make friends with anyone and she has a personality that draws everyone to her. She also has the greatest mom-sense of all time and can put any baby to sleep, anytime, anywhere, and can feed anyone, anytime, anywhere.

She has the patience of a saint and has a calming effect on anyone. If someone is upset in my mother's presence, they will calm themselves within minutes of just being around her. She's someone very special. She's simply the best and I love her dearly.

It was sad leaving my Dad again too, but he and I had already had the chat we needed to have on a fishing trip in Canada the month before. Pop and I were out in the middle of this gorgeous Ontario Lake in about 50-degree weather, not too long after sunup. It was a beautiful morning and we had just casted out our jigs in the water. Everyone, at least once in their life, should get to experience the beauty of an Ontario lake in May. It's breathtaking. There is absolute stillness and absolute calm, but there is a ton going on. There is wildlife everywhere, animals are constantly checking things out, and life is moving. It's dead silent, but it's the busiest place you'll ever be.

Now my Dad is not one to talk of emotions. He's not one to talk of feelings. My Dad, whether he wants to admit it or not, is an old school Vietnam veteran badass. The more I got to know artillery soldiers and ex-artillery soldiers, the better I got to understand my Dad's personality. I could see the exact same traits in them that I saw in my Dad. Their personality is to drive, drive, drive. Their mentality is to take care of your own, push forward no matter what, and always cover your flank. You will never find a human being with more internal drive and guts than you will a current or former soldier who is infantry or artillery. My Dad has lived his life like that. Due to that mentality he has been completely successful and has been a wonderful and devoted father who, fortunately, instilled some of that in his family.

While we were in this beautiful scenario in Canada, it was dead silent. Well, except for me smoking a Marlboro Medium which my dad detested and would shake his head at.

My Dad, without looking at me, said, "Hey, are you going to be all right over there again?" I was taken aback that my Dad, the ultimate hard ass, would ask me a question like this.

I thought about it for a second and I responded, "Dad, this is what I do, and I do it very well with my friends. We all have unfinished business and we need this. I'm going to be just fine."

Pop was quiet for a moment or two and he said, "Well then I guess you better get back over there and finish your business."

We went back to enjoying the quiet and it was never brought up again. That old artillery sergeant knew the deal all along, I think he just wanted to hear me say it out loud.

This June morning my folks came up to the unit, Bob's mom and stepdad Dave came up, and some of the other families made it up too. The unit administrators had set up some tables and chairs and they had some cake and coffee for us. The active staff and the civilians shook each of our hands and wished us the best of luck. It was a very classy thing that they did for us. I remember as we were getting ready to load the vans in the back of the building, when SSG Garcia showed up.

Ron Garcia was someone that took care of me when I was an E-1 private and I was assigned to his platoon. We remained close throughout the first tour and after. I remember he shook hands with Bob, Ryan, and I, and gave us hugs. That really meant a lot to me. This man took a day off of work to drive up to the unit to see us off. Respect doesn't get any deeper than that and Ron Garcia is the definition of respect.

I also remember hugging Jean Drenth and shaking hands with Dave. Dave then gave me a big hug too. I really liked Dave, he was a great guy, and he was super kind and nice to me. Every time I would pick up Bob, and Dave would be outside working on something, he'd run over to say hello and chat with me. I remember him a few times pulling me aside and asking me if I could get Bob into the pipefitters with me. I would tell Dave that I'd talked to Bob about it, but he just wasn't interested. Dave would tell me to keep trying!

We loaded into the vans where we were taken to O'Hare Airport and we would fly out to Philadelphia. Of course, we had a couple of hours until the flight left so Bob, Ryan, a few others, and I headed over to the bar and had a few drinks to pass the time.

Hours later, we landed in Philadelphia and then we caught a shuttle bus to the post. I'm not sure what expressway that is along the eastern seaboard there, but it is a very cool thing to see. There is an old shipyard on the right-hand side that holds old Navy ships ready to be scrapped. As you drive on, on the left side of the expressway, you can see the Eagles stadium, the Phillies stadium, and some other landmarks. It's a really nice piece of scenery.

When we got to Ft. Dix, we were given housing assignments and we showed up to a giant set of old-style barracks. The barracks had been remodeled recently and we were in a large 12-man room. There was air conditioning, we had wall lockers, and the living conditions were very good. I remember we had the rest of the day off and we spent the day organizing our gear and getting ready for processing the next day.

In the room were bunk beds. I took the top bunk and Bob took the bottom bunk. The barracks, at that time, were pretty much vacant except for a few stragglers who didn't deploy with their units for whatever reason. Later that day we went to the dayroom that had a pool table, some couches, and a nice sized TV. That was the first time I saw the movie Blade Runner. It was one of Bob's all-time favorites and he and I sat there and watched the whole thing.

The next morning, we got up early and went for breakfast at the chow hall. Fortunately for us, the dining facility was the next building over from ours. After breakfast, we loaded into a passenger van and headed off to our in-processing.

In-processing was not nearly as crowded as the one at Ft. McCoy had been, but there were still a lot of soldiers moving through it at this time. There were a lot of stations, with a lot of paperwork, and some basic medical checks. I remember when we got to the shots station, we were only required to get one or two shots. The nurses then asked us if we wanted the Anthrax booster shot. I asked why this was optional and the Army nurse told us that the shots had never been approved by the FDA. Due to this, the Army no longer made the booster mandatory.

Bob, smartass that he was, asked the nurse if the Anthrax shots were the reason that soldiers from our first tour had been growing tails. The nurse looked surprised at what Bob had said and asked him to repeat himself.

Bob, continuing to be a smartass, responded, "Hey Suthard! Pull down your pants and show this nice specialist here the scar from your tail! She doesn't believe you grew a tail in Bagram." Suthard, not skipping a beat, undid his pants and showed the scar where he had his tail cut out in Bagram.

This poor young nurse looked horrified. To this day I'm not sure if she was horrified at the fact that people were growing tails, the fact that Bob was perfectly comfortable staring and pointing at his friend's ass, or if she was in total shock at the amount of body hair that Suthard possessed. Either way, it was memorable, and Lester Dodson was laughing so hard that he almost urinated himself. SSG Roberts was upset, of course, and yelled at Suthard to pull his pants back up.

By "tails", I am implying a medical issue that Ryan Suthard had at Bagram on our first tour. On his tail bone he had a cyst that had grown, and consequently he had to have it medically removed. We referred to it as his "tail." Oddly enough, at least two other soldiers also ended up with the same issue shortly after that tour concluded.

We all refused to get our Anthrax booster and we proceeded to get a few shots from another nurse. This nurse was very attractive, by the way. She was smiling and started asking me about where I was from and making small talk. She introduced herself to me as SGT Bonilla, she was a fellow E-5, and I dare to say that she was hitting on me. She didn't seem to mind that there were others in line behind me either, she was taking her sweet time. She was about 5 feet tall, had dark hair, she was olive skinned, and was from New York. She was a Yankees fan and so was I.

We were having a pleasant conversation until I got yelled at by Roberts to keep moving. I had no choice but to say goodbye and move on. Andrew Blanco, who knew everything about opposite sex attraction and men's fashion, came running up to me. "Drake, you idiot. Did you at least get her number? That girl was smoking hot!"

I told him no, I didn't, and that I didn't mix it up with other GIs because it's bad for business. He couldn't believe what I told him, and he called me a dumbass for the rest of the day. In hindsight, Blanco was right. He was always right. Even when he was wrong, he was right.

CHAPTER 30

THAT'S NOT A LATRINE

4th of July in 2005 fell on a Monday. We were given the weekend off and additionally we were given Monday off in observance of the holiday. On post, the shops and stores were all closing up on Sunday and Monday, so if you wanted to get anything for the weekend you needed to run out on Saturday in order to get it.

Ft. Dix had a no-alcohol policy in the barracks. You could drink anywhere outside of the barracks, but it was forbidden inside the building. Across from our barracks was an abandoned bus stop. There were two large benches placed alongside a large, wide-open sidewalk. The stop number had long been taken down and there was no action in this area anymore. It was perfect.

In compliance with the rules of Ft. Dix, we didn't drink in the barracks. We would buy our alcohol from the Class Six (military liquor store) and then take it to the bus benches to consume. 4th of July that year was no different.

Knowing that things would be shut down on Sunday and Monday, several of us loaded up into our duty van and drove to the class six. There we bought a full weekend's supply of ice, beer, hard liquor, and coolers. We kept the coolers in the van and wrapped them in blankets for insulation. We also went to the commissary on the Army side of the post and loaded up on hot dogs, buns, burgers, sausages, and other foods like chips. The cold items we brought back to the building and asked permission from the desk sergeant of our barracks to keep them in his refrigerator. He was totally fine with it, so long as we brought him some when it was cooked up.

Like all other military posts, the one at Dix had an MWR Center. Some military posts had wonderful MWR centers where you could sign out items like sports equipment, kayaks, tables, chairs, or tents for yard parties. And some, like Ft. Dix, even had barbecue grills that you could sign out! We signed out a grill and a folding table to be brought back on Tuesday. We were all set!

Not all of our soldiers were around this weekend, however. Most had left on Thursday afternoon after we were released from duty. Roberts, Schlitz, Globke, and Cain had all decided to take a trip that weekend to New York City. They rented a car and took off after dinner on Thursday. SFC Anderson and SSG Sanchez were also not there. They had flown home for the weekend. The remaining soldiers were Bob, Ryan, Blanco, Lester Dodson, and me.

That Saturday we did not dip into our supplies. We partied at the enlisted club and had our meals there and at the chow hall. By noon on Sunday, it was on! We set up our table in front of the bus benches and got the grill fired up. We brought our coolers out from the van and cracked into our favorite drinks. We grilled and partied all afternoon and into the evening. We had so much food that we would give some to passersby and we also made sure to take care of the poor desk sergeant who was stuck on duty. We kept it up until late into the night on Sunday and then packed our stuff up and headed in to sleep.

Monday was the 4th and it did not disappoint. We hit it early that day because we knew the rest of our detachment would be coming back later that evening. Our plan was to be done drinking by five that evening so we could get some rest and be ready for the next day's training. That was as far as our plan got.

By Monday evening we had our whole detachment out on the sidewalk partying with us and eating up the last of our food. Dan Jabs, a friend of ours from another company in our battalion, came walking by. We didn't even know he was on post! He joined the party with us along with several others.

SSG Roberts had a few drinks with us, but he was concerned at how much the rest of us were drinking and he was also concerned if we would be back in the barracks at a reasonable hour to get some rest. The poor guy was still in culture shock with our partying capabilities at this point.

Most of the partygoers were smart and removed themselves from the party to get some rest at about eight o'clock. Bob, Lester, Blanco, Ryan, and I all stayed outside and kept going. And going. And going. And going. This was business as usual for Bob and I and we were glad that Suthard, Dodson, and Blanco were joining in with us. We had cleaned up our food stuff, grill, and table earlier in the day, but we sat out at that abandoned bus stop until 1am. We made sure that there was nothing left to drink.

When we came back into the barracks, all of us were well done for. We had to help each other up the three flights of stairs to our room. I was seeing double, Bob was cackling his familiar high-pitched drunken laugh, Lester was laughing uncontrollably, and Suthard and Blanco were trying to be responsible. All of us spilled into our beds knowing that we would have to be up in just a few hours for training.

About 20 minutes after lying down in my upper bunk, I started to hear the bunk shake and Bob getting up front underneath me. Instead of turning left to head out the door into the hallway, Bob turned right and headed toward the other row of bunks. He made another quick right and opened up the first wall locker. As I was trying to figure out what Bob was doing, I heard it. Bob's urine stream was hitting against the metal in the locker.

Dodson, without skipping a beat, screamed out, "Hey! That's not a latrine!"

Bob responded with a grunt and then stopped pissing. All of us that had been drinking earlier were now dying laughing as Bob, embarrassed, ran to get paper towels to clean up the mess. Fortunately, it was an empty wall locker!

A few hours later we had to get up for training. Bob and I grabbed our shaving kits and towels and headed down to the latrine to take a shower and get cleaned up. After we had finished getting cleaned up, we stepped back out into the hall to begin the walk back to our room. SSG Roberts was furiously pacing around the hallway, waiting for us. As we stepped toward the door to our room, he stopped us and locked us up at parade rest.

Roberts did his best drill sergeant impression as he bladed his hand and pointed it in our faces while screaming at us, "What in the hell is wrong with you, Allen? You pissed in a wall locker last night! You're out of control, both of you are out of control with your drinking!"

I couldn't help myself and I burst out laughing. Bob followed my lead and also started laughing. This infuriated Roberts more.

Roberts stuck his bladed hand in my face now. Furiously, he said, "Do you think this is funny? This isn't funny! There could have been somebody's stuff in that wall locker! This is not funny. Why do you think this is funny?"

Stifling a laugh, I caught my breath and responded, "I think it's absolutely fucking hilarious, Sergeant!"

Bob and I burst out laughing again and Roberts gave up. We both walked back into the room where everybody else except for Anderson and Sanchez were laughing. Roberts didn't give up there. He lobbied hard to SFC Anderson to ban drinking for the rest of the mobilization.

SFC Anderson called a formation later that day condemning the urination in the wall locker. While he was talking, I did the best I could, but I erupted laughing again. Anderson formed a huge smile on his face while trying to stifle his own laugh. Roberts had steam coming out of his ears!

Anderson then cut a quick speech. "You're all grown men, you're all NCOs, and you're all going to make your own decisions about how to live your lives. So long as you show up to work and do your job, I don't give a shit what you do the night before. If someone pisses in another wall locker, though, we're going to have a problem."

Never again did Bob, or any of us, piss into another wall locker. This wasn't the end of our out of control partying, however.

One Saturday night, Bob, Suthard, Blanco, and I decided to go up to the enlisted club on post. The enlisted club happened to be on the Air Force side and was about 5 miles away from our barracks. We loaded into our assigned passenger van and Blanco drove us up to the enlisted bar. We got some food, drank some beverages, and played some video games. It was a large place and it had a really nice bar. Leave it to the Air Force to do it right!

Well, sure enough exactly what we didn't want to happen, happened. The four of us got absolutely annihilated at this enlisted club. The jukebox was taken over, the bartender was greased to crank up the volume, loud singing was done, shots were being thrown back, and this mild quiet good time turned into a loud, wild, great time.

I remember playing some Sinatra and Elvis Presley on the juke and dancing with the local girls. I tried getting Bob to dance with this one looker, but he wasn't having any of it. She wasn't Jamie Hasenfang and he was having too much of a good time making fun of people and hammering down drinks with Blanco and Suthard.

Before we knew it "Last call!" was being shouted out and we were buying last minute drinks.

We had been at the bar for about 7 hours by the time it closed. I'm pretty sure our tab came out to be well under $100 for the four of us. Again, this was an enlisted bar, drinks were ridiculously cheap. The friendly Jersey girls were trying to get me to go to an off-post club with them, but I wasn't willing to take the risk this early in the mobilization. I remember I exchanged numbers with a couple of these girls, and I did meet up with them at the bar again a few weeks later.

When we got out to the parking lot, I insisted on calling a cab to get back to the barracks. Blanco yelled obscenities at me and ordered us all in the van. He claimed he was fine to drive, and I wasn't going to argue. We hopped in the van and the first thing Blanco did was pull a bottle of beer out of his pocket and put it between his legs. The next thing he did was light up a cigarette. There's no drinking or smoking allowed in government vehicles, of course. He then fired up the engine, punched the gas, and proceeded to drive 65 miles per hour down the road back to the barracks.

I was scared for my life as Blanco was playing chicken with cars at intersections and was taking corners at 50 miles an hour. I pleaded with him to slow down and he called me a "pussy" and told me to "shut up." I turned around to look at Bob and Ryan, who were in the back seat, and they were laughing and thought this was the funniest thing in the world.

I was fully convinced that at any given moment the van was going to flip, and we were all going to die a horrible, fiery death. Blanco sipped his beer and smoked his cigarette as he continued to run through red lights and stop signs on the way back to the barracks. When he pulled into the parking lot, I got out of the van as fast as I could, ran up to the barracks room, and thanked God I was still alive. Behind me all I could hear was Bob and Ryan laughing and Blanco cursing me out for being such a "pussy."

Back in the room I gunned down some water and then I went to the latrine, brushed my teeth, and headed to bed. A few minutes later Bob and Ryan, still laughing, came into the room and they also went to sleep. After a few more minutes I noticed that there was no Blanco. I didn't think much of it and turned over and drifted off to sleep.

About ten minutes later we were all woken up in the room by the blood curdling scream of a woman. I immediately ran out of the room with Ryan and Bob. We heard the scream coming from the floor below us, where the females' rooms were. When we got down to the floor, we saw Blanco stumbling down the hallway smoking a cigarette and walking with his beer in his hand still. We met up with him and got him back to the third floor.

We asked him what the hell was going on and he told us the story.

He said, "I went to the bathroom to take a dump. I finished up and I'm washing my hands. After that, I opened the window, lit up another smoke, and was on the phone with Fabi (his wife.) All of a sudden, this broad came walking in the bathroom and I yelled at her and told her she's on the wrong floor. I mean what the fuck is she doing on our floor?"

Blanco didn't realize that he hadn't made it all the way up the flight of stairs to the third floor. He also didn't realize that it was he who was in the wrong bathroom, illegally drinking in the barracks, and illegally smoking a cigarette in the barracks.

After this day, I referred to that van ride only as the "Demon Hell Ride."

CHAPTER 31

THE FT. DIX DEATH MARCH

Things at Ft. Dix, New Jersey were a well-organized disaster, to put it bluntly. It was endless courses and ranges and training and certifications and on and on and on. There are a couple of ranges that stand out in my mind all these years later. I'd like to touch on them and their utter ridiculousness.

All training being done at Ft. Dix was to send full companies down range to Iraq. There was never once a mention of any other theater of war taking place at the time. Never once did we hear the words Afghanistan, Kuwait, UAE, Bahrain, or any of the other areas that detachments and units were training up for. Everything was about Iraq.

Now, I can reasonably understand that in 2005 probably 75% of the men and women pushing through Dix were headed there, but it got old quickly. Another issue with this training was that everything was fear mongering. They were showing videos of blown up American soldiers' corpses on the streets of Iraq and other videos of their mutilated bodies being dragged around. One video, which I found most disturbing, was a video of some terrorist group showing off their collection of fingers, hands, jaws, and other shredded up body parts of dead GIs from IED attacks. These terrorists proudly displayed the deceased's ID cards and ID tags next to their body parts.

I remember taking a smoke break after this training and there were dozens of soldiers standing around outside the building in silence. There were a lot of young soldiers there who hadn't been deployed yet, who were already scared, and after watching those videos they were now absolutely terrified. I remember overhearing their whispered conversations and seeing how their morale was completely shot because of what they'd just seen.

This last video irritated Bob very much. He went off on a rant at the smoking area. Some of the training cadre was there, also smoking, and Bob really started letting these "slick sleeves" have it.

Bob told them, "Well, this is great training. We're all going to die in Iraq. I'm not even going to Iraq, but I'm 100% certain that now I'm going to die there. What the hell is wrong with you people? Why are you beating down morale and showing shit like this to E-1 privates who should be getting built up right now?"

There was no answer from the training cadre.

Bob was right. It was terrible, counterproductive training. I understand the need to show deploying soldiers the seriousness of where they were going, but this was over the top and unnecessary. We all learned a lesson that day about how to be an NCO and how to train people for effectiveness, not to kill their morale.

Soon after this training, on other ranges, we qualified on our rifles, pistols, and shotguns. Not a single one of us in the detachment had a problem qualifying. We were all first-time-gos and we all qualified sharpshooter or expert on all weapons. That didn't keep us from having to spend twenty hours straight on the range, however, and we had to wait until it was pitch black for the night qualification on the rifle. I remember one of our guys had a difficult time shooting in the dark and we all helped him push through. We were out on that range until at least midnight and we had to be on another range early the next day.

DET 4 didn't get much sleep that night, obviously, and I think we may have slept the few hours we could in our vehicles. I remember shaving in our vehicle's mirror the next day and brushing my teeth in a tree line.

The next range was the dumbest thing I ever did in the Army. Now, I did a lot of dumb things, but this one took the cake by far. Ft. Dix in July is hot. It's very, very hot. When we got to this range in the morning, we started receiving our briefing and instructions. It turns out the range that we were on was a road march range where we were going to have to clear "enemy" villages.

I want you to note in your mind that by the time we started the actual range after all the briefings, it was after ten o'clock in the morning and the heat was about 90 degrees and rapidly climbing. It was Heat Category 5 which means that you are supposed to take several breaks an hour and hydrate on a regular basis. Frankly, a range like the one we were on should have been shut down. It wasn't, however, and we took to the road to complete this 10-mile road march. We had a high speed young 2LT with us who was our evaluator and who had a slick sleeve on his right shoulder. Bob loved him immediately and nicknamed him "Lieutenant Asshole."

I want you to realize that everybody in our detachment at this point had been in either Iraq or Afghanistan except for two guys. We all had experience. Our experiences were different, but we had "down range MP senses" that develop

271

with being in certain places over periods of time. You learn what to look for, what feels right or doesn't, and what the appropriate response is. We knew how to handle ourselves in situations because we'd been in them already.

As we're moving down the road, 2LT Asshole was following us when we came across our first enemy village. They had local people from New Jersey, many of Arab descent, dressed and acting as local nationals. I think the first group we came upon that lovely, hot as hell day, were staging a "protest" that was "getting violent."

SSG Jim Roberts stopped the patrol some distance away and evaluated the scenario. Without saying a word, he split us up through hand signals and positioned us in fighting positions off the road. We had weapons drawn and we were locked onto the group of "protesters." Roberts motioned for the representative of the group to meet him down the road. He did. When they came to the center, Roberts told him that this group of local nationals should disperse and move off the road. The man voiced his resistance. Roberts told him that if he and his people did not disperse off the road and return to their homes, we would open fire and then we would move their bodies off the road.

The man's face was in shock and 2LT Asshole was up in arms yelling at Roberts. Roberts then fired three rounds into the air with his rifle (blank rounds, of course) and the man ran off. Soon enough his people dispersed and left the road. It was a terrific sight to see and this 2LT lost his mind and started throwing "what if" scenarios at Roberts.

Roberts got really pissed and told him, "Sir, this is how things are handled and done, and I just did it. Now we're going to move on down this road with or without you."

And that is exactly what we did. After every one of these "villages" that we came across there was a water buffalo and every single one of these water buffalos were empty by the time we got to them. We didn't have any water.

Shortly after we cleared the first "village", we stopped on the side of the road to rest. Doc Cain, as up front as he always was, stood up and started walking away. 2LT Asshole asked him where he was going.

Cain said, as bluntly as ever said, "Fuck this. I'm a heat casualty and I'm going to go stick my ass with an IV in your medic tent."

We all busted out laughing as this 2LT threatened to hold him back if he didn't complete the training.

Cain's response was, "What are you going to do, sir, send me to Afghanistan?"

The balls on that guy!

The rest of us got up and kept moving on. I can't remember how many villages we visited that day, but we handled each one the same way. We handled them with the threat of brute force or straight brute force and things ended quickly. I recall at one range we apprehended a rowdy villager and used zip ties to bind his hands and feet. The 2LT was screaming at us about how we handled the situation wrong and why did we have zip ties? We explained we were MPs, we always have zip ties, and that's how we handle situations like that. At the end of the village was another empty water buffalo and we left the poor mock-villager tied up on the side of the road. I'm assuming at some point someone cut the ties, but who knows.

By the time we got to Mile 7 or so with no water, tempers began to fly. Blanco finally yelled out a loud and resounding "Fuck this!" and sat down, dropped his Kevlar helmet, and took off his body armor.

It was easily over 100 degrees at this point and we hadn't had water in a very long time. The 2LT started screaming at Blanco to get up and then our other acting platoon sergeant, SSG Sanchez, stepped in. He and Blanco went back and forth for a good 5 minutes. Bob and I laughed hard at this and soon after I coined the phrase "Azteca Blood Feud" to describe the terrible relationship between Blanco and Sanchez. Things were never the same after that and the two didn't get along for the rest of the tour.

After this heated exchange, Blanco put his gear on, got back up, and we finished this ridiculous and stupid range. We nicknamed it appropriately the Ft. Dix Death March.

When we got to the end of the range, we found another water buffalo with no water in it and we were all seeing red now on top of the shiny sparklers we were already seeing from dehydration. What came next was the biggest kick in the groin possible.

To finish off the death march was now another range complete with overhead machine gun fire and explosions. The course was a good 100 yards long and included low crawling, team movements between points, and other obstacle course type activites. It was over 100 degrees, we'd been out in the sun for hours with no water, and now we were being required to sprint, low crawl, climb, fire, and fight our way through a range the length of a football field. Lester Dodson and I partnered up and went through this range first. It was awful. We were both in great shape at the time but both of us were gasping for breath and half-dead as we reached the 50-yard point. We were in the midst of two-man rushes when Lester didn't respond to my call. I looked back at him and he was half-passed out.

I started screaming at him and, suddenly, I saw Lester get the second most pissed I'd ever seen him. He started screaming out obscenities towards the trainers on the range and at the range itself. He came to his feet and was a madman, a man on fire! I had no choice but to start screaming with him and charging too. We finished out the final 50 yards of that range in a blinding rage. We unloaded several magazines with blanks and then attacked dummies at the end of the range as if it were hand to hand combat. The trainers looked at us like we were insane and, frankly, they weren't too far off at that point.

After the death charge, Lester and I walked up a short hill where we found trees and a water buffalo that was actually filled with water! We were completely spent as we filled up our canteens and slumped down under trees and pulled our gear off. I remember I lit a cigarette and Lester asked for one too. I think that was the day he started smoking again. That full range would have been the biggest bullshit range I'd ever seen even if it had been 50 degrees out. Make it 100 degrees out and it was the king of bullshit ranges!

Slowly others started coming in from the final course, all looking half dead from dehydration. About the fourth team that came in was Bob and Ryan. Nobody said a word and it was pretty much polite nods, grunts, and groaning because we were all so spent. Ryan filled up his canteens and then joined us under the trees. Bob started to fill his canteens too, but then something happened. Bob made this horrible retching sound and vomited all over the stem and valve of the water buffalo. It was a massive explosive puke that emptied Bob's stomach. It was also a horrible, smelly puke that immediately invited flies and bees to it. It was all over the water dispenser and there was no way to fill a canteen without getting puke in your canteen or on your hands.

Lester began laughing hysterically and I joined him. We laughed even harder as the other teams came walking like the dead to the water buffalo and almost vomited themselves at the sight and smell that they found there. Nobody touched the water buffalo due to the damage that Bob had done to it. You'd figure that at least one of us would have gotten up and washed off the puke with our water, but we didn't. It was funnier to stand there and watch everyone's expressions as they came up and saw the drying vomit.

Bob, as pissed off as one could possibly get, slumped down under a tree and just sat there by himself. His skin was fire engine red and he was as shiny as ever. Bob's skin would turn shiny when in the sun. He was a sunburned, dehydrated mess who had just vomited all over a water buffalo. He was not happy with what had taken place, and his silence was deafening. Bob just sat there staring off into dehydration-space and not saying a word. He wouldn't respond to any of us calling to him and he wouldn't even look in our direction. I finally got up and walked over to him and dumped half a canteen of water over his head. Then I did something that I knew would re-charge him. I lit a cigarette, pulled a drag, and then stuck it in Bob's mouth. Bob sat there staring off into space again and the cigarette never left his mouth. He'd take a drag about once every minute. Slowly he came back to life and started drinking some water that we gave him because, of course, none of us were going to clean his mess off the water buffalo's nozzle so that he could fill his canteens. That would have stopped us from laughing, pointing, and making fun of everyone else coming off the range and finding the surprise waiting for them at the water point.

After all the teams came back in, they made us all go into the briefing tent again, but this time for a debriefing. It was about 140 degrees in this tent and everyone that had just gone through the range was pissed off. The Army likes to do After Action Reviews (AAR) where they ask for your opinion on the training that you just received. This was a big mistake by the training cadre for this range. Keep in mind that it wasn't just our detachment there, there were probably another thirty or so soldiers that had also had to endure no water on this bullshit range. We all let the trainers have it and we really gave them an earful. The trainers claimed they didn't know anything about the water buffaloes being empty on the range and that they had ordered 15-minute rest periods after every mile on the range. Obviously, the rest periods never happened along with the water buffalos never having water.

About the time this explaining and excuse making was going on, Doc Cain came walking into the tent with an IV in his arm and holding the IV bag up with his other hand. He was asked if he completed the course and he responded that no, he hadn't. The cadre then told him he'd have to come back the next day and finish the course.

Cain responded, "Let me tell you jackoffs something. I had to go to your medic tent because I'm a heat casualty because you had our asses on your stupid range in Heat Cat 5 with no water on site. There's about six others back in that tent and you don't even have any medics in there."

The cadre looked confused and then asked how he got treatment then.

Cain, without missing a beat said, "I'm a Combat Lifesaver. I found your goody bag in there and stuck myself and then I stuck the others in there too. They're all too weak to make it in here and some asshole puked all over the water buffalo so they can't even get water."

We lost it in our seats laughing at this.

Cain's rant continued, "If you idiots think I'm coming back to this range tomorrow, then you must be stupid."

We all left that range that day pissed off and miserable. When Bob finally got out of his dehydration trance later that evening after dinner, he hurled words describing that range that I'd never heard said before. He was furious. He was so pissed that it was actually funny, and he had the whole detachment dying with laughter. It was, without a doubt, the dumbest thing I'd ever done in the Army.

CHAPTER 32

MPS LEAD THE WAY

After a couple weeks of doing regular ranges at Ft. Dix, everyone in our detachment, except for our detachment commander and our two 31 Echoes (Bob and Ryan Suthard), had to go to Ft. Leonard Wood, Missouri for two weeks of training. This school was to give us the MOS of 31E. By mid-2005, the Army had changed MP designations. 95B was now 31B and 95C had been renamed to 31E. Our detachment was heading to The Beast in Afghanistan in order to be "subject matter experts", so it was important that we picked up the official MOS of 31E.

I've heard many stories of what took place at Ft. Dix while we were gone, and they are all legendary. I will focus on the most prolific. Bob caught poison Sumac (whatever that hell that is); Ryan Suthard got stuck at a range for two days and nights while three pieces of brass, or shell casings, were searched for; and lastly Bob managed to party hard in the barracks while on quarters and got away with it.

During the time spent in his medical quarters, Bob managed to insult and intimidate neighbors on the floor that were upset with his loud music and hard partying. When they came to the door to complain about the loud music and illegal partying taking place, Bob would open the door and yell expletives at them and threaten to assault them if they didn't leave. He even went to the extent of nicknaming one of these neighbors "Specialist Dickbag." Bob and Ryan even composed a song about SPC Dickbag. I got a chance to hear the song and it was quite entertaining. If you were to ask Ryan today to sing it for you, he still could.

I don't think there's any need to go further into what took place while we were gone, all you need to know is that this was just classic Bob.

Halfway around the country, the rest of us had flown into St. Louis, Missouri from Philadelphia, Pennsylvania. We had been given instructions from the training school at Leonard Wood that a shuttle bus would be available from the airport to take us to the post. When we landed, we grabbed our bags and headed toward the USO (United Service Organization) where we were to receive instruction on our shuttle.

After we dropped our bags inside the USO, Blanco and I stepped out to find a place to smoke while SSG Roberts and SSG Sanchez learned more about our shuttle. Our other soldiers just took seats in the waiting area. While Blanco and I were walking toward an exit at the airport, a priest that was obviously traveling himself, came walking over. We were in civilian clothes, but he had seen us with our green duffel bags in hand earlier when we were headed into the USO. He was no taller than us, had a slim build, and appeared to be in his early 60s. He had gray hair and kind, blue eyes. He asked us if he could talk to us for a few minutes and we nodded yes. Both Blanco and I were Catholics and Blanco's own father was a deacon. Of course, we had time to talk with this priest.

Father Smith was his name and he told us that he had been in Vietnam.

Blanco asked him if he had served as a chaplain during the war, but Father Smith shook his head no, smiled at us, and said, "I was just like you two. I was young, I was strong, and I was fearless. I ran as hard as I could in the war to get through it. After the war, I realized I wasn't so strong, and I realized I had a lot of fear."

Father Smith went on to tell us that after he was discharged from the military, he re-evaluated his life. He turned to God for mercy and he turned back to the church. Within a year, his decision had been made that he wanted to spend the rest of his life in God's service. He talked to his parish priest and began the process to begin a religious life.

Father Smith asked us where we were headed, we told him we were headed to a training school, and he wished us the best of luck. We shook hands with him and when he was shaking hands with Blanco, he switched over and started speaking to him in Spanish. When we parted, I asked Blanco what Father Smith had said to him.

Blanco had a look of surprise on his face when he responded, "That man spoke perfect Mexican-style Spanish. I mean perfect. He told me to always go with God."

Blanco and I finally made our way out to have our cigarettes, and then re-joined our detachment in the airport USO when we were done.

It was about ten o'clock in the morning because we had picked up an hour from the east coast. Despite the attempts of our two staff sergeants to get information on the shuttle, the people at the desk of the USO seemed to know absolutely nothing about the shuttle. SSG Sanchez had a number for the training school and called it, but he was told to sit tight. Still, no shuttle. This back and forth went on for a good two hours. We ran out and picked up some sandwiches for lunch and brought them back to the USO. The confusion was still taking place about the shuttle and I could see the frustration and anger on the faces of Roberts and Sanchez.

Cain had finally had enough. He stood up and proclaimed, "Well, fuck this. I'm walking down to the rent-a-car place and getting us a van."

20 minutes later, Cain pulled up to the pick-up area of the airport with a van. We loaded our gear into the back of the van and then climbed aboard. I don't know how Cain navigated from the airport to Ft. Leonard Wood since most phones weren't yet equipped with wifi, but he got us there. We took off from St. Louis at roughly three o'clock that afternoon and pulled through the gates of Ft. Leonard Wood at just after six in the evening.

SSG Sanchez got out at the main gate, checked in with the guards, and found out where the training school was located. We drove to the training school which turned out to be an old company CQ building. We stayed inside the van as SSG Sanchez walked into the building. A few minutes later he emerged with a duty sergeant. The sergeant hopped into a military car and guided us to where our barracks were. Once inside, the E-5 duty sergeant gathered us around and explained to us some basic rules.

He said, "As you already know, you're on a training post. This means that you cannot smoke in public, you'll have to use the designated smoking areas. You may also not consume alcohol on or off duty while you are in training. Also, it is in your best interest to stay away from basic trainees. You may react to their greetings, but do not engage in lengthy conversation with them. The closest training barracks that you should try to stay away from is over there."

The duty sergeant then pointed to the large barracks directly behind our building. Ironically, these were the same barracks that I had stayed in for basic training five years before!

The building we were staying in was a one-floor, open-bay tin hut. From what I understand, these were originally built during World War II. There were no latrines or showers in the hut. Those were located in another building a few doors down. When we stepped into the hut, there were three men already inside. One was a young corporal from the same unit in Minnesota that the soldiers in our detachment were from. The second was an E-2 private who was brand new to the unit and was sent to the school to pick up the 31E MOS. The third man in the barracks was my old friend SSG Scofield. Man, was it good to see him! He immediately hopped up out of his bunk, we shook hands and we gave each other a big hug.

The duty sergeant provided us with sheets for our bunks and told us to relax, get settled in, and that we should be ready to leave for training no later than six in the morning. He let us know that an off-cycle drill sergeant would be around in the morning to pick us up and take us to breakfast.

We spent the rest of the night making up our bunks, pressing our uniforms, shining our boots, and storing our gear in our footlockers. I shared a bunk bed with Blanco, taking the bottom bunk this time around.

The next morning most of us awoke about 4:30, got cleaned up, and put our uniforms on. Most of us had been MPs already for years, so we knew exactly how sharp to look for a school to set a good example. Just before 6am, an E-6 drill sergeant showed up at our barracks and stepped inside. He was an average sized black man who defined the look of a drill sergeant. Once he saw that we were mostly NCOs with combat patches, that our beds were snapped tight, and that our uniforms looked just as good as his; his demeanor changed from a hard ass to a demeanor of camaraderie.

He introduced himself as Drill Sergeant Powell and he shook hands with those of us who were NCOs. He did a quick check over the barracks and he apologized to us for having to march us to the chow hall for breakfast. He said he would talk to the MP school to see if it was okay that we drove or marched ourselves. Powell also gave us a reminder of how to act if we came in contact with trainees.

Drill Sergeant Powell then said it was time to step off and we followed him outside where he put us in a formation. We marched, without cadence, the half mile or so to a large, brand-new brick building that served as the chow hall. This building had plenty of space to feed two companies at a time and it was a far different experience, and a major step up, for trainees than what I had experienced 5 years earlier.

After breakfast, Drill Sergeant Powell marched us over to the building we had been at the evening before. He wished us luck with the school and told us he would see us again the next morning. SSG Sanchez took over the formation from Drill Sergeant Powell and now stood at the front.

Things got interesting here. Out of the building came a master sergeant, an E-8, who was about 5 feet 9 inches tall, was slightly overweight, and had a cropped black flat-top haircut. He addressed us as underlings and talked to us like we were basic training privates. He did his best to intimidate us about how tough his school was going to be and how we needed to evaluate ourselves right then and there to see if we thought we had what it took to make it through. All of us had our eyes glued to his blank right sleeve. All of us were starting to get angry.

If this wasn't bad enough, a Command Sergeant Major then came out of the building and addressed us next. He was a tall, very fit black man in his mid-40s. He had a drill sergeant's patch on his chest but also had a slick sleeve on his right arm. This command sergeant major walked around our formation without saying a word as he inspected our boots, inspected our uniforms, and checked that our faces were shaved properly and that our hair was tight. After his inspection, where he found nothing, he then continued the verbal trend of dressing us down like we were day one privates. He was explaining to us how we may not be cut out to be MPs and we were going to have to prove that we deserved to be in his school. After he finished treating us like the filth of the earth, he asked if any of us had questions.

Jim Roberts spoke up, "Sergeant Major, with all due respect, I do not think you are going to find a group of students that are more motivated to be here than this one. All of us here are volunteers for this school and all but three men in this formation have already done at least one tour in Iraq or Afghanistan. Eight of us standing in this formation are on active duty orders right now finishing up our training to leave for a deployment to Afghanistan. Every man in front of you already carries the 31B MOS. We know what MPs do because we are MPs. And what is it we do, MPs?"

All of us took Roberts's cue and knew exactly where he was leading us.

We all screamed out in unison, "MPs lead the way!"

The command sergeant major's expression changed on his face. A slight smile came over his lips as he nodded toward Roberts. He then looked over at the master sergeant that had torn us down earlier and said, "Carry on, Sergeant." The command sergeant major walked back into the building and we never heard from him again.

The master sergeant's demeanor softened also. He had SSG Sanchez break our formation and we formed a line and went into the building one at a time. Inside the building we verified and signed off on paperwork. One of the staff sergeants working at a desk was a lady that had been in MP school with John Wiley and I at Arlington Heights from 2001-2002. It was nice to see her and I chatted briefly with SSG Hernandez as I moved through the stations.

CHAPTER 33

THE SCHOOL

Before we started our classroom work for the 31E school, the first thing we had to do was qualify on the shotgun. Even though we had just passed a shotgun course a few weeks before and showed the instructors our paperwork, the MP school at Ft. Leonard Wood required us to do it again. After breakfast on the third day, a duty pickup truck was sent to get us from the chow hall and take us to the range. These trucks had benches in the beds and you could comfortably seat a dozen soldiers in them.

Once we got to the range, we unloaded out of the pickup truck one at a time. We made a formation and checked in with the range NCOIC. He was a Latino man named SFC Juarez. SFC Juarez was a tiny man in his mid-30s that spoke fast. He was thrilled that we were such a small group because this was his only group for the day. That meant an early quit for him.

Juarez also had a 10th Mountain patch on his right shoulder. When we broke the formation to draw weapons, he walked next to me. Without saying a word, SFC Juarez slapped me on the back, pointed to my 10th Mountain patch, and then shook my hand.

We went to a short building where we drew six shotguns and drew six rounds each from another E-7 who was inside. Our training group would have to take the shooting test in two spurts, because there weren't enough shotguns for each one of us. The rounds we were given were spray rounds, identical to what we had used in Ft. Dix.

The targets were not pop-up targets, but they were paper targets. We were instructed to fire on the targets about ten meters away. We expended our rounds, cleared our shotguns, and then placed them on the ground.

I don't remember the exact count, but to qualify you had to have at least 30 penetrations or so on the paper target. None of us had any difficulty qualifying.

Shotgun qualification ended that day and we were driven back to our barracks in order to drop off our gear. We headed back to the chow hall for lunch. After lunch, we were marched by Drill Sergeant Powell to a mock city.

This mock city was used by the MP School at Ft. Leonard Wood for MP training. Our training group was herded to a building that was designed as a U. S. Army disciplinary barracks or in civilian terms; a military jail. The details were terrific all the way down to which type of handcuffs and shackles were supplied.

In the front section of this building was a classroom, and that afternoon we were introduced to four instructors, who were all E-7s. We got to work right away.

For the next 11 days we were trained on how to operate a U. S. Army stockade that would be used to detain U. S. Army prisoners. Our trainers were knowledgeable, they were eager to answer any questions we had, and they appreciated how we were always willing to push later into the training schedule. Our trainers had told us the first day that if we wanted to, we could push later into the training day and then have our last day off before we left the school. We all thought this was a great idea and we went for it.

We were trained on things that were procedural. We were taught how to do many important tasks in the field. And since all of us were 31B already, a lot of what we were taught was a refresher. It made it all that much easier on our trainers. A big part of the class was learning how to do searches. This included people, vehicles, property, cells, and more. Another big part of the class was how to do forced cell movements for unruly prisoners. Fortunately, most of us had real life experience with all of these things.

A mutual respect grew with our trainers throughout the training. None of them had yet to be deployed and they asked us a lot of questions about overseas detainee operations. They took notes and said that they were looking to add this information to the curriculum of the school. They even went as far as to ask if any of us might be interested, after our tour, at coming back to Ft. Leonard Wood on active duty orders for a year to be trainers. Some of our guys considered this and exchanged phone numbers with the instructors.

On our last day, we were given paperwork certifying us as having completed the 31E school. We shook hands with each one of our instructors. Both the instructors and us students had nothing but positive feedback for each other. Even the prick master sergeant from the first day shook our hands and told us it had been a pleasure having us at the school.

We now had earned the last day off. We weren't scheduled to fly out until the next afternoon at three o'clock. Drill Sergeant Powell stopped by the barracks that morning just as he had done every morning. We asked him about local places to eat, clubs to visit, etc. and he gave us a rundown of things to do around the post and off-post.

I couldn't resist the temptation to go back to my old barracks, so I asked Drill Sergeant Powell if he thought it would be okay for me to do so. He said he didn't see a problem with it and told me he knew the drill sergeants over there and that he'd call ahead and let them know that a "SGT Drake" would be stopping by at some point that morning.

About an hour later, in uniform, I strolled down the sidewalk and headed over to my old barracks. From what I could tell by the one banner in front, the training company in cycle was in their 4th week of basic training. One banner in front meant that there was only one platoon on site. I figured that they must be doing training in their classrooms.

I walked into the CQ office in the building and there was an E-6 drill sergeant sitting behind a desk. He was a stocky powerfully built black man, and his name tag said Johnson. Instinctively, I snapped to parade rest before I spoke.

"Drill Sergeant Johnson, my name is SGT Drake and I'd like to take a look at my old barracks."

Johnson stood to his feet and stuck out his hand while saying, "Drill Sergeant Powell let me know you would be coming. Knock off that parade rest bullshit and shake my hand, Sergeant. Welcome back to B-82!"

I shook hands with Drill Sergeant Johnson, and I told him there was just one thing I wanted to see, and that was a mural that my platoon had paid to have painted on the third-floor classroom. He smiled and said he'd take me right up there.

As we were walking on the third floor to the classroom, my assumption that trainees would be in the classroom doing training was incorrect. Instead of doing classroom training, the basic trainees were in the process of scrubbing down the barracks. As we walked through, the trainees showed the proper respect and yelled out "Make way!" and "At ease!" and were snapping to parade rest against the walls. It was the exact same thing I was taught to do 5 years earlier.

When we got to the classroom, the mural was still in place and I got a smile out of seeing it again. My platoon was called the "Mad Dogs" and this mural had a bunch of dogs in uniforms standing around a large doghouse. It was fun to see it again.

Drill Sergeant Johnson insisted that I see the rest of the barracks and that we walk each floor. Who was I to disagree with him? The trainees were doing a good job on each floor, the place looked clean, but of course Drill Sergeant Johnson let them know the place looked like "dog shit" and was the "worst" he'd ever seen. Again, this was just the Army's way of breaking down new recruits.

I finished my tour with Drill Sergeant Johnson after we had gone through the whole building and we ended up back at the CQ office. We shook hands, parted as friends, and wished each other the best of luck. When I left the office and walked down the short hallway to exit out of the building, there were two young privates sweeping the hall's floor in front of me. One had his back to me while sweeping and I invoked my best Drill Sergeant Garrett when I screamed out, "Get out of the way, Private Shithead!"

After my stroll down memory lane, I returned back to our barracks and changed out of my uniform and into my civilian clothes. I had something important that I wanted to do.

There were two things you could always rely on SSG Scofield for. He was never without a knife and he was never without his trusty airborne Zippo lighter. Now SSG Scofield didn't smoke, he was just old school and carried that lighter to burn off loose threads on uniforms and to heat shoe polish.

On this second to last day at Leonard Wood, I asked Papa Sco, which many of us affectionately referred to him as during the first tour, if I could borrow his lighter. He said "sure" and he handed it over. I took his lighter to the shop at the PX and had some inscriptions made on it. On the front of it I had the dates of our Afghanistan tour written and his full name and rank. On the back I had "Papa Sco" written.

When I brought the lighter back to him and showed it to him, a big smile came across his face. He gave me a big bearhug and he wore that smile the rest of the day. I could see that the lighter inscriptions really touched him. It was the least I could do for a guy that mattered so much to me.

After the lighter exchange, I checked in with our other soldiers. Dodson, Blanco, and the others were going to head off post for lunch. I really wanted a beer and so did the private, E-2, that was with us who was named Denton. Denton and I walked down to the little PX at the corner of the road and we caught a cab up to the bowling alley that was on post.

When we got to the bowling alley, it was desolate. Denton and I ordered cheeseburgers for lunch and we were excited when that day's special was 22 oz. Budweisers for $1.00. The bowling alley had TVs with ongoing baseball games that we watched. Denton was a nice, 21-year old kid, and he asked a lot of questions about overseas. He had been warned by the others in his Minnesota unit that they were due to be deployed again within the next 6 months or so. I told him all I knew, from my experiences in Afghanistan, and I suggested he speak with the NCOs in our training group that were in his unit and had been to Iraq already.

Not only did the bowling alley have a bar and lanes, but it also had a giant arcade area. Denton and I kept on drinking Budweisers as we entered the arcade area to play some games. After a few hours of playing games, watching baseball, and putting away tall glass after tall glass; the other guys from our training group showed up with the rented van. They joined us in this arcade and we all partook in the fun.

Jim Roberts, who was the least wild of us all, mentioned that Drill Sergeant Powell had told him about a popular club off post and he wanted to check it out. I was pretty liquored up at this point along with Denton, so we immediately agreed to go. Everyone else did too. Our training group loaded up in the van and took off for the club.

The club was no different than any other off post club. It was packed full of GIs who were looking for action. By action that means drunk action, sex action, and fighting action. You had to be very careful in these places because these soldiers would get a few cocktails in them and would fight over anything.

Luckily for us, we didn't have any problems that night. We drank shots, we drank Long Island ice teas, and we really cut loose in that club. It was the first time I had ever seen Jim Roberts really open up and have a good time. I was seeing three of everyone by the time we left the bar with my blurred vision and Blanco had to help me walk back into our barracks.

When we got into the barracks, we woke up the others that hadn't come with us. It was after 1 in the morning and everyone, except for our driver, was drunk as skunks. I remember SSG Scofield got out of his bed and was helping a few of us make it to our bunks. He was laughing, shaking his head, and saying, "Nothing ever changes, does it?"

A few days before this, we had two new soldiers move into our barracks. Both of these soldiers had formerly been in the Air Force and were new to the Army. One was an E-3 and the other was an E-4. They were at Leonard Wood and assigned to a special school to learn about the functions of the Army. Both of these new soldiers were cocky, arrogant, and we didn't like them at all.

These two new soldiers were awoken by our shenanigans, they climbed out of their bunks, and they began voicing their displeasure with our drunken state. Looking back on it, I don't blame them, and I would have been just as upset if I had been in their shoes. They had training in the morning and didn't need to be woken up by our nonsense.

It was a mistake on their part, though, and they should have stayed in bed with their mouths shut. Lester Dodson walked over to them and put his finger in their face. He had veins bulging in his neck and had gone from a peaceful, happy-go-lucky drunk, to a war machine.

Lester fired off, "I'd suggest you two mother fuckers shut your faces and get back in your bunks before I rip your arms off and beat you to death with them!"

They did as they were told.

The next morning was not a good one. When I woke up, I had the worst hangover of my life and I couldn't keep any food or liquid down until after we finally got on our plane after three in the afternoon. I looked the way I felt, too, and I was questioned by the airline at check-in if I was okay to fly. Fortunately, they let me board the plane.

That day was the last time I ever saw SSG Scofield. We loosely kept in touch over the years on social media, but we never got together again. Sadly, Terry Scofield passed away from cancer on December 1, 2020, at the age of 54. I took the news very hard. When I was notified of his death, I was walking the hallway of my workplace. I quickly ducked into a custodial closet and locked myself in. For the next twenty minutes or so I let my emotions out. Rarely for the past seventeen years had a week gone by that I hadn't thought about that last big bearhug from Papa Sco or heard his voice in my head giving me some kind of advice or guidance.

Papa Sco was someone that I looked up to and I really appreciated how well he treated all of us young soldiers on that first tour. He was a good man with a good heart and the world is less of a place without him.

CHAPTER 34

THE FOB

Upon our return from Ft. Leonard Wood, us newly brandished 31Es received some bad news. We would be forced to leave our very comfortable barracks room and go live at the FOB (Forward Operating Base.) The FOB at Ft. Dix was an area where the Army had spent millions of taxpayer dollars to build a forward operating base just off post. We quickly loaded up our gear and headed out to this FOB.

What was strange about the location of this training area was that we had to drive on regular city roads in order to get to it. I always felt uncomfortable when we'd be stuck in traffic in full gear in the back of a Humvee troop transport. Not to mention we had our weapons on us. It was one thing to do this in a foreign country, but it was an odd feeling to do it in our home country.

When we pulled up to this FOB for the first time, I was blown away with the accuracy of it. The Army had created the real deal setup complete with a slow-down gate entrance (that means zigzagged concrete barriers.) It was quite impressive. The good impression stopped right there, however.

Once we entered the FOB, we saw zombies walking around. We saw the lifeless eyes of poor SOBs that were condemned to the FOB for their entire Ft. Dix mobilization train-up. You could see these people were living in misery day in and day out. I just never understood the need to kill soldiers' morale and make them completely miserable right before they were heading somewhere where they'd most likely be miserable for the next 12 months. It just didn't register with me.

In the FOB, you were required to wear full gear at all times, carry a weapon(s) at all times, and you had to respond to 8,873,920 mock rocket attacks per day. Another 10,234,098 occurred at night. You couldn't get more than 2 hours of sleep per night. Everyone was in a heightened state of panic-fury and it was all-out ridiculous.

Should I tell you about the latrine situation next? Of course, there weren't enough latrines for the amount of people in the FOB, so there were ridiculous wait times. And yes, you had to be in full gear in order to use the latrines.

It doesn't stop there, either. The chow hall was a stand-up chow hall where there was no seating. You had to eat standing up. In order to even get in, you had to endure ridiculous lines that could take you up to an hour to get a hot meal. The meals were glorified T-rations that had been heated on a field stove too. T-rations were the type of food that may or may not have actually been real food and were still edible in their packaging 20 years after production. Every soldier I talked to in these lines was a zombie. I talked to some folks that had been stuck in that FOB for over two months. It was pointless for anyone to be in that training environment for that long and I felt awful for them.

After not wanting to wait 45 minutes to urinate, some of us found a hole in the floor of the vacant tent next to ours. That became the DET 4 urinal and it served its purpose well. I guarantee you all these years later that there is still no vegetation growing there. How, you may ask, did we mask the smell in the New Jersey July heat? Simple. We smoked cigarettes illegally in the vacant tent and we also poured bleach down the urinal hole. We were outlaws to the bone, I tell you.

Now that we were at the FOB, the big-time training started. Again, it was rare that a single one of these trainers had a patch on their right shoulder which means that they hadn't been anywhere and hadn't done any of this stuff for real. They were strictly training off of doctrine and not real-life experience.

Every time I think of one of these trainers, I can hear Bob's voice yelling out in a groan, "Oh great, another fucking slick sleeve!"

Although our detachment was not a group of special forces operators, we were a group with a lot of experience that really knew our fields well and knew what we were doing. We were good MPs. Except for Schlitz. He was an idiot.

One night while condemned to the FOB, I had to urinate in the middle of the night. Of course, I wasn't going to put on all of my gear to walk to a port-o-john, so I walked into the tent next door with the hole in the floor. When I walked in, I found Schlitz with some female GI in there. Thank goodness they had their clothes on! I announced to the two of them that I was dropping my pants, peeing, and smoking a cigarette. If they wanted to watch, they could, otherwise they could get the hell out of the tent and start acting like professional soldiers. They left.

So back to the big-time training. After not sleeping all night because of mock rocket attacks in which you were forced to run to concrete bunkers in full gear, you then had to attend roughly 14 hours of training and ranges per day. I could see why these soldiers at the FOB for months at a time had become zombies!

The first big-time training we had to attend was vehicle convoy training. This consisted of a serial of vehicles fully mounted with gunners. You had to drive through a course, which was wooded, and they would shoot firecrackers at your vehicle or mock local nationals would stand in your way to set you up for an ambush.

Ryan Suthard and I were assigned as the serial commanders of our vehicle serial and we split duties as commander and driver of our vehicle. I got us into trouble right away when "local nationals" stepped in front of our convoy and I increased speed and kept driving toward them. Ryan also gave the order for the rest of our serial to do the same. The local nationals moved and so did our ears as we got screamed at by the evaluator in the backseat of our vehicle. We were chastised about how "down range" we wouldn't be able to do that.

The other thing that stuck out about this range was when we received fire from the right side. I was the serial commander at this point and did as I was trained. Suthard and I identified that the fire was coming from the right side, only the right side, and from an isolated machine gun nest. I figured if we kept driving down the road, there could be an IED setup waiting for us.

I responded to the single machine gun nest attack in MP fashion. I ordered the vehicles in the serial to drive toward the threat and to fire upon the target - completely lighting up the attack area. (We were shooting blanks.) It was a thing of beauty as our Humvees drove off the range and straight at the machine gun nest set up. Oh, we got in big time trouble for that! We were told to immediately drive to the end of the range.

At the end of the range, a 6 feet 2 inches tall master sergeant came running to our vehicle and ripped open the driver door and ordered us out. Ryan and I got locked up at parade rest by this master sergeant, who was the NCOIC of the range, and he laid into us. After he let us have it, he ordered us to stand at rest and then asked, calmly, why we did what we did. Ryan and I took turns explaining that in our MP training and in our rules of engagement in Afghanistan, we were required to neutralize a lesser threat. We had acted accordingly. The master sergeant, totally calm now, explained that although we were doing the right thing according to our training and our experience, damaging his range was not permitted. We let him know that we understood and then we were then dismissed.

Ryan and I laughed all the way back to the waiting bleachers of the range. We sat there waiting for the rest of our detachment to go through the course.

One by one our group came back to the bleachers scathed like us. Each of them had also taken an ass chewing for doing the exact same thing that we had done. Fortunately, Bob did not get dehydrated on this range, but I do recall him throwing his Kevlar after being laid into for doing the right thing in training. Expletives came out of his mouth when he got back to the bleachers and all of us shared his sentiment.

After spending about 7 days out at the FOB, SFC Anderson decided that he'd seen about enough of the bullshit. He pulled us out of the FOB, and we went back to our comfortable living conditions in the barracks. Part of the deal, though, was that we had to make it look like we were still out at the FOB. We would be up at three-thirty or four in the morning on some days in order to get out to the ranges to make it LOOK like we had been at the FOB overnight. Some days we'd drive back to the FOB just to turn around and leave it a few minutes later. It worked perfectly!

The next range that we attended was some kind of a simulated firing range. I don't know exactly what it was because I never participated. I had that unique radio skill and the range was looking for help operating the radios. When the range opened that day and they were giving us our initial briefing, the NCOIC asked for a volunteer with prior experience who could operate their radios that day. I volunteered.

I was given instructions of where to report, and I went to this TOC (Tactical Operation Command) that they had set up. It was a small wooden building with a tin roof and it had push out windows that were wide open in the blazing July heat.

At the door, I was met by a staff sergeant who showed me the operation. There were two radios setup, one for the post and one for the range itself. There were also code cards that changed at certain times. The protocol was something I was familiar with and I sat down at the opposite radio of the staff sergeant.

I slapped on the headphones and opened up the logbook, becoming the radio operator for the range. The traffic that came over the radio was typical range radio banter. There were discussions of weather, range conditions, troop movements on the range, and consistent radio checks for different points on the service.

For the rest of the range day, I was assigned to continue operating that range radio. This radio shack did not have any kind of air movement outside of the opened windows. Eventually the staff sergeant took a fan in the room and placed it in front of the building's door, which he propped open. This at least brought some air flow while pulling the hot New Jersey air inside. Not long after I had taken up my position, a young captain came walking into the room. The staff sergeant and I rose to the position of attention, but he told us to sit back down and get back to our work.

I learned that he was the OIC of the TOC and he would randomly look over our reports and, on occasion, ask us for a status update on the range. He was a chain smoker who sat at a desk and lit up one cigarette after the other. That was okay with me because I was a heavy smoker myself at the time. We puffed away in this little building.

About 3 hours into this range, a major came walking into the building, relieved the captain, and set up shop. Quickly, our smoking privileges were revoked and about every 15 minutes this major would scream out "INCOMING!" and make the staff sergeant and I pull off our headphones and jump to the floor. I think he really enjoyed doing this. The problem was that while we were without our headsets, nobody was monitoring the radios. The major was making us stay on the floor for a few minutes at a time until he decided to give us the all clear. The staff sergeant and I tried explaining to him that we were missing transmissions and we had to stop taking off the headsets. He arrogantly waved us off with his hand.

After the next time we were picking ourselves up off the floor, the staff sergeant put his headphones on, and he heard the tail end of a transmission that had been repeated several times. The calling party was not pleased that the TOC had missed the initial messages. The staff sergeant was irritated now.

"Sir," he said, "You've got to stop this 'incoming' stuff. We are missing messages and command is not pleased."

The major got angry with the staff sergeant and told him that when he wanted his opinion, he would ask for it. The major let him know that HE was the OIC of the TOC.

This was all fine and dandy until there was a real injury on the range and I was on the floor playing 'incoming' for the major's jollies. I missed the transmission and barely caught the third repeat in time.

About 20 minutes after this incident occurred, a lieutenant colonel came flying into the TOC demanding to know why transmissions were being missed. The major folded his arms and shot a dirty look my way. I didn't say a word, but the staff sergeant answered for me.

"Sir," he snapped, "the transmissions are being missed because the OIC of the TOC is yelling 'incoming' and making us dive to the floor. We have to pull our headsets off in order to do this, he's keeping us on the floor for a few minutes at a time, and we are missing transmissions because of it."

The lieutenant colonel was really pissed now and looked over at the major. Between clenched teeth he said, "Is this what is taking place here, Major? Are you making these men throw themselves on the floor over some mock rocket attack?" The major sheepishly nodded yes.

I'm not going to tell you the words that came out of that lieutenant colonel's mouth, but it wasn't pleasant. Needless to say, that major was sent out of the TOC immediately and the captain and I lit back up 10 minutes later.

At the end of the range our entire detachment was filthy head to toe. I don't know exactly what they had to do that day, but they looked like beaten animals. I remember Bob was silent and had that "enough of this bullshit" look on his face that he would get.

On the back of the open Humvee while driving back to the barracks that evening, Bob broke the silence between drags of his cigarette by invoking Orlowski and stating, "Well, free meals!"

CHAPTER 35

HEADBUTTS AND HOT TUBS

Mobilization for deployments in 2005 was a pretty simple thing. You had to do certain ranges and make certain requirements in order to "certify" for deployment. I have a hard time believing that anyone, outside of medical problems, was ever held back from deploying for not passing a range at a mobilization site. At this time, Iraq was barely two years old and Afghanistan was only in year four. The wars were still new, and training was doing its best to adjust to what was taking place in theater.

Toward the end of our train-up at Ft. Dix our detachment was knocking out final ranges and we were sleeping every night in our luxurious barracks accommodations. That meant hot showers, clean sheets, clean clothes, phone access, and hot food each night. It also meant we didn't get woken up every half hour to mock explosions and be forced to hide in bunkers. Our only sacrifice was that we had to get up extra early in order to get out to the ranges before they realized we were never at the FOB in the first place. It was quite a scientific approach to the matter, and we had become experts in it.

While living in the barracks, we discovered a Chinese takeout place that had the best Chinese food I'd ever had in my life. One of us would take the orders from the guys in the detachment, we'd pool our money together, and then we'd wait downstairs in the day room for the delivery to show up. I swear to you that from phone call to delivery was only about 12 minutes. I have no idea how they got the food cooked, driven onto the post, and then to the barracks in that fast of time, but they did it. And it was great tasting, top notch stuff. It was none of that re-fried rice that had been heated and then re-heated again and again throughout the day. Bob, and I coined a phrase for the delivery. I'm not exactly sure of its origin; but, in a sing-song, mock Chinese accent he'd say, "We make you food fo you so faaaaaaast!" To this day every time I get Chinese food, I hear Bob say that in my mind.

Another thing we ordered a lot of was pizza. It'd be the same process; we'd pool our money together and someone would run down to the day room to wait on the order. One day we had gotten done with training very early and Bob, Ryan, and I had walked down to the Class Six and picked up some beverages.

We sat at the abandoned bus stop across from the barracks and legally drank. We drank enough just to get goofy and then we headed back into the barracks. The three of us decided that we'd order a pizza and Schlitz came around and asked if he could get in on the pizza too. We told him that'd be fine. Schlitz then left the barracks (probably to meet up with some girl somewhere) and Bob, Ryan, and I sat playing the computer game Civilization while half-drunk.

About twenty minutes later the pizza showed up. I ran down to get the pizza and then I brought it up. Bob and Ryan immediately paid their cut. We ate conservatively, waiting for Schlitz, and the guy never showed up. As a result, we killed the rest of the pizza. About an hour later Schlitz showed up and started asking about the pizza. I happened to be playing Civilization at the time and I decided to create a new city called "Nopizzabluesbullshitsky." Bob, Ryan, and I busted out laughing after I typed it.

Schlitz was really upset about the pizza situation and then became even more upset when we started laughing over the new city name in the game. Schlitz, idiot that he was, would have this really weird reaction when he'd get upset. He'd start breathing really hard, like borderline hyperventilating, and then stick his chest out and ball up his fists. This was one of the first times we'd seen this, and it made us laugh at him even harder.

What finally put an end to it was when Blanco came walking up to Schlitz and said, "Schlitz, you fucking idiot, you didn't pay anything for the pizza and you disappeared for an hour-and-a-half. They ate the pizza. Big deal. Walk over to the chow hall and get something to eat and stop bitching."

It was like a lightbulb went off in Schlitz' head and he left and went to the chow hall. Again, what an idiot!

At this point the training cadre in charge of the FOB, and all the ranges, would hit the roads leading to the training areas early in the morning and set up "booby traps" and "IEDs" to further screw with the zombies coming out from the FOB. As I've said before, our detachment knew how to think outside of the box because we were experienced. We would leave at different times, we would take different routes, and we avoided every single one of their stupid IEDs and attacks.

One of my favorite things that we ever did was leave at five o'clock one morning for a range. As we drove down the road in black-out mode (no lights), we found one of the cadre's vans running on the side of the road with two NCOs dead asleep inside of it. They must have gotten to the area earlier than expected and were killing time with a nap. We couldn't just leave things be. In our truck we carried a great deal of 100 mile per hour tape, cord, and other stuff you randomly need in the Army. A couple of us hopped out of our vehicle, took out the 100 mile per hour tape, and wrapped it around the van so that the cadre wouldn't be able to open the doors when they woke up.

Another favorite of mine was when we pulled up to the FOB one night after being blasted by the hot sun all day. None of us were in any mood for BS. All we wanted to do was bring our tactical vehicles back to the FOB, hop in our van, and then head back to the barracks. As we pulled up to the FOB there was a mass "local national protest" taking place in front of the gates. We were receiving radio transmissions that we weren't allowed to enter onto the post because of the protest.

Jim Roberts was in charge of the serial that evening, and he wasn't pleased. Roberts had spent 12 months in Iraq running convoys and he had zero tolerance for this kind of activity, training or not. He gave an affirmative response to the radio transmission and then ordered the vehicles in our serial to increase speed. We drove straight at the gate doing about 40mph and all the "local nationals" moved out of the way. When we got to the gate, Roberts ordered the guards to open the gate and we drove right onto the post without any trouble. Needless to say, the cadre were pissed off at us because we didn't play by their rules and we did things logically and the way you'd do it in country.

By late July, we had completed all of our medical checks, all of our certifications, and almost all of our ranges. One of the last ranges that we had to attend was a building-clearing range. The skill set required for this range was absolutely nothing new for us and we knew exactly what to do. We were MPs and we knew how to do squad movements and how to clear out buildings. Ft. Dix had built a mock downtown city area and we had to move from one side to the other and clear specific buildings. We worked how we were trained and coordinated before we moved. We knew how we would take each building.

On some buildings we would split and enter through two floors at once, in other buildings we would go in all together. We made plans and knew what we were doing, and we put those plans into action. Ryan, Bob, and I had specifically cleared hundreds of cells, rooms, and buildings together both in training and for real in Afghanistan. We could go through this kind of work like a hot knife through butter. We operated so well together, in fact, that we rarely said a word and would do things by hand signals or taps on the back.

The training cadre lost their minds!

While on this range, we were doing exactly what we were ordered to do. The trainers on the range went absolutely crazy, however, because we weren't doing it their way. Specifically, we weren't doing it the way their TM (Training Manual) from 1986 said that it was supposed to be done in the Cold War. I kid you not, they were using a training manual from the 1980s that did not apply to Mideast urban warfare.

We didn't snap back at the cadre, but we didn't back down. We continued doing things our way, for a little while. At one point we were moving building to building and Doc Cain was in front of me. I had Bob and Ryan Suthard behind me. We were peeling off one by one and moving to the rear of another building. We had planned this out and we were following the plan. Suddenly, one of the members of the cadre ran up and yelled out "SNIPER!" and pushed over Cain. He then yelled out, "You're dead! Just lay there!"

We were already exposed anyway, so if there had been a real sniper present, that sniper would have been able to pick us off at random. I ran over, grabbed Cain by the back strap on his gear, and began dragging him as I went for cover toward the back of the building. Bob and Ryan peeled off doing the same and once we reached the back of the building, we continued on the mission.

This E-6 trainer followed us back there and then went insane screaming at me, Bob, and Ryan telling us that we should have left Cain and we shouldn't even have moved at all because of the sniper. Ryan, calmly, started explaining to the staff sergeant that we were exposed anyway and that we didn't leave our wounded or dead.

In the midst of Ryan's explanation, Bob ran off and re-entered the building from where we came. The other members of our detachment were already in the building and had begun clearing it. As Ryan, Cain, and I are arguing with this instructor, the next thing we know is that we see a rifle come out of one of the windows and we hear blank rounds start firing. The instructor ran around to the front and started screaming at Bob, who was on the second-floor firing rounds.

"What the hell are you doing!?!?!" the instructor screamed in anger.

Bob, without skipping a beat, yelled out, "I saw where the rounds from the sniper were coming from, Sergeant, and now I'm killing that mother fucker!"

We lost it and busted out laughing! At this point, the cadre threw their clipboards down and stormed off the range. After Bob had expended all 30 blank rounds of his magazine, he and the rest of the squad exited the building, we re-grouped, and we walked to the ending point of the range. We filled our canteens and smoked cigarettes waiting for our next instructions. We never received any because our instructors had left the range.

About an hour went by when we finally saw a tactical vehicle pulling onto the range. A command sergeant major and two other senior NCOs got out of the Humvee and came walking up to us. We all formed up and snapped to parade rest immediately for the CSM. We figured that we were in real hot water now.

It turned out that he simply wanted to know what was going on and why the cadre was not on the range. We explained what had happened and he told us to stay where we were. We saw the command sergeant major get on his cell phone and about ten minutes later the training cadre came back to the end of the range. They were hot and were bitching up a storm about us to the CSM saying that we were refusing to train.

SSG Roberts finally asked permission to speak and explained to the CSM and to the cadre that we were simply operating the way we knew how. The cadre's methods of clearing buildings were outdated, old, and the TM they were using for instruction no longer applied.

The CSM asked us questions about exactly what we had been doing and how we had reacted. After this exchange went on for about ten minutes, the CSM told us that we had passed the range and that we were to leave the range immediately. We returned to our tactical vehicles and got the hell out of Dodge!

The commandant of Ft. Dix at this time had a policy that everyone would get four days at home before being deployed. Our ship out date had been set for August 1st, so we were granted leave the week before. The way the arrangements were made really worked out in our favor.

You were allowed four days AT HOME and travel time did not count. This meant that we were released at eleven in the morning on a Wednesday and we weren't required to be signed back in until nine o'clock at night on the following Tuesday.

All flights were out of Philadelphia and the earliest we could get a flight out back to Chicago was at 6am on Thursday morning. We bought our tickets over the phone. Lester Dodson found this long of a wait time to be unacceptable and he was convinced that he could get an earlier flight out and take advantage to score extra time home. That Wednesday when we were released, Dodson went straight to the airport to try and get as early of a flight as possible.

What did the rest of us do? We partied. We partied hard. I remember we closed out the enlisted club at about one in the morning and then went back to the barracks. We slept until about two-thirty and then we got up, showered, and drove out to Philadelphia. When we got to the airport, we hit the terminal bar and who did we see pacing the terminal? You guessed it, it was Lester! He, unfortunately, was not able to get an earlier flight and he had spent the whole night in the terminal.

That extended weekend home is a bit of a blur to me, but I remember spending a lot of time with friends and family and I remember going out every night and partying hard with Bob. I also had a few day's fling with a beautiful girl that I had gone to high school with. It was good to spend a couple of days with her.

Bob and I were special drinkers back then. As I've said before, we had a lot of things in common and a lot of common interests, but our greatest common interest was drinking. We just really enjoyed getting smashed, talking Pashto, playing the jukebox, and hanging out together. We especially liked sitting at the end of the bar and seeing everyone coming in and going out.

One night during this four day leave Bob and I got invited back to a friend of mine's house to keep the party going once the bar closed. Bob and I had stopped and picked up extra booze earlier on figuring we'd end up on one of our patios at some point before the sun came up. We left the bar and drove over to this guy's parents' house and brought our booze with us. There ended up being about twenty people at this party and it was a really great time. There was a hot tub and there were gorgeous girls in the hot tub including the girl I had the fling going with.

Bob and I had our beer in coolers about 50 feet away from us where there was a bonfire going. In the hot tub, we passed around a bottle of Wild Turkey. Bob wasn't interested in any of the women in the hot tub despite them being interested in him, however. They weren't Jamie Hasenfang. And yes, we had borrowed trunks and hopped in the hot tub.

I turned to Bob in the hot tub and said, "You know what? In about six months we're going to be sitting in the jail on an overnight shift with birds shitting on us, and we'll be talking about this night."

He agreed.

About every half hour one of us would get out of the tub to make the trek down to the coolers to get more beer. It was Bob's turn in the cycle to get more beers, so he hopped out of the tub and started making the walk. I was watching him as he walked up to the cooler.

One of our other friends was acting like an idiot yelling and screaming by the bonfire. His name was Ron. I heard Bob yell for Ron and motioned for him to come over by Bob. I knew what was coming. Bob grabbed Ron by the neck and hit him with a head butt. The guy went straight down like a ton of bricks.

As I was dying laughing in the hot tub, Ron got back up after a couple of seconds and started yelling at Bob. So, what did Bob do? Bob grabbed him by the neck and head butted him again. This time the guy stumbled backwards and went head over heels over a bench and was knocked out cold with his legs up in the air. He lay like that for a quite a while as Bob returned back to the hot tub with our drinks.

The ladies we were with were quite impressed with Bob's actions. What they didn't realize was that Bob was being merciful. If Bob had wanted to, he could have ripped Ron to shreds and there wouldn't have been anything Ron could do to stop it. Bob was mean and fit enough at that point and random violence never bothered Bob. What the ladies in the hot tub were impressed by was business as usual for us back then. Ron got lucky.

CHAPTER 36

AKS OUT, WHEELS UP

When our four-day pass was up, Bob's mom gave us a ride to the airport to fly back to Philadelphia. It's never easy leaving your family, but I can tell you that it does get easier the more you do it. I think it gets easier on the family too. I don't recall this time being as hard as the first time, but it's never easy to say goodbye to little kids and I had a very young niece and nephew at this time. Bob had such a hardness about him that I'm not sure how he felt about leaving his family, especially his young brother and sister. I'm sure it bothered him, but he was never the type to show emotion and even less the type to talk about it.

When Bob's mom dropped us at the airport, Bob and I had a little bit of time and we hit the bar and had a few drinks. We were joined shortly by Andrew Blanco, who was sick and had a deep cough going, and soon Lester Dodson showed up. I don't recall any delays or issues with this flight, and we took off as scheduled from Chicago to Philadelphia.

When we landed in Philadelphia, we had already established a meeting point at Jack Dempsey's restaurant just down the road from the airport. SSG Sanchez had stayed back and was playing shuttle driver with our duty van. He picked up the four of us and dropped us off at the restaurant. I'd like to tell you a little bit about this place since it was one of the coolest places I'd ever been to. It was a sports bar and restaurant with a pure boxing theme, obviously. There were fight posters and pictures around the whole building along with a lot of other unique memorabilia. As a boxing fan, I found this to be a treasure trove of boxing history. Blanco liked boxing too and he and I walked around the whole building checking out each of the posters, pictures, and gear. This bar also had a different layout than I was used to, maybe it was an east coast thing? The restaurant had a giant bar in the middle of the building that people could sit at from either side. The tables were set up all around it. The chairs were all leather (or fake leather), the place was carpeted with red carpeting, and it was dark in there with real dimly lit lamps. Even though it was probably one in the afternoon, it felt like it could have been ten at night. The place had a sense of class and charm to it and wasn't something I was used to seeing growing up in the Midwest.

We all took advantage of being in this place and we ate and then started drinking since we weren't going to be on duty until the next day. We had a good time in that place and after a few hours we had made friends with all the other folks in the bar and we were buying each other drinks. Bob and I did our usual and took over the jukebox, shelling the crowd with rock 'n' roll classics, singalongs, and all-out jam sessions. The bar had turned into a jovial atmosphere and there were smiles all around. We may have only been in our early 20s, but Bob and I knew bar culture and were very comfortable in these surroundings.

As time went on, all the others from our eleven-man detachment that had gone home for the pass started coming back to the restaurant one at a time. By six o'clock that evening we said our goodbyes to everyone in the bar, shook hands with the regulars, finished dances with the bartenders, and loaded into our duty van. We began our trek back to Ft. Dix up the expressway on the seaboard. As I said before, I really enjoyed that ride. It was such a unique view after growing up in the flatlands of the Midwest. After a couple of hours, we were back at our barracks in Ft. Dix, New Jersey.

The following day was our load up day because the next day was August 1st and that was our ship out day. Our detachment went to Home Depot and purchased lock boxes for our gear. The guys from Minnesota recommended this and they said they had better success using boxes on flights during their Iraq tour. It turned out that they were absolutely right. The airports would much rather deal with these boxes than with loose duffel bags and gear. They were thrilled when we checked in with them.

Our detachment had been given a listing for gear regarding the max amounts of boxes and duffels. It was all based on weight. We spent the rest of the day spray painting our duffels and these boxes. We loaded up our duty van and took our gear over to a loading station where we were able to weigh everything out. We also had to put each of our rifles and pistols in locked cases. There were specific instructions on how to do all of this and none of this was a problem for us. We worked together and made it happen. As a matter of fact, things worked out so well that all we had to carry by hand was one duffel bag each and a carry on. Although most of us were young in age, we were experienced soldiers by this point and knew how to handle our business.

Bob and I had even taken another, smart step prior to all this while on pass. We had made this suggestion to everyone else too. Back home we went to

K-Mart and loaded up on hygiene products. You could never totally count on the PX in country to have what you needed when you needed it. It was best, if possible, to load up beforehand and send it out to yourself.

Bob and I had loaded up on $200 worth of shaving cream, razors, antiperspirant, shampoo, soap, foot powder, and more. We also bought hard, locking, plastic bins for these essentials to be shipped in. We went to our local post office and mailed them to MSG Holder. MSG Holder was already in country and would be our NCOIC when we got there. We sent him an email and he agreed to accept the packages on our behalf.

DET 4 only carried the bare essentials on our trip to get us through a couple of weeks or so. We also thought ahead and bought about 4 cartons of cigarettes each. I smoked Marlboro Mediums at the time and Bob always liked his Marlboro Reds. We remembered from the first tour that sometimes in Bagram there would be shortages on certain brands, so we made sure to stock up on what we liked. We pooled our cartons together in one bin and also mailed that bin to MSG Holder. It was a smart move and I remember within a week of being back in country, all of our plastic bins showed up. That load of hygiene products lasted the whole year and the cigarettes lasted a few months. We could be forward thinkers at times!

Later that night we met travel busses in a designated lot on the post. We joined a full company in loading up on these busses. Again, since there were only eleven of us, this was easy. We loaded up in no time and we were on the busses and asleep as the company we tagged along with fought among themselves over who was going to load up what gear. They were also having skirmishes over the other endless problems that companies have when they are transporting a large number of people and equipment.

I can't recall how long the drive was because I slept through most of it, but we drove from Philadelphia to Baltimore-Washington International Airport. It was morning when we got there. We brought our gear into the airport off of the busses and went through our appropriate cordoned off area at the airport. Again, this was really easy for us because our numbers were so small. Our gear was checked in no time and we were through the gates and into the terminal. Our flight was leaving in a few hours and a bunch of us headed to get breakfast.

After about an hour we started to wonder where Schlitz, Roberts, and SFC Anderson were. This hour rolled into another hour before finally the three of them joined us at the departure terminal. Do you want to guess why they were late? Despite the 2,872,342 times we were told to check our weapons, clear our weapons, and check each piece of our gear for any loose rounds; and despite the 2,872,342 times we did this, SCHLITZ STILL HAD A ROUND IN HIS DUFFEL BAG!

Do you know what happens when you show up to an airport with a round in your check-in bag in 2005? The FBI puts you in a room and interrogates you. WHAT AN IDIOT! Somehow Schlitz got out of any kind of major trouble, however, and the FBI released him. It wouldn't be the last time he did something incredibly stupid and it wouldn't be the last time he was in trouble.

We loaded on this dedicated flight with the company we came to the airport with. I remember that Bob and I got a window seat next to each other. Bob did his usual back then and popped some sleeping pills and was in and out of sleep for the next 7 ½ hours as we flew to Frankfurt, Germany. I remember I had brought a couple of books to read for the travels back to the Ghan.

The book I read on this leg of the trip was called "Walking a Golden Mile" by pro wrestler William Regal. The book had some very funny stories in it, and I passed over the book to Bob a couple of times so he could read some of the funny stuff. One story that Bob and I enjoyed was the time that Regal took a ride with another wrestler to a show. Regal didn't know this wrestler very well, but a free ride was a free ride. While riding in the car Regal learned, the hard way, that this man suffered from Turret's. He kept going crazy yelling and screaming and almost crashed the car dozens of times.

Bob and I would laugh about that story for the rest of our friendship. Bob also liked to re-enact it sometimes when he was driving. He would start screaming and yelling and would jerk the steering wheel in different directions. Bob did this once when he was driving a Gator in Bagram, the Gator almost rolled, and he almost killed both of us that day. The best part was that I didn't expect it at all and when he did it, I almost hurt myself from laughing so hard – right after the Gator went back down on all four wheels.

Our flight had a layover in Frankfurt for a couple of hours. If you're a good soldier, then you do good soldier things with this time. You shave, you take a bathroom sink shower, you eat, and then you smoke as many cigarettes as you can because you're not exactly sure when the next one will be. Bob and I and the others did just this.

I noticed while in Frankfurt that I started feeling really tired and very achy. As Blanco was starting to feel better, I was starting to get sick. It turned out his wife Fabi had been ill and he had caught it from her. I was coming up next now on the Fabi virus.

As we waited in Frankfurt and my health began to deteriorate, word came down that we would now be taking a bus to Rammstein and we would fly out from there to Turkey. We all loaded onto the bus and took the couple hour drive to Rammstein. While driving to Rammstein, Bob and I both remarked how the woods looked exactly like northern Wisconsin. Once we finished the hour or so drive to Rammstein, they fed us and then we loaded onto another plane.

I can't remember the exact time it took, but I think it was about another 5 hours from Germany to Turkey. We landed in Incirlik, Turkey at an Air Force base in the middle of the night. I was very ill at this point with a fever. When we got off the plane, they bussed us onto the post and assigned us temporary housing. They told us up front that it would be days until a bird would be ready to fly us out on the next leg of our journey. The housing was modular housing and it had very nice living conditions. We had bunks with mattresses and sheets, a TV in the room with a DVD player, and we had access to restrooms and showers right in our housing unit. We couldn't have had better living conditions as we waited for our next flight. The Air Force really did housing right!

I've always said that Incirlik, Turkey is the most beautiful place I've ever been. I was there in the summer and I was also there in the winter / spring and the temperature was the same. This Air Force base had swimming pools, there were palm trees everywhere, and it was just a very pleasant place to be. This time around in Turkey I didn't see much as I was bedridden ill. I had a very bad fever to the point where Doc Cain wanted to take me to the hospital, but I refused. We were in Turkey for four days total and I spent three-and-a-half of those days in bed.

Cain brought me meals and Bob supplied me with flu and cold medicine from the PX. I had a really bad virus and I was completely shut down. I was in and out of sleep for days on end. Looking back on it, I'm incredibly lucky I didn't get dehydrated. Finally, on the 4th day the illness broke, and I started to recover. When I came to, our room looked like a tornado hit it with carryout food boxes, booze bottles, and beer cans all over the place. DET 4 took advantage of the great living conditions and access to alcohol and partied like rock stars while I was completely out of it. I don't recall any of their partying, but from the looks of it they had a great time.

We eventually loaded up on another civilian plane and this time we traveled another four-to-five hours to lovely Manas, Kyrgyzstan. As stated before, Kyrgyzstan is a former Soviet Republic that in 2005 still looked and acted like it was 1985. We traveled through here while en route to Afghanistan on the first tour, but I didn't get much of a look around then. Our company was there for only about 15 hours. This time we had a three-day layover waiting for flights into the Ghan.

A bunch of us walked around the Air Base and it was pretty much a tent city still with only some permanent structures in place. Bob and I went and got haircuts and the Kyrgyz women that were doing the haircuts also offered scalp and shoulder massages. We were not interested mostly because the women had thicker chest hair than we did. Lester Dodson happened to come into the shop at the same time as us, however, and he took advantage of the offer. Bob and I laughed and made fun of Lester for the look on his face during his massage.

From what I could tell, the national language of Kyrgyzstan was Russian, and I bought a t-shirt of the Kyrgyz flag that had Russian writing on it. I still have that t-shirt somewhere. It was the strangest fitting shirt I ever owned, and eventually I cut the sleeves off of it. Later on in my life, I used it as an undershirt for hockey. Bob bought a t-shirt that had an AK-47 across the front of it with Russian writing. Neither of us ever figured out what it said, but we imagined it said something along the lines of, "This is AK-47. It is good rifle."

Every military post has an MWR Center. That means a place where soldiers can use phones, get coffee, watch television, and laugh. MWR stands for morale, welfare, and relief. In some countries this can be a large, elaborate facility and in others it can be something as simple as a tent. In Kyrgyzstan, it happened to be an old Soviet enlisted bar of some sort. It was a really interesting place. Bob and I went there one night to look for phones to call home. What we found was that this old bar had been turned into a coffee house. The physical bar itself still existed and you could sit on stools and drink your coffee. There were Soviet unit insignias and flags all over the walls of this little facility along with old photographs of Soviet soldiers.

If you were into history, this was a great little place that was stuck in a period of time that had long passed by. Bob and I, being history fans and admirers of the Soviet military, really liked this place. I'm pretty sure that we studied every piece of nostalgia in the joint before and after our phone calls. To this day that place really sticks out in my mind because it gave a deep insight into the enemy of the Cold War. They were soldiers, just like us, and probably headed to

Afghanistan just like we were.

We ended up spending about three days in Kyrgyzstan waiting for flights into the Ghan. Eventually, we got word that we were up for flights out the next morning. There was a company-sized element traveling in country and we were going to piggyback with them. The company and our detachment both reported to the holding area for the flight out to Afghanistan. At the holding area, we were broken down into flight serials. This was no different than what we had experienced on the first tour.

Our detachment worked with the company and we loaded our gear onto pallets for the Air Force to bring over to the C-130s. We were issued FCLs and we were down to bare equipment for the flight in.

Early the next morning, we separated into our serials and loaded busses to head out to the flight line. Our detachment happened to all be on the same serial, the first flight. Unfortunately, there was a really heavy rainstorm taking place as we loaded the bus. It didn't look good for flying out.

The busses that we were loaded onto were again Aeroflot busses complete with the blue hammers and sickles on them. There was also a Kyrgyz soldier driving the bus and his uniform, you guessed it, was still a Soviet uniform from the 1980s. On this bus driving onto the flight line, we were once again transported back in time to 1985.

If we doubted we were in 1985, we got further proof with the song that came on the radio next. It was a Russian language radio station and after a DJ made an introduction, the theme from Ghostbusters started playing. Bob and I lost it laughing and Bob said, "Hey you know what the DJ just said, right?"

I responded no.

Bob said, "He said 'Hot new track from America, Ghostbuster by Ray Parker Jr.!'" Bob got me laughing pretty good with that one! Bob didn't speak Russian, of course.

We drove around the flight line and then finally pulled up to our bird. Our detachment had been very lucky to all end up on the same flight serial, so loading the bird was going to be easy for us. There were 30 of us in total on this bus waiting to load onto the plane. The bad rainstorm was still raging, and the bus driver would not let us off the bus. We could see the pilot and crew in the aircraft, and they were obviously waiting for the storm to die down before flying. We were stuck on this bus for about 3 hours before the storm finally started to die down. Many of us had to urinate badly and we kept asking the driver to let us off the bus, but he wouldn't budge.

Eventually, Blanco had enough. He popped the back door, the emergency door, and we all hopped off the back of the bus. The driver was in a fury screaming at us in Russian. All of us smokers lit cigarettes and walked over off the tarmac to relieve ourselves into a ditch. While we were finishing up, a 1980s Soviet Army jeep of some sort came flying up toward us with a blue light flashing and with three Kyrgyz soldiers carrying AK-47s. They started screaming at us in Russian and broken English to get back on the bus. One of them tilted their AK-47 down and Blanco, without hesitating, pulled out his pistol. Things elevated very quickly! Man, was Blanco pissed!

At this point, we caught a break before an international incident could occur when the flight crew came running out of the bird. They came sprinting toward us, waiving off the Kyrgyz and telling us that we could board the plane. Blanco put his pistol away and we boarded the C-130. I fear what would have happened had that flight crew not interceded!

C-130s are notoriously cold so it's a smart move to break out blankets. Everyone who was experienced did just that. In a matter of minutes, we were wheels up and heading back to the Ghan. Bob and I had waited for this day for 16 months and now it was finally here. We were going back to where we belonged.

CHAPTER 37
BACK IN THE GHAN

When the C-130 touched down at Bagram Air Field in early August, 2005, the four of us that had been there before, were surprised when the back door opened. Yes, we got nailed with the unforgiving heat of the Afghan sun, but this time it wasn't nearly as dusty, and this time we saw green. The drought that had gone on for seven years in Northern Afghanistan was over. There was now foliage, grass, and leaves on trees. You could see green in the mountains surrounding the Air Field and you could see green around the base.

We went to the PAX terminal and waited for the forklift to bring over the pallets containing our gear. The eleven of us claimed our gear quickly and we were then met by MSG Holder. We were not required to attend any new-in-country training and MSG Holder had some people with him with vehicles. We loaded up our gear in the vehicles, and he took us over to the giant transient tent near the main roadway of the post. I remember as we were driving and looking around, we saw that a lot of the international element that was on the post before was now gone. I also found it odd that there were people in civilian clothes EVERYWHERE! Things had definitely changed since we had been gone.

We entered the transient tent, claimed cots, and chained our gear up as best we could. MSG Holder then took us to The Beast where we turned our rifles in, but we kept our pistols on us, which was protocol. We then took a tour around the post on foot.

Things had changed, but they hadn't changed too drastically. Where there were tents with wooden structures inside before, the living conditions were now, mostly, b-huts. All of the main areas were still there but there were some additions. Where the PX was located the area had expanded to include separate buildings that contained small shops. The coffee shop had also expanded and there were picnic tables set up with shade-netting above and there were dozens of people, almost all civilians, sitting around smoking cigarettes and drinking coffee 24 hours a day.

I don't care who you are, when you've just traveled across time zones for days on end and then end up 10,000 feet up in the Hindu Kush, your body is a bit off. It takes a few days to fall in line and then it takes a few weeks after that to completely regulate. All of us felt the jet lag and felt this strain on our bodies. Unfortunately for Lester Dodson, he was the latest casualty of the Fabi virus that Blanco had brought back to New Jersey.

MSG Holder gave us two days off to settle in. He also gave us five days to get rid of the uniform patch on our left arm and to put the current command's unit patch in its place. He provided us with the new patches, told us training would start in three days, and for us to settle into our temporary housing in the giant transient tent.

The first night there was a rough one. The transient tent did not have any kind of insulation and it leaked the elements right into it. When you come from 95-105 degrees during the day and then down to 75-80 degrees at night (which Northern Afghanistan is notorious for) it can really take a toll on your system. You feel like you're going to freeze to death. All of us were wrapped up like burritos with our Gortex cold weather gear on in our sleeping bags.

Poor Lester Dodson had now gone from sick to really sick. He was actually starting to hallucinate and a few of us decided that we needed to get him some medical attention. He was in bad shape and getting worse in the lousy conditions of the transient tent. We were able to connect with MSG Holder, and he brought a doctor over to take a look at Dodson. We left Dodson bundled up and we carried him and then put him in the back of a vehicle where he was taken to the hospital for the evening. That's about the sickest I've ever seen someone at that young of an age. That flu really hit him the hardest.

Here's the other thing that happens when you first fly into country: you can't sleep worth a darn for the first few days because your inner clock is so messed up. I remember being up in the middle of the night with Doug Globke, smoking cigarettes, and then taking walks around the air base with Doc Cain. We found a 24/7 internet café on post and we both messed around in there for a while. You're like a zombie and it's tiring on the body.

By the time the third day hit, we were at The Beast for the first time in a long time to begin our training. Lester had finally rejoined us, and he was on the mend. Man, did he still look terrible. He had dropped at least 15 pounds and his face was shrunken in.

That first morning back at The Beast, we turned in our weapons and then entered into the building through the sally port. Bob Allen, Ryan Suthard, and I paused as we saw a large picture of SSG Mowris in a frame on the wall. There was an inscription underneath his picture explaining who he was, his decorations, and his KIA date. It was a touching moment for the three of us and something we were very glad to see had been done.

From there we walked out onto the floor of the facility for the first time since April, 2004. Oh, how things had changed!

To begin with, the general population cells now had plumbing in them. Also, renovations that had begun while the HHC was in command had been completed. There were no longer holes in the roof, there were no longer birds and rats and mice running around the building, and the gaps in the giant doors had finally been sealed off. The place still smelled bad, but not nearly as terrible as it had in June of 2003. Lastly, the rules had changed. There was no longer tight control over everything, and detainees were now allowed a great deal of freedom. With that freedom came a price and that price was the safety of guards.

The cells were loud now because talking was allowed. Something odd happened when Bob, Ryan, Doc Cain, and I stepped out on the floor of The Beast. The place went silent. Familiar detainees began running up to the cell walls to look at Bob, Ryan, Doc Cain, and I. They recognized our faces and we recognized theirs.

Years later, Lester Dodson said you could "hear a pin drop in the place" as we walked across the floor and went to the designated area where we were to begin our training. I don't think it was fear the old detainees had, but I think it was the respect of authority. They remembered how tightly things had been run and they were now concerned that things may return back to that way. Needless to say, the four of us were celebrities among the population for the next couple of weeks.

Something had happened in The Beast just two weeks before we had arrived. There was an escape in which several detainees safely got out of The Beast and off of Bagram Air Base. To this day, I have no idea how this could have possibly happened.

I remember sitting in Ft. Dix, NJ when we were given a special brief over the SIPRNET (secured internet.) As they showed us the faces of the detainees, I recognized some. Ryan recognized a few also, but Bob recognized all of them and remembered their detainee numbers, the circumstances of their capture, and where they had originally been from. The man had a remarkable memory when it came to that stuff. We then watched the video these former detainees had posted online where they had described how they had escaped the facility.

Things just didn't click with all this and the circumstances didn't sit well with us. We all had theories and Bob was convinced that it was an inside job. To this day, we still don't know, and I doubt we ever will know.

Many months later, I was sitting down and smoking a cigarette outside of our office in The Beast. Bob came up to me and threw a printed piece of paper in my lap. It was a picture of a dead Arab man with a hole in the middle of his chest the size of two fists. You could see through the hole. Bob asked me if I recognized the name. I told him I didn't. He had a big smile across his face as he read off the detainee number and the biography of the former detainee. He was one of the Bagram escapees and he had been found dead in an insurgent training camp in Iraq. His body was found by an infantry platoon that went in to clear out the training camp area that an A-10 had lit up just a few hours before. While searching the dead bodies, the platoon found his BTIF release papers in his pocket. This specific detainee had caught .50 caliber rounds through his chest. Justice had been served and nobody was happier than Bob.

Going back to August, 2005; we were being re-indoctrinated into the facility by a young staff sergeant. He was about 5 feet 5 inches tall, of Filipino heritage, and you could tell that he took his PT very seriously. His name was SSG Fernandez.

SSG Fernandez was a sharp guy, but his training did not have a very polished delivery. MSG Holder stopped by a few hours later and he put a quick end to the training. That evening we found ourselves with work assignments.

All of the soldiers that had not worked the facility before were assigned to guard force shift work. The four of us that had worked the facility before were assigned to operations or training. Ryan Suthard got assigned to go to Kandahar right away to support the sister mission down there. Bob and I were assigned by MSG Holder to the training team and we were tasked to come up with a training program. We were told that we would be a part of, and we were to work with, the Mobile Training Team.

Doc Cain got assigned to the operations office where he began desk duty. I don't know if he enjoyed it or not, but Cain was REALLY good at that duty. Captain Hildegard, who was the OIC of operations, thought very highly of him. Bob and I also worked for Captain Hildegard, but indirectly.

It was weird losing Ryan so soon, but it was the nature of the work. He was really excited to head down there and he took it as a pat on the back to be assigned the special duty. All of us had passed through Kandahar on the first tour and it was known as a first-class shithole back then. Their holding facility for detainees was nothing more than an open field with c-wire and some tents. The living conditions for the guards weren't too much better. Bob and I got stuck there once for a couple of days on the first tour and the guards we dealt with were understaffed and walking zombies.

I was afraid Ryan would be going into those conditions and I felt bad for him. My assumptions of the conditions of "down south" turned out to be 100% incorrect.

Bob and I went to work with a staff sergeant that we both immediately formed a bond with. His name was SSG Fournier. SSG Fournier was a tall, slim black man in his mid to late 30s with a well-trimmed mustache. He had been deployed before in the first Gulf War with the 25th Infantry Division and this was his second tour of duty. We learned very quickly that the training program was composed of this staff sergeant on his own and he was glad to have our help.

Over the next few weeks, we put together a self-defense program, a cultural awareness program, an Afghan history program, and we reviewed and made the existing programs even better. I really enjoyed this work and so did Bob. We got to put our knowledge and skills about Afghanistan to use. Everything that we spent time learning about back home came pouring out of us and into this work. It was very gratifying.

All of our new programs were immediately approved, and the command seemed very pleased with our work. MSG Holder was our direct NCOIC and, he too, was very happy with the work we were doing.

He pulled me aside one time and with a mouth full of chew said, "Did you and Allen ever leave this place?"

I responded, "You know we did Master Sergeant, we all left together in

'04."

He looked at me again and said, "That's not what I asked. I asked did you and Allen ever leave this place?" as he pointed to his head.

I caught his drift this time around and said, frankly, "No, Master Sergeant."

He smiled and said, "That's what I thought and that's why I'm glad you're back."

One of the advantages of the new style and ways of The Beast was that there were several civilian interpreters on staff per shift and they had their own office area. Their office area was what used to be our old break room.

Bob and I spent a lot of time with these interpreters. The first time we walked into the office area we rattled off, "Salaam, shaem a salah-khan?" which meant "Hello, how are you gentlemen?"

We introduced ourselves in Pashto to each of the interpreters. Bob and I went around the room and shook hands with each of the interpreters individually. After the handshake, we immediately put our hands over our hearts. They were pleased at our attempts with Pashto and they happily shook our hands and returned the symbol of respect and friendship; the hand over the heart.

They really liked our interest in the culture of the country, Pashto, and the history of their former country. All of these men were American citizens that had fled Afghanistan in the late 1970s and early 1980s during the Soviet War. These men were treasure troves of knowledge and information. They were so excited to have guys like Bob and I interested in their stories. We spent dozens and dozens of hours talking with and learning from these men. They gave us books to read, phrases to remember, and they worked with us to make sure that we were telling the right history of Afghanistan in our training program. It was a pleasure working with these gentlemen.

After the first two weeks we were finally out of the hell of the transient tent and we moved into our new b-hut as the detachment we were replacing rotated out. The b-hut didn't have enough room for all of us, so our detachment was split up among three b-huts. Each hut had rooms built out of plywood and 2x4s. It was up to you how to customize it. Beds were available if you wanted one.

I went out and found some old ammo crates and I borrowed a hammer and nails from the R&U (Repair & Utilities) shop of The Beast. I made shelves out of the ammo crates and stood them straight up in the air. I then found flat plywood and nailed the plywood on top of the shelves. I created a bunk bed of sorts and picked up some mats to roll out to create a mattress. It was a pretty nice little setup and I also found an old steel desk that was being thrown out. I gave a pack of cigarettes to civilian contractors to put this desk in their truck and bring it back to our hut. Bob did something similar with the ammo crates for shelves, but he did draw a bed.

We were settled in, things were going well, and our first month back in The Ghan flew by.

CHAPTER 38

CONVOYS AND MOBILE TRAINING

We fell into our routines very quickly on this tour. What we were doing was not new to any of us and things clicked back into place. After a few weeks, Captain Hildegard changed things up a little with the Mobile Training Team. He had me split my time working directly for him in operations and working for the mobile training team. Bob also volunteered, and enjoyed, working the floor of the jail once again. He still remained a part of the Mobile Training Team, however. SSG Roberts had eventually been sent down to Kandahar to join Ryan Suthard.

Something I forgot to mention in the last chapter was that a few days after landing back in country, MSG Holder selected Blanco and I to go out on a vehicle convoy for a detainee release mission. I want to point something out that anyone who has been down range will know and understand. You are really messed up the first couple of weeks back in country. Your plumbing is all out of whack, your sleep is all over the place, and you're just an absolute mess. You're especially a mess ten thousand feet up in the Hindu Kush mountains. Due to this, I had to pee about every hour, on the hour, the first two weeks back in country. This made for a very long and, at times, embarrassing convoy mission when I had to urinate in a bottle in the truck every hour. I couldn't help it, but my body had just not regulated out yet.

I hated convoys. I hated them with a deep passion. I always felt like we were sitting ducks with huge targets on our backs on these missions. When you're air mobile in a helicopter you have an advantage, but when you're driving in a vehicle you don't have much advantage except for being heavily armed. I felt trapped in convoys and despised them. They made me very nervous and I never got over that nervous feeling. Everything else I experienced in my two tours I had gotten used to and they became second nature, but convoys never did.

Blanco and I joined the active component, attended all the briefings, and we went along on this release mission to the heart of Kabul. This convoy was smooth in operation, but slow and tedious in travel. I was uncomfortable the whole time due to having to urinate every hour, and my general disdain for convoy travel. One thing that sticks out to me from this convoy is we were driving through some back alleys to make our way to the meeting point. A kid ran out into the middle of the road and threw something under our vehicle. The driver didn't stand a chance of moving in time had it been an explosive. Luckily for us, it was just a water bottle filled with rocks, but that didn't stop our .50 caliber gunner from almost sending that child and everyone around him to their maker.

Man, did I hate convoys.

This convoy mission ended up going off without a hitch. Unfortunately, I peed in about 8 water bottles during the mission, though. The other soldiers in the truck were looking at me funny by the end of the mission. I was glad it was done and, luckily, I'd only have to do a few more of these convoy missions. Blanco broke his cherry with this first one and I was glad I was there with him for it.

337

For the Mobile Training Team, we got our first mission handed down to us and we would be out and about for roughly two weeks. Bob was passed over for this training mission, and I was assigned to the team with SSG Fournier, a male specialist, and a female specialist. We flew by helicopter to forward operating base after forward operating base. Most of these FOBs were in pretty rough shape. Many had run out of any kind of water for bathing and some didn't even serve meals. These poor SOBs had nothing to eat but MREs on a daily basis. Other FOBs had only one meal a day served.

Most FOBs had tents for living conditions, but others had bunkers or b-huts built. Every one of these FOBs that we visited to train had infantry soldiers pulled out of the field to learn proper handling of detainees. To this day, I have the highest level of respect for these men. They were the backbone of the military and the best our nation has to offer. It has always brought me great sadness to hear of these men perishing in battle.

When we were training the 82nd Airborne in Ghazni, I got friendly with another E-5 during the training. On one of our breaks we stepped outside for a cigarette break. This E-5 was about 6 feet tall, 165lbs, with a skinned head and a neatly shaved face. He had that emaciated, been out in the field too long, infantry-look to him though. His name was Sergeant Jackson.

SGT Jackson looked to be in his mid-40s. It was not uncommon to see older infantry soldiers stuck at E-5 in those days. We began chatting and he asked me how old I was. I was 23 at the time and I asked Jackson how old he was, fully expecting him to say 44 or 45. He responded to me that he had just had his 27th birthday not too long ago. I couldn't believe it.

Jackson went on to tell me that this was his fifth tour to Afghanistan or Iraq since 2001. He told me how great of an idea he thought it was to have MTTs come out to train his soldiers. He complimented me on how good the classes were and how important the information we were training his men on was. What Jackson said next has stuck with me ever since and I'll never forget it.

He told me, "You know this is great information, but I'm going to tell you the truth. I give two warnings and then I grease them. If they don't do what I tell them to, they don't get a third chance. I've lost too many men to take that risk. Just last month they killed our medic and I've been blown up twice. Here, just check this shit out."

With that, Jackson took off his uniform top and pulled up his brown t-shirt. His back and arm looked like that of an alligator's skin. The scar tissue was bumpy and rigid. SGT Jackson's skin coloring in these areas was a combination of cherry red, to yellow, and then to white. He had obviously suffered severe burns from an explosion.

After Jackson pulled his t-shirt back down and put his uniform shirt back on, he once again told me how he appreciated our training, but that he didn't take risks anymore. He repeated himself that they got two warnings and then he greased them.

SGT Jackson was the real deal.

Years later, I recall when President Obama approved a cut to sixty thousand combat arms soldiers. This cut mostly affected infantry soldiers. I often wondered if SGT Jackson was one of those cuts. I couldn't imagine a man like that doing anything but being a soldier and being an NCO. He was good at what he did, obviously, his men respected him, and he had an instinct to survive that many of us will never understand.

If he did get cut, do you really think he lasted in life bagging groceries or pouring concrete for a living? Frankly, I couldn't see that man doing anything but what he was doing.

At the end of the two weeks of mobile training and not being able to shower in ten of the fourteen days of that time, we returned back to Bagram. After the helicopter landed and I stored my gear, I immediately went to the operations office to let CPT Hildegard know that I was back. I also ran into MSG Holder as I was leaving the office, and he ordered me to head straight to the showers and to burn my uniform.

MSG Holder said to me, "Drake, you smell like a mule that has rolled around in dog shit."

As I was walking back toward our b-hut that morning, I saw Andrew Blanco. He stopped me and he had a really serious look on his face. He told me that Bob had not left the b-hut in days, that he wasn't talking to anyone, and Blanco said he was worried about him.

I immediately walked back to the b-hut with Blanco and I banged on Bob's door. He had it locked and he wasn't responding. After a few attempts like this with no response, I kicked his door open and found Bob asleep in his bed with his headphones on. His living area was filled with piss bottles, empty MREs, and it had the smell of dirty clothes. Frankly, this didn't surprise me, and it wasn't uncommon for Bob back then. Bob liked solitude, it's when he would do his best artwork, but this seemed extreme.

I shook Bob awake and asked him what the hell was going on. I asked him why he hadn't been in to work and why he wasn't responding to people looking for him. He didn't have much of an answer, so I didn't pry. I told Bob that I was going to go take a shower and that he was going to get out of bed and do the same. He did what I said, and we went and got cleaned up.

After our showers, we put on clean uniforms, and then we went and got breakfast together. Bob acted totally normal and like nothing had happened. In fact, he seemed happy to see me and we made fun of people in the chow hall. That's when I knew he was fine; his humor was still there.

Bob then reported to work that day and every day after that. Looking back on it all these years later, I think Bob went into a little depression there when he was separated from his two closest friends for a couple of weeks. I would experience a similar feeling when I would get sent to Kandahar about a month later.

For the next few weeks, the Operations OIC ordered me to fill in with the guard force because he didn't have anything for me to do for a while. The Mobile Training Team wouldn't have another mission until the spring because training missions were not carried out over the winter.

As I joined the guard force in late September, 2005, I was assigned to the second shift. Bob had himself transferred over from the first shift right away so that we could work together. It was just like old times. Bob and I made sure we were put on the same team and that we did the same rotations. We often volunteered for the worst duty of all, which was patrolling the catwalks. Bob and I liked the peace and quiet up there and we took the time to practice Pashto for hours on end. We would walk the lengths, shotguns in hand, and then meet in the middle and quiz each other on greetings and phrases.

Bob and I also ran showers together again and we hadn't lost our efficiency in the least. We ran work details together, we did escorts and transports together, and we made sure to spend all of our breaks in the interpreters' office asking questions and taking in the knowledge they were willing to pass over to us. It really felt like '03-'04 again.

Bob and I worked together all night, took all of our meals together, smoked cigarettes, and drank coffee outside the b-hut when we came back after breakfast in the morning. Although we worked the second shift, we had no problem switching over to the first shift to help out, if needed. Sometimes we'd work 24 hours straight if it was necessary. We just really enjoyed being guards together again.

I'll always remember that month we worked together. I think at that point in our lives both of us would have been more than happy if that month had extended on forever. When you have a friendship like Bob and I had, there's just something that clicks. We lifted each other up, we made each other better, and we were both at our very best when we were working together.

In early October of 2005, our Operations OIC, Captain Hildegard, decided to pull Ryan Suthard and Jim Roberts from Kandahar and to send SSG Sanchez and I down there to relieve them. I was more than happy to continue working with Bob as a guard, but the captain had different plans for me.

I would spend three days in Transit Hell trying to get down to Kandahar. Transit Hell is when you'd stay in the flight terminal all day and all night waiting to get a flight to your destination. You'd have your name on an Air Force manifest sheet and you'd wait for your name to be called. It was a long, drawn out process as your name would constantly get pushed down as higher priorities would be taken first.

In Transit Hell, you also couldn't leave the terminal because if you weren't there for a roll call, you'd automatically be bumped from the system. It sucked. I hated Transit Hell.

CHAPTER 39

THE ROMANIANS AND HEALY

In early October, my time in Transit Hell came to an end as I was able to catch a seat on a C-130 that brought me down to Kandahar. I would spend a week there working with my old friend Ryan Suthard and learning what I could from him. SSG Sanchez would follow me shortly to relieve SSG Roberts.

Although I'd been down to Kandahar already a few times on this tour on pick-ups and drop-offs, I noticed a big difference in temperature when I came back down there again this time. Bagram was cold come October. Bagram was located in the Hindu Kush mountains and saw temperature extremes. In October it was usually in the 40s and it wasn't rare to see snowstorms. When I landed in Kandahar it was in the 70s mostly and sometimes it would heat up to the 80s.

The housing in Kandahar was far superior to that of Bagram. This airfield had modular housing and it was very nice. Each housing unit had about eight separate rooms. The rooms were large and could accommodate up to four soldiers comfortably. These rooms were complete with wooden wall lockers, beds, and furniture. Each housing unit also had its own showers and latrines. This was a major improvement in living conditions compared to Bagram, which was still using port-o-johns, shower houses, and b-huts.

As far as the jail that I would be working at, it was a large steel building with an interior structure that was a collection of independent cells. Each cell was only large enough for one detainee and each cell had its own toilet. In the non-jail areas, there was running water with indoor plumbing, an oven, a refrigerator, cable television, and a phone. We also had our own duty vehicle complete with MP markings and lights. These were very good living conditions and equally good working conditions. I got the impression from Ryan that he was sad to be leaving Kandahar.

Our job there, two of us per shift, was to in-process and out-process captured enemy detainees. We also supervised the guard force that watched over the detainees. You HAD to know what you were doing to run this jail. We were responsible for this whole operation. It was crucial to know how to operate all of the processing equipment, how to do the paperwork properly, and how to keep proper records. If you did anything of these things wrong, it could have disastrous results on the overall mission.

There was skill involved in this job with no room for error. It was no joke since this was the starting point for captured enemy combatants. I took my duties very seriously and so did the others.

I never had the pleasure of meeting the OIC of the jail. There was one, but none of us knew who he or she was. We had an NCOIC, though, and he would stop in once a day or so. He was a huge former infantryman who had a full chest of jump wings, an air assault badge, a combat infantryman's badge, and a former drill sergeant's patch. Master Sergeant Williams was an intimidating man.

I learned very quickly that as long as you kept your nose clean and did your job, MSG Williams would leave you alone. If you messed up, however, he was all over you.

My first introduction to his bad side was when Ryan was driving me around the airfield showing me where everything was at. We were in the MP vehicle and I was smoking a cigarette. Technically, there was no smoking in government vehicles, but most everyone would smoke in them anyway.

When we got to our destination, the hospital, where Ryan was going to show me around, this master sergeant came riding up in his utility vehicle and asked me if I had been smoking in the vehicle. I hadn't seen him behind us, so I told him that it was an old butt in my hand. That was a big mistake. He locked me up at parade rest and laid into me. I deserved the ass chewing and he was in the right to lay into me. After that I never did anything again to upset him. In fact, I respected him a great deal because he treated the others and I fairly. If I saw him on the street today my first reaction would probably be to snap to parade rest.

MSG Williams also had another job on the airfield where he was the Equal Opportunity NCOIC and being the NCOIC of the jail was his second job. I got the impression that he did not want to be bothered with the jail. He would stop in for about twenty minutes a day, check the logbooks and receive the report, and as long as everything was good, he'd be on his way. He knew we could handle things and he left us to it. That's the way every good leader should act.

After SSG Sanchez joined us down in Kandahar, we took him around and showed him all the important places. SSG Roberts also spent a lot of time with him going over the duties and responsibilities. Three days after this train-up, Ryan Suthard and Jim Roberts headed back to Bagram.

Although Roberts and Suthard had done their best to train us, there was still a lot to learn in Kandahar and we had to learn it quickly. It was a large airfield and it was difficult to remember where everything was. The Army didn't manufacture maps, after all, for fear that they could end up in the hands of the enemy. You had to mentally map out where everything was.

There are a lot of things that go into running a jail such as supply, logistics, transportation needs, and coordination. Another big part of the job was working with the Air Force and Army to schedule air mobile for flights. Like I've said before, this job was no joke.

For the first few weeks SSG Sanchez and I worked tirelessly. We also had three active duty soldiers who had been stationed in Kandahar for a while who helped us out. One was an E-5 whose name was Sergeant Post and then there were two specialists named Graziano and Randall. I took the second shift and Graziano ended up being with me. SSG Sanchez stayed on the first shift with Randall and the other E-5.

For all of the great living conditions of Kandahar, the food situation was a very poor one. To put it plainly, the food was awful. There were only two accessible chow halls to regular soldiers, and both required a long wait in line to enter. There were many other countries on the airfield at that time and they also ate in these same chow halls.

Everyone hated the Romanians. Everyone. The Romanians were always the first ones in line, they were all overweight, and they treated every meal like it was a full meal with courses. Every other country respected the chow hall. You got in, ate as fast as you could, and then got out so that others could eat. The

Romanians just straight up didn't give a shit. There could be lines of five hundred people waiting outside, and they would still sit back in their seats and eat slowly and talk away. There was also a rumor that they were stealing fruit and mailing it home. They were selfish, they were obnoxious, and nobody on the post liked them. It was no coincidence that their housing had been located directly across from the water reclamation area, otherwise known as the shit ponds.

At this point in time, the airfield was in a transition. The British Army was getting ready to take over the airfield in just a few months. They were already starting to take over the secondary chow hall and they had also taken over a portion of the hospital. The British were everywhere. I enjoyed working with them too. They always had smiles on their faces, and they all tended to have a witty sense of humor. They would constantly point at my last name on my uniform and tell me I had an English last name and that I must be English. I told them I wasn't aware of any English ancestry, but that didn't stop them from calling me "cousin" and other English terms for family I don't quite remember. Although most I could understand well, some had heavy accents that were difficult to follow.

One thing we never did in Kandahar was turn in our laundry to be done for us. They had laundry facilities on the airfield that you could use free of charge. It was another plus up from Bagram. There were about four large tents full of washing machines and dryers. It was a good setup. I'd often grab a book or a magazine and head off to do my laundry while off shift.

Almost every single time I'd run into British nurses from the hospital at this laundry facility. We were at the hospital often with our duties and I'd gotten to know some of the nurses by name. Every time, they'd sucker me with their good looks and charming accents into giving them rides back to their compound. Every, single, time. A couple of the nurses, in particular, were very friendly and would invite me into their compound for meals or to watch soccer matches or movies. I never took them up on it because I knew where that was headed. I didn't need to deal with an international love affair! All these years later, I'd like to have a talk with my 23-year-old self over that decision. Duty is one thing, but experience is another!

There was a lot going on in this job in Kandahar, but we didn't always have detainees in the jail. Sometimes we'd go on dry spells for four-to-five days straight without detainees. SSG Sanchez would then pull us from nights and make us work the day shift doing manual labor by scrubbing down the facility, painting, and training. I had no objections to the labor or training, but I did have my objections to leaving the second shift. We should have stayed on two shifts for coverage purposes in case a call came in. It was silly to break off and all go to one shift. Almost every time that we did this, detainees would arrive in the middle of the night and Graziano and I would have to scramble to head in.

SSG Sanchez, as much as I respected him, would do stuff like this all the time and it would drive me insane.

When there were detainees in the jail it was our job to in process them. The next step would then be to make sure that the capturing unit that was guarding them, was trained. We had to teach them how to do checks, how to keep logbooks, and how to safely handle themselves while conducting detainee operations.

Most of the time in Kandahar, the captors of the detainees were special forces. The Special Forces unit on the airfield had a team of 6 MPs assigned to them which included two female MPs. We worked with these men and women often and I liked them. They were good soldiers. The NCOIC of this group of MPs was a master sergeant who was at the end of his career. His name was MSG Elliot, he was a black man about 6 feet tall, and he kept himself at a trim 190lbs. MSG Elliot was a class act. He and I spent a lot of time talking together and I had a great deal of respect for him. He really knew his stuff and knew how to handle his business. He also looked after and took care of his people.

One of the female MPs that was assigned to this group was named Healy and she was a specialist. She was about 5 feet 4 inches, she was in very good shape, and she had blonde hair and blue eyes. She had a southern accent of some sort and she was a nice girl. She was right around my age by a year or two. Healy was a very pretty woman and she was a very pleasant person to be around.

Healy was always working shifts in the jail, usually nights, with us. She was a good soldier and dedicated to her craft. After working together for a few weeks, Healy got promoted to sergeant. Graziano and I even attended the ceremony, which was conveniently held in the garage area of our jail. Healy and I were now the same rank, she was now an NCO.

Once she got upped, Healy was now in a supervisor's role and she worked more closely with Graziano and I. She would take meals with us in the middle of the night, I'd loan her our truck to drive back and forth from her compound, and she'd even watch football games and movies with us during downtime. As I said before, we also had a phone that you could call out on and she'd use our phone often to call back home. Healy was a nice girl and a good soldier, I enjoyed working with her, but it ended there for me. I had zero interest in getting wrapped up in a romantic relationship with a fellow GI. I had learned my lesson back on the first tour.

Over time, I noticed Healy was spending more and more time around me. I had a feeling what she was up to. If I stepped out to have a cigarette, she'd join me. If I was going to run to the PX, she always asked to come with me. If I was at the chow hall and she saw me, she'd make sure to sit down next to me. Healy would also always insist that she came with me when we would have to do pickups or drop offs at the flight line. I felt the vibe and I knew exactly what she was doing, and it made me very uncomfortable.

One night after SSG Sanchez had us scrubbing the jail all day, detainees came in at night. Graziano and I had to get dressed and drive back to the jail where we met the capturing unit and we processed the detainees. Healy and her team showed up to take over the guard duties, since it had been a special forces' capture.

Graziano and I had been up all day, so I told him to get some sleep for a couple of hours. When he woke up, he relieved me, and I sat down on our couch to take a nap myself. When I woke up about an hour later, Healy was also on the couch with me. She had wrapped herself around me like we were lovers and she was sleeping on my chest. I immediately leapt to my feet and shoved her off of me.

Angrily, I said, "Healy! What the hell are you doing?"

Healy responded, "Well, we're both single and we're both the same rank.

351

There's no problem if we get together."

I couldn't believe this with Healy and, in my opinion, this was totally unprofessional. I responded, "Look, Healy. I'm flattered, but I'm not interested. Nothing is going to happen between us and we need to remain professional as NCOs. This is not being professional. Anyone could have walked in here and seen this and gotten the wrong impression."

That put an end to this puppy love thing that Healy had going on. Once again, I'd like to have a talk with my 23-year-old self. Duty is one thing, but experience is another. Healy was a nice girl and easy on the eyes, and it might have been worth a shot!

CHAPTER 40

HAPPY, WHO THE FUCK ARE YOU?

On Thanksgiving 2005, Graziano and I stayed at the jail after our shift ended. That morning we had gotten a batch of detainees in right at shift change. We stayed over to help out the day shift to process the detainees and then we finally got back to our housing and got to bed around eleven in the morning.

At one o'clock that afternoon SSG Sanchez came into our rooms, woke both of us up, and told us to get cleaned up. We had been invited by MSG Elliot, the NCOIC of the MPs assigned to the special forces group, to have a Thanksgiving meal at the Special Forces compound. I told SSG Sanchez that we'd much rather sleep, and we could eat together later. Not to mention, Special Forces did not like outsiders in their compound whether there was an invitation or not. Sanchez ignored my protests and he ordered us to get up.

Graziano and I got up, got cleaned up, and we climbed into the truck and headed with the others to the Special Forces compound. When we arrived at the compound, the Command Sergeant Major of the Special Forces group was greeting soldiers at the chow hall entrance. He was shaking hands and saying "Happy Thanksgiving" to everyone that passed through.

I was first in line from our group of people and he looked at me, extended his hand, and said, "Happy, who the fuck are you?" He didn't look too happy that an outsider had gotten into his compound.

I then explained that MSG Elliot had invited us. The CSM began questioning us and questioning why we were there. This was a very uncomfortable situation and was exactly what I thought would happen. Eventually, MSG Elliot came out from inside the chow hall, vouched for us, and the CSM let us pass.

When we got inside the chow hall, we had a nice meal with MSG Elliot, Healy, and the others in their team. Like I said, they were all good people and we enjoyed spending time with them. Fortunately, it appeared that Healy had gotten over her case of puppy love.

After this afternoon meal, Graziano and I were allowed to head back to our housing to sleep. We agreed that we'd get up at four o'clock that afternoon so that we could get together with the others and eat again. We stuck to our plan and we were picked up by our other MPs that night and we drove over to the chow hall that was now being run by the British Army.

The British had done a good job and they had all the tables put together in one long line, family style. We waited in line for over a half hour and then finally got a seat inside. We sat down at open spots at the table between the British Army, the Canadians, and some Australians. We shook hands with the other soldiers, and we wished each other a Happy Thanksgiving. It was kind of funny how the other countries took to our holiday, but they were very friendly, and we enjoyed eating with them.

Do you remember how I told you that the Romanians were obnoxious and not well liked? Well, they didn't disappoint us this night either. There were lines of people looking to get a hot meal this Thanksgiving night and everyone was eating quickly so that the other soldiers outside could get in. Not the Romanians. They were being their usual rude selves and were laughing, joking, talking loudly, and enjoying their hours-long meal.

At our table some of the British soldiers were from Northern Ireland. One guy, in particular, looked like a nasty cuss covered in tattoos. The Romanians were REALLY pissing him off! I could see him seething and getting angrier and angrier.

This British soldier, from Northern Ireland, finally stood up and yelled out, "That's e-fooking-noof! I've had enoof of these fooking wankers! It's not even their fooking holiday! There're lads out there in the cold trying to get a meal and these fooking animals are sitting there fooking them over! Right! That's enoof!"

This soldier stood up, blew his stack, and started screaming at the Romanians. Graziano, SSG Sanchez, the others, and I just sat there in amazement as he hopped over the table and started storming towards the Romanians. Several Romanians stood up and started yelling back and this prompted the other British Army soldiers to stand up. We were poised to see a brawl between the Romanian Army and the British Army! After a few minutes of insults being hurled and some light pushing, soldiers got in between the two groups and things simmered down.

I sat there thinking to myself: it's an American holiday, being celebrated in a British chow hall; in Kandahar, Afghanistan; and I just almost watched Northern Irish soldiers come to blows with Romanians. Where else would you get this kind of entertainment?

CHAPTER 41

DID YOU CHECK THEIR IDS?

In December, 2005, the command of The Beast back in Bagram rotated out. They were replaced by a National Guard unit along with an Air Force Security Forces component. It was an odd, hybrid mix and I was not there for the train-up or command change. This only affected us in Kandahar because the three soldiers we had down with us also rotated out. Replacing Graziano, Randall, and their sergeant were three soldiers from the National Guard unit that had arrived in Bagram.

SSG Sanchez received their flight information, and I hopped into our truck and drove down to the flight line to pick them up. Due to our MP status, we were permitted to drive directly onto the tarmac and up to the aircraft, all we had to do was turn our blue police lights on.

As I pulled up to the aircraft, I introduced myself to the load master and verified the soldiers I was looking for had been on the manifest. I called out their names, told them to grab their gear, and to then meet me at the truck.

As they came walking up, two of the soldiers were specialists by the names of Norton and Hernandez. There was also a staff sergeant with them by the name of Harrison. I introduced myself to each of them, shook hands with them, and then helped them load their gear into the back of the truck. I drove them back to our housing area, got them settled in, and then I brought them back to our jail.

At the jail, SSG Sanchez introduced himself and both of us brought these new soldiers up to speed on the operation. MSG Williams also stopped by to meet the new soldiers. All three were scared to death of him just like SSG Sanchez and I were. Right then and there, I knew we'd have no problems with these new soldiers.

SPC Hernandez was assigned to me on the overnight shift and SSG Harrison and SPC Norton stayed on days. We didn't have any detainees present on this day, so we all stayed together for the rest of the day. The next evening, however, Hernandez and I would get our start together.

Hernandez was a small guy. I'm a small guy, but he was even smaller than me. He was about 5 feet 2 inches with a muscular build, and he was originally from Puerto Rico. He was a really nice guy and we got along from day one. Hernandez had only been in the National Guard about two years at this point, but he was very smart and was already a fully capable MP. He didn't have any problems picking up on the details of our work and he quickly learned how to handle the machines and equipment that we used for in-processing.

Our first night on shift, Hernandez and I got a call on our secured line from the special operations compound that we should expect detainees on site within the hour. I had zero concerns, this was business as usual at this point, and I made all the proper coordination with military intelligence and the hospital.

About an hour after the call, we heard a knock at our back door. I verified it was the capturing unit and then I opened our large overhead door so that they could back their vehicle into our facility. The team had arrived driving a troop carrier Humvee with a cover on it and, once they backed in fully, I closed the door again.

There were four members of the capturing team who climbed out of the bed of the truck and there were two more who were in the cab of the Humvee. These were special forces operators and they were in rough shape. Their uniforms were tattered, soiled, and filthy. Each man had long hair with a beard, and their eyes were sunken in and their jawbones were closer than normal to the skin. It was obvious to me that these men had not slept, nor had they eaten regularly, in some time. As they began dropping their gear, I noticed that they smelled absolutely awful. I also noticed that each of these men had blood all over their uniforms. One operator's entire right leg of his uniform was stained red. I wasn't sure if the blood was his or where it had come from, and I didn't ask.

Healy and her team showed up soon after and they worked with us to get the two detainees that the operators had brought in processed. I will not convey the details of an in-processing, but it involves three parties: MPs, medical personnel, and MI. We handled our business and got the detainees into their cells. Hernandez operated without flaw and I was really impressed at how quickly he picked up on things.

When I returned to the open area of the jail where the operators were standing around, I asked them if they were hungry. They responded yes, and Hernandez and I got our oven fired up with some frozen pizzas. We also shared soft drinks with them, cigarettes, chewing tobacco, water, and anything else we had. These men were worn out and they thanked us over and over again for the hospitality.

One operator stood up and spoke, "SGT Drake, I'm Lieutenant Martinez. May I use your facility's secured line?"

I responded, "Yes, sir. Let me show you where it is."

I took LT Martinez upstairs to our office where the phone was. He thanked me and then closed the door as I left.

About 15 minutes later, SGT Healy came out into the open area to let me know the shift arrangements for her team overnight. We talked briefly, and then I turned my attention back to the operators.

I said, "Gentlemen, I'm not sure where you're based out of, but SGT Healy here stays at the Special Forces compound on the airfield. Would you like for her to take you over there where you can take showers and change clothes?"

One operator responded, "Sure, that sounds good. Give us about 20 minutes, okay? We have to wait for the Lieutenant, and he may take a while."

I nodded that I understood, and I went back to talking to Healy and Hernandez. Our work had been completed for the night, but I wanted to make sure that these operators were taken care of. As I said, they were in rough shape and I felt a duty to make sure I could help them out as much as I could.

It was around three o'clock in the morning and the SF team was still waiting on their lieutenant when SSG Sanchez came walking into the jail. This was not an uncommon thing for Sanchez to do. He would come into the jail at all hours of the night to use the phone or to watch television. He also did it because he was a control freak. Even though I handled everything well, he still had to have his head over my shoulder. It drove me crazy and by this stage of the deployment,

I was growing sick and tired of being stuck in Kandahar with Sanchez.

SSG Sanchez and I walked over to a side area and he started asking me questions about who the operators were and what was taking place. I was prepared to brief him at our shift change at seven in the morning, but he wanted to know right now, so I gave him the full briefing. He found no problems with our procedures, but he double checked all the paperwork, unnecessarily.

After his paperwork check, he glanced over at the rifles and pistols that the operators had.

"Why aren't those weapons locked up in the cage, Drake?" He asked.

We had a policy where we would have guests to the facility lock up their weapons in our makeshift arms room.

I responded, "I'm not too concerned about these operators, Sergeant. These guys are in rough shape and their uniforms are all bloody. As soon as their lieutenant finishes his phone call, Healy is going to take them over to the compound."

SSG Sanchez got angry with me and fired off at me with, "Did you check their IDs? You should have checked their IDs!"

I was irritated now and responded, "If you want their weapons and their IDs, then you go ahead and talk to them. These men have obviously been through enough shit tonight and I don't find it necessary to give them anymore. Why don't you just let them relax? They're probably going to be out of here in a few minutes. Their paperwork was straight, Hernandez and I in-processed their detainees, and everything is on the up. There's no reason to bother these guys."

"Rules are rules," Sanchez said as he turned around. Hernandez, Healy, and I watched with a collective groan as Sanchez went around and demanded the operators turn in their weapons and show him their ID cards. They did as he asked, but you could tell they were irritated. We received several "What the fuck?" looks and all I could do was shrug my shoulders.

About the time SSG Sanchez was locking up their weapons, Lieutenant Martinez was coming down the stairs and told his team it was time to mount back up and get out of there. He shook hands with me, thanked us for everything, and then he looked at his team with a blank look on his face.

"Where the fuck are your weapons, boys?"

CHAPTER 42

CHRISTMASTIME IN AFGHANISTAN

A couple of weeks after the incident with Special Forces, SSG Sanchez and my working relationship was at an all-time low. He was now staying at the jail almost the entire overnight shift and sleeping in our TV room. When he wasn't sleeping in the break area on our shift, he was micromanaging my every move.

At this point in late December, SSG Sanchez and I had been working together in Kandahar for almost 3 months. In all that time, there was never a problem or an error in our operation. Our paperwork was always straight, the guards were always doing what they were supposed to be doing, and in-processing and out-processing procedures had been carried out flawlessly. I couldn't wrap my mind around why now he was suddenly acting like this, and it was driving me crazy.

I was concerned that SSG Sanchez was needlessly burning himself out. There was no reason for him to be putting the hours in at the jail that he was. Whenever I would ask him why he was staying at the jail most of the night, he would say, "I don't have all the gadgets that you guys do, so I come here to relax."

The only problem was he wasn't relaxing, he was continuing to do more work.

Two days before Christmas that year, we were holding quite a few detainees in our jail. The decision had been made that a significant number of these detainees needed to be transferred to Bagram. SSG Sanchez told me that he wanted me to be the NCOIC of the transportation team and to conduct the operation.

I did as I was told. I made all the arrangements needed and I took three of the Special Forces' MPs with me. We flew out on Christmas Eve on a C-130 transport plane back to Bagram.

We did not have a dedicated flight and on top of the cargo in orange that we were transporting, the bird was loaded with other gear and equipment. There were also around a half dozen passengers also on the plane. Several times during the flight we had to stop people from trying to take pictures of the detainees. This included the flight crew! I understood that this was a unique thing for them that they didn't see every day, but it was common sense that doing something like taking a picture of a detainee broke operational security.

When we landed in Bagram, we were met by a transport vehicle from The Beast. Driving the transport vehicle was Doc Cain and with him was SSG Roberts. I shook hands with both of them, hugged them, and wished them a Merry Christmas. I then introduced them to the other MPs that made the trip with me. My MPs and I climbed onto the vehicles with our detainees and we drove over to The Beast where we signed custody over to the Facility OIC.

I took the MPs with me for a tour around The Beast and introduced them to all the men of my detachment. I kept them the hell away from Schlitz. While checking in with SFC Anderson, he let me know that SSG Sanchez had called on the secured line and told me to stay up in Bagram until the day after Christmas. I appreciated that from Sanchez, and I was looking forward to seeing Bob, Ryan, and all the others.

When we finished our tour of the facility, it was dinner time. None of these MPs had ever been to Bagram before, so they followed me to the chow hall. After dinner, I took them back to the Air Force terminal and got them on the manifest for a flight back to Kandahar. Luckily for them, there was a flight leaving in just a few hours. There would be no Transit Hell experience for these young soldiers.

There was a specialist with them by the name of Chase who I had faith would be a good NCO one day. I told Chase that the two other soldiers were now his responsibility and I wished him a safe trip back to Kandahar. I shook hands with the three soldiers, wished them a Merry Christmas, and provided them with the phone number to KFDS for a pickup when they landed.

From the terminal, I walked back to my b-hut where I hadn't slept in almost three months. Outside of seeing that my little room was being used as a storage area, I was glad to be back in my old bunk, and I was glad to be back in the company of my good friends. I had been unhappy in Kandahar for some time at this point and the isolation of the mission down there was really getting to me. I missed my friends.

When I had left for Kandahar back in late-September, Schlitz had a room in our b-hut. None of us wanted him there and he didn't want to be there either. I was pleased to see that he was no longer living in our b-hut. Schlitz had left and moved to another b-hut where SSG Roberts was staying. In his place was Mike Leathers. Mike Leathers was a fellow E-5 that had belonged to one of our sister companies in the 327th Battalion. I didn't know him before this tour, but I liked him from the first minute I shook hands with him that night.

Leathers was in country with another 11-man detachment that had come to Bagram from the 300th command. They were known as DET 5.

It felt great to see Bob, Ryan, Lester, Blanco, and Cain that night. We all sat around chatting and smoking cigarettes into the late hours of the night. It was a special Christmas Eve that I'll always remember because I felt so relieved to finally be away from SSG Sanchez.

On Christmas Day, everyone in my tent was off. Because I wasn't involved in the operations of The Beast at this time, I'm not sure how this was arranged. All I was told was that The Beast, for probably the first time in its history, was now actually overstaffed with personnel due to the numbers from the National Guard company and the Air Force component.

We all spent Christmas Day eating three meals together, drinking a lot of coffee together, smoking a lot of cigarettes together, and watching Schindler's List together. It was the first time I had ever seen Schindler's List and I have watched it every Christmas since.

At night we all walked up to the MWR center on post and waited our turns in line to call our families. I was sad to be away from my blood family for Christmas, but I was also very happy to be with men I considered my other family for the holiday.

This was a special Christmas for me and one that I'll never forget.

CHAPTER 43

THE WHALE MOVIE

After Christmas, I caught a flight and headed back to Kandahar. When I landed, SSG Harrison and Norton picked me up on the flight line. They drove me back to the barracks and then told me that SSG Sanchez wanted to see me right away.

I dropped my gear in my room and then hopped back into the truck to head over to the jail. When we got to the jail, SSG Sanchez was in the office and told me to close the door behind me when I came in. The look on his face told me that this wasn't going to be good.

"What the hell were you telling people up there about me?" he asked.

"What do you mean, SSG Sanchez? I visited SFC Anderson and CPT Hildegard and they asked about you. They asked why they were getting emails from you at all hours of the night. They also asked why whenever our office calls up there, it's always you on the phone no matter what time of the day it is. They were concerned that you were overworking yourself. I told them that, yes, you work a lot of hours, and I was also concerned about you."

"You're lying to me!" he exclaimed. "You made up some story that I'm working 24 hours a day and now they're mad at me!"

I wasn't smart enough then to know how to play politics. I should have kept my mouth shut in Bagram when I was asked about Sanchez. I should have smiled and just told Anderson and Hildegard that everything was fine. I didn't do that, and I had answered their questions honestly. This was exactly what I was afraid might happen.

The truth is Sanchez was burning himself out. He was on edge, he was stressed out, and he was making what should have been a really easy duty into one that we all dreaded walking into each day.

I chose my next words wisely, because I knew I was in really hot water for doing nothing but being honest.

"SSG Sanchez, I have a high level of respect for you" I said. "I think that you and I have done good things here in this jail together. We've run a solid operation and we work well together. If you think that I'm trying to stab you in the back or go around you, then you've got my character all wrong."

SSG became enraged, "I question your character after this! Get out of my office!"

This was the final straw for me. I could no longer stand Sanchez's controlling, overbearing ways. I was a perfectly competent NCO who had never let him down and I didn't deserve his paranoia.

A few days after this I sent an email to our detachment commander asking to be transferred back up to Bagram. I had been with SSG Sanchez for over three months at this point and our relationship had deteriorated to the point of being unrepairable.

Despite the word of concern sent down from command, SSG Sanchez continued his ways of staying at the jail all day and all night. Around this time AFN (Armed Forces Network) TV was showing a movie about a dysfunctional Samoan family. The specifics escape me, but the film revolved around a young girl from this family that had a fascination with whales. AFN showed this movie frequently and at all times of the day and night. We nicknamed it "The Whale Movie."

SSG Sanchez was obsessed with this movie and would watch it whenever it was on. He would be at the jail overnight, half asleep on the couch, with the movie on. Hernandez would go in there to watch TV while on a break and he would turn the channel. Sanchez would snap awake and yell at out, "I'm watching that!" He must have watched that movie 20 times and nobody was allowed to watch anything but that stupid movie when it was on.

As my anger grew, I started sending weekly emails to our detachment commander requesting a transfer. My emails went unanswered.

January moved to February and life continued on in Kandahar. My attitude started changing to a negative one because I did not like the situation I was in with SSG Sanchez. I was also having the soldiers on the day shift, Norton and SSG Harrison, constantly complaining to me about Sanchez. Their bitch was that he was always on them and no matter what they did, it was never good enough. I knew the feeling and I did my best not to get involved. As my attitude was turning negative, though, it was becoming very difficult to not agree with these soldiers. Another contributing factor to my attitude at this time was that I really missed my friends back at Bagram. I felt isolated at Kandahar and it was getting tiresome.

February rolled along with the same pace and I had now spent a solid four months in Kandahar. SSG Sanchez never changed his ways and continued on his marathon pace of work hours undermining every task we did and every move we made. The only way you could get away from him was when you were in your room off hours or had to take a transport mission to Bagram. I did both as frequently as I possibly could. I also continued sending my weekly email asking for a transfer.

In late February, I led a transfer mission to Bagram and did the usual where I stopped in to see SFC Anderson. CPT Hildegard, our Operations OIC, had been relieved by an Air Force captain that I never got to know too well. I'm not certain he even knew we had another jail in Kandahar. While visiting with Anderson, he let me know that he was sending someone down to relieve me in early March. This was music to my ears!

In early March, I picked up my replacement on the tarmac of the airfield and brought him to housing and then over to the jail. I had known SSG Manson from back home in the unit. He was a member of one of our sister companies and had volunteered as part of DET 5, the second 11-man detachment that came to Bagram after us. He was with the same crew of soldiers as Mike Leathers.

When Manson asked me about SSG Sanchez, whom he knew before from Iraq, I acted unprofessionally and went off. I let my nearly five months of frustrations out. I talked badly of Sanchez and how he had ruined the morale at the jail. Manson didn't say a word back, but I could tell that he was disappointed with the way I was speaking of someone he had previously worked with. If I could travel back in time and change the way I acted that day; I would. It was not the way an NCO should talk about another NCO. Despite his methods and our differences, SSG Sanchez was a good NCO and the right man for the job to run that jail. I respected him very much, I was just tired of working for him.

Around the same time that Manson showed up, the rocket attacks started coming. Just about every night, the airfield was coming under fire. Similar to what I had experienced at Bagram, these rockets sometimes hit things on the base and other times they did not. You just never knew, so it was always best to find a concrete bunker to sit in and ride it out.

Later that month, the insurgents managed to dial in the rocket attacks and hit a chow hall near the flight line, killing several civilians, American soldiers, and international troops. It was an absolute shame.

After a few days when Manson was settled in, I traveled to the jail for the last time. I shook hands with all the other MPs and said my good-byes. Hernandez, who was a great guy and I knew was going places in his military career, gave me a hug and thanked me for showing him the ropes. He and I had worked very well together, we were a good team, and I was going to miss working with him.

On the same token, I was beyond excited to finally be leaving Kandahar and to be heading back to Bagram to be with my friends again.

CHAPTER 44

BACK IN BAGRAM

When I got back to Bagram in early March, 2006, I was met with a handshake and a hug as Jason Cain met me at the flight line with a truck to help me haul my gear back to our b-hut. After getting all my gear re-settled, I headed up to The Beast to check in with SFC Anderson.

I thanked Anderson for bringing me back to Bagram and he shook my hand. SFC Anderson welcomed me back to Bagram and told me that I needed to check in with the Operations NCOIC about my work assignment. MSG Holder had long ago rotated out while I was still in Kandahar, and there was a new Air Force E-8 who was holding the position of NCOIC. I went to his office, introduced myself, and stood at parade rest waiting to hear where I'd work. He asked me a few questions about what I had done in the past at the facility, and then, without hesitation, he told me that he was assigning me back to the guard force on the day shift. I was more than happy to go back to the shift because Bob was there along with a few others from our detachment including SSG Roberts.

I found out shortly that SSG Roberts was no longer with us at this point. Roberts's home unit had been deployed to Iraq on a one-year tour. Roberts asked permission from the command to be released from his current tour in order to join his home unit in Iraq. They approved his request. I feel badly that I never got to shake his hand when he left. For as roughly as our relationship started, in the end I think we had a mutual respect for one another and we were friends.

Roberts's idiot friend Schlitz was still around, however. He had somehow weaseled a promotion to E-6 and he was a one-man office in The Beast taking pictures for IDs and making ID badges for the jail. It was a pretty good job for him because it limited his interaction with people and kept him away from screwing anything up.

The next morning, I was back on the guard force, but this time around Bob and I were not able to get ourselves on the same work team. We would still take all our meals together, but it just wasn't the same working without him. What also wasn't the same was the pace. When it came time to do showers, the Air Force and National Guard unit making up the guard force just didn't move quickly enough for my liking. The shower rotations were taking twice as long as they should have been taking and key details were also being missed, such as searching cells when detainees were out of them.

As a sergeant, I had the duty to get E-4s and below in gear. I did just this. I started doing my best to train these young soldiers and airmen the proper techniques to do certain tasks in the jail to promote maximum safety. Bob was trying to do the same thing, but when I'd cross him on the floor, he'd often give me that frustrated Bob look and shake his head in disappointment.

I worked as part of the Guard Force for about four weeks. During that time, I met with the soldiers from the other detachment, DET 5. Three of their soldiers were on the guard force, including my new roommate Mike Leathers, while the others had taken over the training, classes, and the mobile training team. DET 5 had even built themselves their own office area in what used to be an old isolation cell block. I got along with all of them and had zero problems, although several others did. Several soldiers from my detachment did not appreciate how DET 5 came in and just took over.

After I got to know some of the senior NCOs in the other detachment, I became friendly with their detachment commander who was named SFC Lansky. He asked me to join them in training new soldiers. SFC Lansky liked the programs that Bob and I had put together and he wanted me to present them. Bob wasn't interested, however, he just wanted to stay on the floor at that point.

Whenever new soldiers or airmen would come into The Beast, I would train them on Cultural Awareness and the History of Afghanistan. On some occasions, I was also asked to give my Unarmed Self Defense course. There was no shortage of manpower during these days for the Guard Force, so when DET 5 needed help with training, I would just make the arrangements with the Sergeant of the Guard. I would then spend the day working with DET 5 helping to train the incoming soldiers and airmen.

During those four weeks, Bob was sent down to Kandahar with two of the National Guard company's soldiers to relieve the three soldiers that had come down while I was still there. I was sad to see Bob go, and I warned him about what it was like working for SSG Sanchez. This time I did it cordially and respectfully, however.

What I figured would happen finally happened. The operations NCOIC decided that I was "too rough" and moving "too quickly" as a guard on the floor.

My style of handling detainee operations was effective, safe, and efficient; but I was found to be too "aggressive." I think that some of the guards may have even called me "mean." It seemed that my methods of running day-to-day jail operations in The Beast were no longer PC enough for the current command. Despite the hundreds of incoming soldiers and airmen I had helped to train, despite the riots I had helped quell with some brave and tough soldiers and airmen, and despite working with my fellow NCOs to get showers and transfer operations back orderly, command felt that I was best suited off of the guard force and in another role.

I told the NCOIC that I was sorry to have hurt feelings, but I had a lot of experience in this field and my way was going to keep them safe. In hindsight, I would have had a better chance of pleading my case to the ass of the camel down at the bazaar.

About the time I was removed from the guard force, Ryan Suthard left to go down to Kandahar to take over the position of NCOIC of the group of MPs assigned to Special Forces. The timing was perfect, and I moved into his old job. What I didn't like was that I had finally gotten back to Bagram after being away so many months, and now within a matter of a few weeks, I was separated from my two closest friends again.

Another thing I didn't like was that the new command in The Beast was doing random urine tests for drugs. I had no problem taking the test, but I did have a problem with it being at three o'clock in the morning and it being a constant thing. Every week I was "randomly selected" for this test.

I wasn't the only one. There was a grizzled, old master sergeant who was handling the operations side of The Beast for the Army. He had a drill sergeant's patch, was airborne and air assault, and wore a 10th Mountain combat patch on his right arm. MSG Bolton was an average sized black man with a shaved head and a demeanor that was very intimidating. If he walked by you and something wasn't right, he was going to let you know about it. MSG Bolton was also "randomly selected" each time there was a urine drug test.

The last urine test we took together, we were both awoken at three in the morning and escorted down to the first sergeant's office to receive our cups. MSG Bolton was hot! He had already been cussing out the young soldier who had gone down to his b-hut to get him and, once he entered the first sergeant's b-hut, he laid into everyone in there.

"What the fuck is this shit? Every time there's a mother fuckin' drug test, my ass and his ass," MSG Bolton was pointing at me, "have to come down here and piss. What the fuck is this bullshit?"

The First Sergeant responded, "The test is random. We have no control over who gets selected, Sergeant Bolton."

"Random, my ass! Give me that mother fuckin' cup!" Bolton growled as he snatched the cup and walked to the latrine trailer with his escort. I was about six steps ahead of him out the door and just caught the tail end of his outrage in the b-hut.

I had beaten Bolton to the trailer and was urinating into my cup with my pants around my ankles when he came into the trailer, still loudly protesting. As I was finishing up, I saw MSG Bolton walk into a stall.

His escort exclaimed, "MSG Bolton, you can't be in the stall! You have to give a sample out here at the urinals!"

MSG Bolton fired back, "Fuck you! I'm going to shit in this mother fuckin' cup! That's going to be my sample!" He continued firing off expletives.

Fortunately for my escort and I, my sample was complete, and we got the hell out of the trailer. From what I heard later on that morning, Bolton gave a fecal sample that day.

CHAPTER 45

PSB AND BS

In this next job, I was given a spot alongside Lester Dodson, Doug Globke, and SFC Anderson in the PSB office of The Beast. PSB stood for Personnel Services Branch. This office of The Beast was responsible for keeping records, running the property room, in-processing, out-processing, and just about anything to do with information on detainees that were incoming, present, outgoing, or gone. At the time I thought it was the easiest job in the Army and all these years later I realize that it was the easiest job in the Army! I was moved into the PSB office in early May.

Things had really changed in The Beast and not for the better. The new PC culture being run by the joint Army-Air Force command led to weekly riots and guards being assaulted on a daily basis. In ten months of operations in The Beast in 2003-2004, we had two attacks on guards. In ten days in July, 2006 in The Beast, we had twenty attacks on guards. Riots were never heard of in 2003-2004, but riots were now a weekly thing and they were becoming more and more dangerous as time went on.

For example, the last riot I was involved in featured detainees swinging stolen handcuffs, waving shanks made out of formed scrap metal, and donning face masks made out of ripped up uniforms that had been soaked in urine. In case you're wondering why the detainees thought it was a good idea to put clothes on their face soaked in human piss, they somehow thought that it would neutralize the riot control gas we used on them. It didn't, but it did soak their beards in piss and that made me laugh pretty hard!

There were ways to avoid these attacks on guards, there were ways to keep riots from happening, and there were ways to take back control of the jail. The command wanted to hear none of it and transferred, removed, or prosecuted personnel that suggested these ideas or implemented these measures. I was one of them and so were some good friends of mine. The command felt it was okay for guards to be spat on, have urine thrown on them, and have feces thrown on them. It was also acceptable for guards to be punched, kicked, bit, and in the case of female guards; to have their genitals groped. This was all okay so long as the guards did not do anything physical in reaction. If guards reacted, they would be punished. A reaction meant paperwork and paperwork could potentially put the careers of those in the offices in jeopardy.

I am certain that our command was under strict orders from the top and I'm certain that they did not come up with these policies on their own. The whole Army detainee operations system had shifted into a PC culture due to the fallout of Abu Ghraib in Iraq two years before. What I was seeing, however, was excessive and unnecessary. Guards working in this facility were now being put at serious risk to their safety due to the rule and policy changes. It was very frustrating, and it angered me very much. I hated watching soldiers and airmen get injured.

I personally witnessed at least a half dozen guards, good people just doing their jobs, get charged with abuse. On more than one occasion it sent me into a rage after I heard about some kid who defended himself now having to fight for his or her career. It was disgusting and by July of 2006, I had seen about enough.

When DET 6, our relief, had arrived, I was ready to be done with the tour and move on. I don't know why I took it so personally, but it just really bothered me to see young soldiers and young airmen in a no-win situation. I loved the Army, I loved being an MP, and I loved my brothers and sisters in uniform, but I was disgusted with the backwardness of the current detention system. The way good men and good women were being treated every day was inexcusable and left me pissed off and burned out.

At the ending point in the tour, I had some interesting jobs in the PSB office. One of them included the monstrosity known as the property room. I had inherited the property room from my friend from DET 4, Doug Globke. Globs had inherited an absolute mess and the property room had been way below standards. Globs had done a good job bringing things up to par and then when I relieved Globs of his duty, he and I really got things in order. We had a solid system in place. I can't write much about this room because that would break operational security, but I will tell you that one thing I learned from working in that property room is that scumbag terrorists travel into the United States illegally from Canada and Mexico often. I don't care what the media says, I saw the proof with my own eyes. It wasn't just a few either, it was a high number. If you don't accept that and if you think I'm lying to you, I have some oceanfront property in Arizona I can sell you. I'll throw in the golden gate for free.

Speaking of George Strait, the property room had a dedicated computer that had the largest collection of George Strait .mp3s I had ever heard. It was magnificent! Every time I pulled duty in the property room, I would rock it out with George and things were good to go! I was familiar with George Strait before that tour, but after spending hours in that property room organizing terrorists' belongings to the sound of his music, it made me a bigger fan.

Another interesting job I had in the PSB was pulling old records for ongoing military criminal cases in court. Yes, some were for American GIs, but most were for the new hearings taking place down in GITMO. One of my favorite records that I had to pull was from one of our first detainees we had brought in back in June of 2003. This detainee was rotting in GITMO because he had personally financed the Taliban and al-Qaeda. This same detainee had now filed a claim against the United States Government through ICRC (International Committee of the Red Cross) claiming that he was tortured in custody in The Beast by being refused medical treatment. The government took his claims so seriously that they sent agents to The Beast to meet with me to pull his record. I was pleased to go over the record with these agents (whose agency will remain nameless.)

Would you believe that when we went through the old log books that a medic had been brought to see this specific detainee over 180 times in his 90 day stay in The Beast? I was pleased to report that my own handwriting was in those logbooks as the guard who was on duty and had contacted the medics.

How many more of these detainees claimed false atrocities in an attempt to be released from their rightful hell in GITMO? I would estimate, from my experience, 98%-100% of them.

The last of these interesting jobs I had in the PSB office was to register new detainees into our system. There were two systems we used: one for the Army and another for the FBI. This was the same system that I had learned and operated in Kandahar, so this was easy for me. We would have to swab cheeks, do fingerprints, and make note of any tattoos, scars, deformations, amputations, etc. I don't even want to tell you how many webbed feet I saw, sixth fingers, sixth tows, third testicles, or ridged foreheads. It turns out generations of marrying first cousins causes serious mutations. In some tribes in Afghanistan, it is mandatory to marry your first cousin.

I was glad to begin training our replacements in the PSB when they arrived and I was also glad to turn the property room over to them. For the last few weeks of the tour, Bob Allen joined us in this office to help with the training. Bob had returned to Bagram from Kandahar after a two-month stint down there. Bob verified he had similar problems with SSG Sanchez, but he didn't really care. He did his thing, Sanchez did his thing, and Bob didn't let Sanchez get to him. The way Bob saw it, if SSG Sanchez wanted to work himself to death then that was his choice to do so.

It was good to be working side by side with Bob again.

CHAPTER 46

ANOTHER ONE IN THE BOOKS

Most of the soldiers replacing us had not been to The Ghan before and Bob and I really enjoyed helping to train them. We did our best to teach them what to look for in order to separate the ethnicities, tribes, and religious affiliations. We taught our replacements the mandatory Pashto they should know and we taught them the golden rule: never put Pashtuns with Arabs in a cell because it won't go down well. We even went around and personally introduced them to the biggest shitbag detainees in the jail, so that they knew who to watch out for. I hope we saved them from a face full of piss or spit.

Soon enough, it finally happened.

A few days before August 1, 2006, Bob and I shook hands with the entire shift of the guard force and made our way out of the jail. We had an emotional goodbye with the interpreters that day. Bob and I respected that culture a great deal and we took great pride in learning it the best we could. We had spent hours upon hours with those interpreters learning everything we could. We exchanged books, old travel guides, old Pashto magazines, Pashto newspapers, and we listened to their stories.

Working with the interpreters at The Beast on this second tour was one of the highlights for me. I truly enjoyed sitting and talking with these men. There were six interpreters assigned to duty in the jail; two men would be assigned to each shift leaving the other two men off at any given time. It was a successful rotation and kept them from the burn out of a twelve-hour shift. This was especially important because if a large number of detainees happened to come, the interpreters who were off shift would get pulled in to help out.

Our interpreters were all male and they ranged in age from mid-40s to mid-60s. All were of Afghani Pashtun descent, although one man was of Afghani Uzbek descent. This man, Mr. Ahmad, was my favorite. He was a large, overweight man with a heavy black mustache and he talked with a slight lisp. He was in his mid-40s and his American English was very good - he only carried a very slight accent. When he did his job, he had a powerful and booming voice that commanded respect from detainees. Back in the States he lived outside of San Francisco, California, the same as all the other interpreters, where there was a very large population of Afghani Americans.

Mr. Ahmad always had a smile on his face just like he always had time to answer my questions and work with Bob and I on our Pashto. He told us his story of coming to the United States. He was sixteen when he left Afghanistan and escaped the Soviet occupation to a refugee camp in Pakistan with his older brother. Out of respect we never asked what happened to the rest of his family, we assumed that they were probably killed in a Soviet bombing or attack.
From Pakistan, Mr. Ahmad and his brother were sponsored by Catholic Charities from Minnesota and brought to the United States. Mr. Ahmad's face would brighten even more when he talked about how nice the people were in Catholic Charities to his brother and him. Catholic Charities helped both men find an

apartment in Minnesota, found them jobs in a restaurant, and enrolled them in English classes. Mr. Ahmad said that within a few months he grasped the understanding of English and within a year, both he and his brother were able to freely converse in English.

Bob and I were impressed by how quickly he picked up the language. From our understanding, American English is not easy to learn. Bob and I both knew parents of friends who were immigrants and still struggled with English after living in the States for decades. I asked Mr. Ahmad how he managed to learn so fast. His face lit up and a big smile came over his face as he said, "Kenny Rogers albums." He closed his eyes, obviously drawing on memories, and smiled even wider when he said, "I just absolutely loved his music, country music, and that's how I really learned English."

It turned out that Mr. Ahmad eventually learned how to drive an eighteen-wheeler truck and became an over the road truck driver. He said he really enjoyed seeing the country and the freedom of travel on the open road. He happily talked about how nice people were to him, how generous they were, and how happy he was to be living in America. Mr. Ahmad said that the proudest day of his life came when he became an American citizen.

Mr. Ahmad would always tell us how grateful he was to Catholic Charities and how grateful he was to the United States for how good the country had been to him. He had been so successful in America that he actually owned his own trucking line with numerous tractor-trailers out on the roads at all times. He was a good man and I really enjoyed spending time with him and getting to know him.

Another one of the interpreters that sticks out clearly in my mind was an older man in his early 60s. He was shorter than me and had graying hair and a gray mustache. He was extremely polite, very kind, and very patient with Bob and I when it came to Pashto. His name was Mr. Afridi, he also lived in the San Francisco area, and he had escaped Afghanistan in 1979 not too long after the invasion. His escape story was something I'll always remember. He, and several others, got into Pakistan by hiding in an empty fuel tanker. He said the smell of gasoline was so strong that he thinks some of the people in the tank may have died on the trip. He said he wasn't entirely certain because when they got to Pakistan it was completely dark and he couldn't see as they exited the tanker. Out of respect, we didn't ask what had happened to his family. All Bob and I knew was that Mr. Afridi had traveled to a refugee camp in Pakistan with an uncle. After staying at the refugee camp for some time, they were able to be sponsored by relatives in California and brought to the States. Mr. Afridi was also involved in trucking in the States.

Mr. Afridi would travel to Kabul often and would bring back small gifts for guards in The Beast that he liked. These ranged from rings made from local minerals to perfumes for female guards. He brought Bob and I old travel guides from the 1960s and 1970s showing what downtown Kabul used to look like. He would also bring back newspapers and read them out loud to us in Pashto, then in English, to help us learn. Mr. Afridi seemed to really enjoy watching us learn and he was a natural teacher.

When we'd visit him in the interpreter's office he would always get excited, tell us how happy he was to see us, and then he'd insist that we sat at the little table in the office. This was my first lesson on Pashtunwali, the code that Pashtuns live by. If other interpreters were sitting at the table, they would get up and sit somewhere else. We were Mr. Afridi's guests and guests came first in their code of honor. In our American moral system, older people always sit before the younger people, but in Pashtunwali guests always come first.

During our visits, Mr. Afridi would pour us tea, offer us small cakes and cookies, and he would sit at the table with us and teach us just like a grandfather would teach his grandchildren. Some days it was Pashto lessons while other days it would be Afghan history lessons. Oftentimes the other interpreters would join us and also teach us. This was not only a language or history lesson, these men were teaching us about Pashtunwali and the code they grew up with in Afghanistan. It was a very good experience. Here were fellow Americans looking out for fellow Americans and passing on their knowledge.

One of my favorite things the interpreters would do is carry on a conversation in English with us and then slip into Pashto. This was the same thing that Babajan would do with us back at the BP station back home. We could usually follow right along and respond in either English or Pashto, and the interpreters would get so excited! They would shake our hands, hug us, and they even taught us this little song in Pashto that was what they sang for celebrations. Sadly, I don't remember it but I do remember the tune.

Although I liked all the interpreters and learned so much from them, Mr. Ahmad and Mr. Afridi really worked the hardest with Bob and I and taught us the most. They had our respect and we knew we had their respect too when we would see them in the jail and they would grasp our hand and walk with us. In American culture this may be seen as an act of homosexuality, but in the Uzbek and Pashtun culture grasping another man's hand while walking was a public show of respect and friendship. Mr. Ahmad and Mr. Afridi were showing the detainees, who were watching their every move, that Bob and I were men to be trusted and respected. We were worthy of having our hands held by Pashtuns and Uzbeks.

Bob and my deep respect, admiration and friendship for each of these interpreters was returned to us that final day in The Beast; the final time we would ever see these men. With tears in their eyes, the interpreters placed their hands over their hearts, then shook our hands, and then embraced us. Some of them even kissed us on both cheeks, a great sign of reverence in the Pashtun culture. They said their well wishes to us in Pashto and, to this day, I always remember what one of those old interpreters said to us.

He said, "You're like us now. Afghanistan will always be in your heart wherever you go. Afghanistan will stay with you forever."

That man told the truth.

After walking out of the jail for the final time, Bob and I joined with the rest of our detachment for dinner. After dinner, all of us were quickly summoned to the courtyard outside the jail where we hastily made a formation.

The battalion commander, the commander of The Beast and all its operations, took over our formation and called us up one by one. He pinned an Army Commendation Medal on each of our chests, saluted us, and shook our hands. I respected this Lt. Colonel a great deal because he was not like the others. He understood that we were trying to do the right thing in that jail.

I took it to heart when he said, "SGT Drake, well done, I'm proud of you and I wish you the best."

The next morning, before we were due to head down to the flight line and register for our freedom bird, Lester Dodson, Bob, and I headed down to the PX to get haircuts, get some coffee, and smoke cigarettes to kill time.

An interpreter that had not been at the jail the evening before spotted us in the parking lot of the PX. He was waving us over to a stand. Back then they allowed local nationals to come on post and sell their wares out of little stands outside of the PX. We made our way over to this interpreter and he told us that he wanted to give us a gift since we were leaving.

He insisted that it was Pashtun tradition that he must give us a gift. We tried to talk him out of it, but he persisted and said that he would be insulted if we didn't accept his gift. He took Bob, Lester, and I over to a stand where a man was selling beautiful scarves. He spoke to this man in Dari, so we didn't really understand what he was saying.

After a brief exchange with many headshakes, the interpreter became heated with the vendor and began yelling at him. After a few moments, it looked like the vendor finally was defeated in the argument.

The interpreter said to us, "My friend here says to take one scarf each to take home to your wife or to your mother."

We each picked out a scarf, shook hands with the vendor, and then we repeated an emotional goodbye like we had the day before. This interpreter was crying as he hugged us, kissed us on the cheeks, and told us we were his dear friends and that he would miss us.

After he left and we were drinking our coffee at a picnic table outside of the coffee shop, Bob looked at Lester and I and said, "That mother fucker never paid that vendor, did he? He just hustled that guy into giving us these scarves for free!"

Lester and I burst into laughter knowing what Bob said was true. It was the Pashtun way, I guess!

I mailed that scarf home to my mother and to this day she says it's the most beautiful scarf she's ever owned.

CHAPTER 47

WHEELS UP, PANTS DOWN

During the last week of July, DET 4 moved out of our b-huts and into some new open bay rooms built out of shipping containers. They were brand new, smelled new, and looked new. They had real beds, wooden lockers, wooden dressers, and wooden floors. These accommodations were definitely an upgrade from the wood huts that we'd lived in for the past year. Not all of us had moved into these huts, however. Ryan Suthard, SSG Sanchez, Jason Cain, and Doug Globke all extended out another six months. So instead of ten of us heading back to the States, only six of us were.

When you're in your final few days in country, things tend to slow down and get really easy. There is no more work to be done, you've already mailed all your excess gear and stuff home, you've sold off what you didn't want to mail, and you're down to the bare essentials. At this point you're focusing really hard on doing nothing but relaxing.

Some of the things I remember most from those last few days in country were eating three meals a day, spending a lot of time down at the PX drinking coffee, and smoking cigarettes for hours on end. I did a lot of laughing and joking with the boys, and I did as little as humanly possible.

There was a movie that was pretty popular at that time called Syriana. Bob Allen had bought it from the PX and we watched it on my computer in our new, fancy room. Of all the things that occurred during those last few days, it's this that I remember most. Well, this and the scarf incident – that crooked Pashtun interpreter! I remember sincerely enjoying watching the film and when it ended Bob and I looked at each other and at the same time we both blurted out, "What the fuck was that?" I've seen that movie ten times since and I still don't understand the point.

In the late evening hours of August 1, 2006, the remaining soldiers of DET 4 walked down to the flight line with their remaining gear. We spent time going through customs, then neatly arranged our duffel bags on pallets along with our crated weapons. Once the Air Force wrapped up our pallets, we then took our place in a fenced-in holding area with a picnic table and some chairs. They called this area the quarantine area and it was a lot smaller than the holding area Bob and I were held in back in 2004.

We had reported that day at about nine in the evening local time and we didn't wait too long, remarkably. At about twelve o'clock that morning we boarded a C-17 bound for Manas, Kyrgyzstan. I remember looking around the airfield one last time and I took in the mountain ridges in the still of the night. I was looking forward to going home, but a part of me was very sad to leave the country. I knew right then, just as the interpreters had said, Afghanistan would always be a part of me.

After the short flight we disembarked in Manas, Kyrgyzstan and we were back in 1985 all over again. It was very early in the morning when we landed.

They had no billeting for us yet and we were expecting to catch another bird to Germany sometime soon. When you're amped up waiting for the next freedom bird, it's very tough to sleep, so there was no sense trying to sleep at the PAX terminal.

Bob and I once again sat in the old Soviet bar that was now the MWR. We once again appreciated the fading pictures of Soviet soldiers adorning the walls along with old Soviet company banners proudly displayed. There was a Russian language radio station on the speakers and I remember hearing some guy yell at his wife from the phone bank - at least we knew that relationship was healthy.

The bar was an orgy of red and yellow mixed with a faded pride of decades past. It was an eerie feeling being in the bar of the former enemy, but it was also a fascinating experience seeing all the old pictures and memorabilia one more time.

When Bob and I returned to the PAX terminal, we were told that we were going to be stuck in Manas for a few days. No civilian chartered plane was due in for a few days. The reason was obvious; some poor SOBs were getting ready to start their journey and we were going to take their bird back home. None of us were happy with the delay, but our spirits were raised once we learned that there was a two-beer allotment per day!

The Air Force assigned us some billeting, which was a small open tent in the middle of nowhere on the post. The six of us went to get breakfast after putting down our carry-ons. We weren't carrying much because the rest of our gear was on a pallet somewhere along with our weapons.

After breakfast, we found out where the tent was where we could draw beer. At 9 in the morning, we each showed our ID at this tent entrance and we were admitted in. We were pleased to see that this wasn't two normal domestic bottles of beer per day. It was a strange European sized bottle of beer that we figured looked like it was about 30 ounces. It also was almost double the alcohol content of an American domestic beer. There were several choices too, and I took a Russian beer that the bartender said was the closest thing to Budweiser – my beer of choice in those days!

We were all tired, jetlagged, and none of us (at least I hadn't) had had a drink in several months. That Russian beer was one of the best tasting beers I'd ever had in my life! By the time we finished our second beer, we were all laughing, joking, and feeling pretty good.

We left the MWR in great moods and we all headed back to our tent. We all hit our cots and we were out cold. A few hours later I woke up, rushed to the latrine trailer by our tent, and vomited. I don't know if it was the beer or the breakfast, but it didn't sit well with me at all. As I was heading back to the tent from the latrine, I noticed that a group of six men were coming into our open tent. They had special forces patches and they were just that: a special forces team rotating back to the States. I shook hands with them and made small talk before finally getting back to bed.

We were stuck in Manas in that tent with no air conditioning for two days before we finally got word that our bird had landed. The Special Forces operators, along with us, headed down to the flight line to report for our bird. All of us, once again, had to clear customs. I remember that after clearing customs, they were

Navy guys this time and total jerks, we were all herded to a grandstand bleacher that had a cover over the top of it just off the flight line.

We waited in those bleachers all day and all night, and all of us smelled horrible by the time that civilian airliner pulled up. I remember that Bob and I stuck together when we boarded the plane and sat toward the rear of the bird. We had a space between us, and that was a major bonus for international flight travel!

When the flight attendants came around to bring us water, we got to talking with this young lady flight attendant who was from California. Bob, in his most professional tone possible, said, "Ma'am, you'll have to excuse us. We smell like animals who sweated all day in the hot sun, then dried, then sweated again." She got a good laugh out of that!

The flight from Manas to Germany was about six hours. The flight showed a couple of movies, but I don't recall what they were. I drifted in and out of sleep, so did Bob, and we woke each other up a couple of times when food or water would come around. Finally, our bird touched down in Rammstein, Germany, and we walked off the plane smelling horribly and holding our day bags. Guess what happened next? Good guess! We had to go through customs again!

When we finally passed customs and got into the flight terminal in Rammstein, they had us quarantine off, but there was an exit where we could go outside to smoke. Bob, Lester, Andrew Blanco, and I chain smoked half a pack of cigarettes outside. We were just so happy to be able to enjoy nicotine again. This quarantined area was makeshift, with just a fence outside the door where smokers could go. All people alike, both military and civilians, were still walking in and out of the doors around ours, they just weren't caged in like we were.

Bob and I did our best impression of the movie Red Dawn when we held our hands up against the fence and yelled out to people walking by us, "Avenge me!" Some people laughed loudly, knowing what we were talking about, while others looked at us creepily and walked by. The creep-lookers were mostly Air Force. The Air Force doesn't know what a good movie is, I guess. I blame their parents.

After leaving the cage outside, I decided to do something about the stink and the beard that was taking over my face. I stripped down to just my trousers in the latrine and took a homeless-man shower in the sink. I also shaved and scrubbed out the pits of my uniform. I had another uniform in my day bag and some t-shirts, but I hesitated to use them just in case we were stuck in Germany for a few days. As I was scrubbing at the sink, of which there were only two sinks with a line of men from our flight piling up behind me, nobody took exception.

I actually got a compliment from a lieutenant as I put soap in his hands and let him wash his hands over my shoulder as I shaved.

After the latrine shower and a shave, the others from DET 4 and I sat in our quarantined terminal with most of the others from our original Bagram C-17 flight. Also, sitting there were the special forces guys we picked up in Kyrgyzstan. The hours went on and on and on, and finally, they corralled us up, placed us in lines, and made us go through customs again. Yes. Customs again. This time it was the Air Force customs and they were nice, but all of us couldn't understand why we were going through customs again when we had been completely isolated since Bagram.

After completing customs, we finally boarded a civilian airliner again. This time, unfortunately, they allowed active duty soldiers and their dependents on regular travel to load with us. The bird was packed to capacity. Bob and I got separated and he was stuck in a seat behind me. I got crammed between two monsters-of-men, one that included a major who was a surgeon to my right. It was the most uncomfortable flight I had ever been on and just two hours into the nine-hour flight, I couldn't take it anymore.

I yelled out to Bob behind me in Pashto and he responded, in Pashto. The surgeon to my right cocked his head and looked at us funny. I told Bob, in Pashto, to let me have a couple of his sleeping pills. I'd never taken sleeping pills before in my life, but Bob was quite experienced with them. The poor guy had insomnia and would be up for weeks straight before finally crashing out.

Bob handed over two small pills of wonder and I tossed them back with a gulp of water. The next thing I knew, I came to and looked in front of me where there was a meal tray, snacks, and drinks stacked up on the folding tray.

The surgeon to my right said, "Hey, are you alright? You've been out for about 5 hours. I checked your vitals a few times just to make sure you're alive. They hit you in the head passing over the food trays and the staff sergeant to your left clocked you in the jaw with his carry on by accident. You didn't budge."

I assured the surgeon that I was fine and he went on, "Just so you know, they just announced we're approaching the States in the next hour or so."

I high-fived Bob behind me and thanked him with a loud Pashto, "Tashakur!" I survived that level of discomfort thanks to his magic pills.

Over the next hour as I caught up on food, the surgeon and I had a tremendous chat. Most people might be repulsed by what we talked about, but I was fascinated with anatomy after working in a funeral home in high school and post high school. The surgeon explained to me arterial and vein structures and explained a lot of his work to me on how he saved lives by closing up wounds where veins and arteries had been damaged. It was an absolutely fascinating conversation and it was a pleasure listening to him explain his trade.

Before I knew it, the pilot announced that we had entered American air space. There was a thundering roar of cheers on board and soldiers were high fiving each other and shaking hands throughout the plane. I threw my hand over the seat behind me and Bob grasped it enthusiastically.

Bob yelled out to no one in particular, "Two down you sons of bitches!"

Our wheels touched down in Dallas-Ft. Worth Airport. When we filed off the plane, you guessed it, they made us go through customs again.

Even though none of us had been anywhere outside of a quarantine for our entire journey, they made us stand in the lines as civilians went through our gear, clothing, etc., and asked us questions. Bob Allen made light of it, naturally, by quoting Ogre from Revenge of the Nerds as a customs agent wanded him down. As the man bent down near his boots, Bob said, "Take a whiff of that, nerd!" Needless to say, we were all quite ripe at this point.

I, on the other hand, did not take things so lightly. I was at my wit's end with customs. There was absolutely no reason that we needed to go through customs again, since it was impossible for us to have taken on any form of contraband. After cursing and swearing for an hour waiting my turn, I finally reached the desk.

The customs agent asked me questions about where I had come from and where I was going as he dumped out my carry-on / day bag and started going through my belongings. I was in no mood for this bullshit. I told him that I had come from a lovely vacation in the Caribbean and that I was planning on visiting the Bronx Zoo next.

The agent didn't like my humor, gave me a dirty look, and started asking me questions about my computer. He wanted to know what was on it and if I had sewn any secret pockets in my bag to hide ammunition in. At this point, I became livid and started taking my clothes off. I heard Bob Allen start laughing hysterically and he was soon cheering me on along with Blanco and Dodson. All three had already cleared customs and were now waiting to see if I would be arrested by the customs officials.

The agent asked me what I was doing as I was pulling clothes off. In a serious tone, I informed the agent that, "I'm going to get naked, bend over right in front of everyone and spread my cheeks so that you can see I don't have anything hidden in my ass. That's what you want, right?"

The look on his face was one of disgust as my uniform blouse came off, my undershirt came off, and I started to undo my belt. The others behind me in line were standing there horrified as I dropped my trousers and stood there in my boxer briefs. I then started to undo the laces on my boots so I could take my pants completely off. The customs agent quickly threw my stuff back in my bag, begged me to put my clothes back on, and told me I could proceed as he handed me my ID and flight ticket back.

I called him a name I won't repeat, put my clothes back on, and then I joined my friends on the other side of customs. They laughed as I continued to curse out customs the rest of the walk.

We got information on our next flight and terminal and we were scheduled a few hours later to board a plane to go from DFW to Philadelphia. While in the terminal, I tracked down and shook hands with that surgeon I had sat next to from Germany and I wished him the best. I have a feeling, all these years later, that that man continued saving the lives of wounded GIs and may still be doing it today. May God bless him and the work he did – he's a real hero in my book.

I had taken another latrine shower in our waiting area, shaved, and this time I put on a clean uniform. When we boarded the regular passenger airliner this time, Bob and I made sure that we sat next to each other.

It was becoming real now and in just a few hours we would be back in Philadelphia and then heading back to Ft. Dix. The mission was finally ending.

Little did we know what was in store.

CHAPTER 48

GI PARTY

When the six of us landed in Philadelphia, SFC Anderson had been provided a phone number to call for a shuttle to pick us up and take us back to Ft. Dix. When he returned from the call, he let us know that the shuttle should be at the pick-up area in roughly an hour.

We split into groups and rotated to go get some food and to call home. The time estimate was pretty accurate, and about an hour after we made the call, a shuttle pulled up. This was a charter bus, but one of the mid-sized busses that could fit about 15 passengers. We loaded our gear into the storage compartments of the bus, and then we climbed aboard.

It was dark outside already, nighttime, and the bus pulled away from the airport and headed toward the expressway to take us up the coastline. SFC Anderson asked the bus driver if he could make a stop at a gas station for us and the driver agreed to do it.

We headed into the gas station and bought snacks and beer, which we brought back onto the bus with us. The bus driver had no problem with it, he said it was perfectly legal, and as the bus merged onto the expressway, the driver put on the movie The Rookie for us.

Some soldiers slept, but the rest of us drank our beer and ate our beef jerky and chips. We were all in a very happy mood and we were glad that this all was coming to an end. We were even cordial with Schlitz, who knew he was riding a thin line. Schlitz was on a thin line because the month before he had gotten demoted back to E-5.

Schlitz' demotion was the result of being drunk and walking around the housing area of Bagram with two married female soldiers. Under questioning, the two married female soldiers admitted to engaging in inappropriate relationships with Schlitz. The Army frowns very much on alcohol in theater and frowns even more on adultery. He was lucky that all he got was a demotion and that he wasn't sent to jail on charges of adultery.

After the two-hour drive to Ft. Dix, the driver pulled up by our barracks around one in the morning. We shook hands with the driver and thanked him for stopping for us and bringing us back. We then unloaded our gear and brought it into the day room of the barracks. SFC Anderson and I went to talk to the duty sergeant.

The duty sergeant gave us a room and provided us with bedding for our bunks.

I asked him, excitedly, "When do we start our out-processing in the morning? Six o'clock this morning or seven o'clock?"

The desk sergeant shook his head negatively and said, "Unfortunately, you can't start out-processing until Monday. The civilians don't work Fridays anymore."

I was surprised at this, thought about it for a minute, and then responded,

"You'd better get the MPs and the hospital ready; because these guys are going to tear this place up with three days of nothing to do and zero alcohol tolerance."

The duty sergeant shrugged his shoulders and said, "Just, please, no alcohol in the barracks."

The six of us went up to our room, fixed our beds, and then stored our gear. All of us went and took our first showers in several days and then we returned to the room where we sat around talking for a while. One by one we all drifted off to sleep.

We all woke up just a few hours later jet-lagged and thrown off by the time change. We sat around chatting for a while and Blanco, Dodson, and I dressed and walked across the parking lot to the chow hall. We took a gamble on if the chow hall would even be open since it was only five in the morning at this point. We were relieved when we walked up and saw that it was open. When we went inside, the dining facility was vacant except for us and we were able to cruise right up to the front.

There was a big hand-written sign that was in front of the grill that read, 'No Eggs to Order.' Since there was nobody else in the chow hall, the three of us began talking to the civilian ladies that worked the facility. We had them laughing and smiling and, wouldn't you know it, they made us omelets on the same grill that had the sign up.

We ate our breakfast that morning and drank our coffee in peace until about 20 minutes later when a company sized element came into the chow hall. We had been lucky to beat the rush and we made a mental note of this.

We slept on and off the rest of that day and ordered out for lunch and dinner. We enjoyed Chinese food for lunch and pizza for dinner. We sat in the day room in our civilian clothes and watched movies also, enjoying the fact that there were very few soldiers in the barracks. After dinner, we stopped at the enlisted club for a few drinks, but it didn't last long as we were all shot from the travel.

When we came back to the barracks that night about six o'clock, there was a knock at our room door. I answered the door and it was a female sergeant, the same rank as me. The fact that she was in these barracks, alone, told me that she was most likely a medical holdover from her deployed unit. This sergeant started telling me that the barracks were filthy and that the next day she was rounding up all the soldiers in the barracks for a cleaning detail. She said she was hosting a "GI Party." She seemed really pleased with herself and obviously bored out of her mind because the barracks were really clean and in good shape already.

I looked at her and said, "fuck off" as I slammed the door in her face.

CHAPTER 49

5 MILES

The next day was a Saturday. We all woke up extremely early again due to being out of whack with the time. This time, Bob joined us for breakfast. It was the same as the day before with the chow hall vacant. We smiled and chatted with the civilian cooks who, once again, made us eggs to order.

We got the hell out of the chow hall as soon as we saw the company sized horde marching up to the dining facility.

When we returned to the barracks, we did our laundry in the machines available in the latrine, took naps, and sat around not doing a whole lot. At about ten o'clock that morning, there was another knock at our barracks door. Bob answered the door this time. When he opened the door, it was the same female sergeant from the night before. Only this time she had a sheet written out and handed it to Bob.

Bob said, "What the hell is this?"

"That's this room's work assignments for the GI party today," was her response.

Bob crumpled up the sheet and threw it in the hallway while saying, "fuck off." He then slammed the door in her face.

A little bit later, Blanco and I took our assigned duty van and headed over and bought some new clothes at the PX since we were low on civilian supply. We returned to the barracks a couple of hours later and threw our new clothes in the wash with our other dirty clothes. After all of our clothes were clean and we ate some lunch, most of us went down to the day room to watch whatever movie was on the TV. We were in and out of sleep and when it got to be dinner time, we all got cleaned up and decided to head up to the enlisted club for dinner.

I drove the van as we made the trek across the post and onto the Air Force side to go to the club. We all went inside, ate dinner, and had a few drinks. The enlisted club also had an arcade and we went into the arcade to play games. After a couple of hours at the bar, it hit us. All that fatigue and jet lag slapped us right across the faces.

SFC Anderson, Blanco, Schlitz, and I decided that we'd had enough and that we were going to head back to the barracks. Dodson and Bob decided that they were going to stay out.

"How are you going to get back?" I asked them.

Bob responded, "It's a military post. There's got to be cabs all over the place."

He had a good point, so the rest of us loaded back into the van and I drove us back to the barracks. We made our way back up to our room at about nine o'clock that evening. We accidently locked eyes with the female sergeant who was making her way into the stairwell on the second floor.

As she opened her mouth to say something, Blanco cut her off with a loud "fuck off!"

When we got back to the room, we all fell sound asleep very quickly.

I sat up in bed suddenly. It was dark in our room except for the emergency exit sign above the door. A loud noise had woken me up. I glanced at my watch and saw that it was shortly after two o'clock in the morning and I looked around to see if the noise had come from any of our people in the room. I then climbed down out of my top bunk and checked on everyone in the room. It wasn't coming from any of them.

I then heard rhythmic pounding coming from the stairwell that was adjacent to our room. The sound was coming stronger now. Blanco woke up and we looked at each other confused. Neither of us had any idea what this sound was. We both made our way out into the hallway in our underwear to investigate.

As we turned the corner and looked down into the stairwell, we saw the source of the sound.

Climbing up the stairwell, one foot at a time and stooped over, was Lester Dodson. In the dim stairwell light, we couldn't quite make it out, but he had some kind of a heavy weight strapped to his back. Lester had sweat coming down his face and his shirt had perspiration leaking through.

We rushed down the stairs to relieve the burden strapped to his back. When we got there, we saw that Bob Allen was strapped to Lester's back! Lester had taken out Bob's shoelaces and used them to tie Bob's hands and feet together. Lester had then taken Bob's belt, linked it with his own, and used the belt to secure Bob to his back. Lester had then leaned forward and climbed the stairs with Bob on his back.

We removed Bob from Lester's back. Bob was so drunk that his legs were no longer working and his speech was very limited between hysterical laughter. We took Bob back to the room and put him to bed. He thanked us and told us that we were "all right guys."

We then helped the ailing Lester back to the room as he was still catching his breath.

I said, "Lester, did you just carry him like that up all three flights of stairs?!"

Lester replied, "It wasn't only the stairs!"

"What're you talking about," I said. "I thought you took a cab from the enlisted club?"

Lester let us know that he learned the hard way that cabs stopped running on post at twelve o'clock. This was new and was not the same as it had been the year before.

I couldn't believe what I was hearing. "You walked all the way back? At what point did Bob's legs stop working?" I exclaimed.

"He went limp after about an eighth of a mile. I strapped him up and brought him back the rest of the way," Lester said.

Blanco's jaw dropped. "Holy shit, Lester! You carried him back over five miles?"

Dodson, now standing up straight, made a funny look on his face. He replied, "Well yeah. What else was I going to do?"

Lester Dodson strapped a grown man larger than himself to his back and carried him five miles and up three flights of stairs that night. That's the definition of a good friend and one hell of a soldier.

CHAPTER 50

THE PUNCH AND THE EYE

The next morning, Sunday morning, we all ended up sleeping later than usual partially because our bodies were adjusting and partially because of the late-night arrival of Bob and Lester.

When I woke up, I looked at my watch and saw that it said six in the morning. I climbed down off my bunk and checked on Bob. He was sleeping peacefully until I shook him awake. When he woke, he looked at me in confusion, and then regained his bearings.

"Hey Bob," I said. "Let's get cleaned up and let's get some breakfast."

Bob nodded and started to get up out of his bunk. As I grabbed my shaving kit and towel out of my wall locker, Bob made it to his feet. I was keeping an eye on him expecting him at any minute to fall back down and go back to sleep. It was either that or I was expecting him to vomit. He did neither. As a matter of fact, he acted like there was nothing wrong.

I took a shower and was shaving at the sink when Bob finished his own shower and came up to another sink to shave.

"Hey man, how the hell are you feeling?" I asked.

Bob responded, "I feel fine. Why?"

I stopped shaving for a minute to turn and look at Bob before I said, "I don't know Bob, Lester had to carry you five miles back from the enlisted club last night because your legs wouldn't work. Blanco and I put you to bed. You were pretty oiled up."

Bob shrugged his shoulders and started putting shaving cream on his face. He didn't look in my direction when he said, "Eh, we've all seen worse. At least nobody pissed in a wall locker."

With that last line, I lost it and started laughing. I just shook my head and finished shaving in amazement of Bob's ability to recover from drinking. I knew he had a way above average ability to recover, but this performance was super-human.

As I walked back to the room, the rest of the detachment was still sleeping. I got changed, Bob got changed, and we headed over to the chow hall together. We had showed up at the worst possible time as the company element that was there the past two days was in the midst of filing into the dining facility. Bob and I got in line with them, but we were wearing civilian clothes and stood out like a sore thumb.

As we rounded the corner of the line and made it to the area with the open grill, I said hello to the lady cooks that I had become friendly with the last few days. They smiled in my direction and I smiled back.

One of the ladies yelled and got my attention with, "SGT Drake, baby, you want one of them omelets again?"

I smiled again and responded, "Yes ma'am, that'd be wonderful. Can you make one for my friend here too?"

She gave Bob a big smile and he smiled back. Without skipping a beat, she nodded and quickly said, "You got it, baby."

One of the guys behind us in line yelled out to the cook and asked if he could get an omelet too. My favorite cook looked at him with cold eyes and said, "Can't you read the sign, son? There ain't no eggs made to order in this line!"

My mother always said honey got the bees, and she was right!

Bob and I finished our breakfast and headed back to the barracks. The rest of our detachment was starting to wake up. Bob and I took the van and went for fresh haircuts and we picked up some starch to press our uniforms. We didn't buy that canned garbage starch, we bought the all-time classic Blue-Flo along with a spray bottle.

When we returned back to the barracks, we pressed our uniforms and prepared them for the start of our out-processing the next day. The rest of our detachment was starting to come alive. One by one they headed to the showers to get cleaned up and then headed out to get food. I think everyone shook Lester's hand and hugged him several times over his feat of strength from the night before.

That evening we all headed back to the enlisted club. We did what we did best. We ate dinner there and then we pounded drinks, leaving one man sober to drive us back to the barracks after. I don't remember how late we stayed, but it was late enough, and we were all pretty drunk. Lester Dodson had volunteered to drive.

Toward the end of the night at the bar, Bob had started messing with Schlitz. At first, he was gently ribbing him, but by the end of the night he was calling out Schlitz on all his BS throughout the mobilization and the tour. Schlitz tried arguing in his own defense, but there was no defense, so he had no choice but to sit there and take it. Our detachment commander, SFC Anderson, was witness to what was taking place. He did nothing to stop it, however, and I'm not sure he had to. Bob finally stopped laying into Schlitz as we finished our final drinks.

When we climbed into the van to begin our drive back to the barracks, Bob and I sat in the far back row while Schlitz sat in the middle row with Blanco. SFC Anderson was in the passenger seat and Lester was driving. Schlitz was still fuming, still pissed off, and he was doing his best to not let it show. Bob started a goofy giggle and then started wiggling his fingers at Schlitz' ear, flicking his ear lobe. Schlitz started his huffing and puffing and became really angry. He told Bob once to stop it and then he turned around in the seat and looked at Bob after the second round of ear lobe flicking.

Schlitz fired off with, "If you do that one more time, Allen, I'm going to punch you in the face!"

Bob got the message now and realized he had pushed too far. 30 seconds later he forgot the message and messed with Schlitz' ear again.

Schlitz turned around, squared up, and punched Bob straight in the eye with a right hand. Bob slumped back in the seat with a groan, and Blanco and I yelled at Schlitz. Schlitz turned back around with a terrified look on his face. I think he was concerned that Blanco or I would come after him.

The area under Bob's lower eyelid had a split in the skin and he was bleeding pretty badly. The cut itself was not that deep, but he had been drinking heavily and his thin blood was running out of the cut. We had some paper towels in the van, and I handed them to Bob and told him to put some pressure on his eye.

A few minutes later, we pulled into the barracks parking lot.

When we got out of the van, I took Bob inside into the day room, where there was a lot of light, and took a good look at his eye. Where his cut was running below the eye concerned me, because blood was flowing so heavily, it was flowing up into his eye. Blanco went and retrieved some ice from the desk sergeant's freezer and Dodson came back down with a towel to put the ice in and to get pressure on Bob's eye. No matter how hard I tried, the eyelid kept filling and overflowing with blood.

"Bob," I said, "look, we've got to get you to the hospital. If you don't get some treatment, your eye is going to swell up to the size of a softball and you could have some serious problems."

"Fuck that," was Bob's response. "I'm not going to the hospital. They'll throw me in jail for getting in a fight."

Blanco chimed in, "Well, why don't you just tell them that someone sucker punched you when we were leaving the bar? This is an Army post; this kind of shit happens all the time."

Bob continued to refuse to go to the hospital. Blanco, who had organized fighting experience, ran upstairs and got some Vaseline. He and I continued to work Bob's eye for the next hour to try and keep the blood out of it. We weren't successful.

Would you believe who walked into the day room during all this? It was the GI party sergeant from the last two nights! She starts asking questions about what happened to Bob's eye.

Lester, without hesitation, yelled at her, "Fuck off!" She did too.

We continued to work Bob's eye and the blood started to slow down. We just couldn't keep it from pooling up and going back into his eye, though. It was a bad cut and his thin blood was making things way worse.

This time I spoke forcefully to Bob. "Bob, I'm taking you to the hospital. You're in a bad way here."

"Fuck that, I'm not going to the damned hospital!" was the response. Bob now left the day room and stormed off back up to our room.

Hanging around the corner of the day room was a very nervous looking Schlitz. I called him over. I could tell he was very leery to come near Blanco, Dodson, and me.

"Look Schlitzy, I don't like you," I said. "In fact, I think you're a scumbag. However, I don't blame you for punching Allen. He stepped over the line, you warned him, and he messed with you again. You'll have no problems with me over this." I then reached out with my hand and Schlitz accepted it.

Blanco and Dodson did not shake hands with Schlitz. In fact, Blanco and Dodson looked like they were going to kill Schlitz as he walked away.

When we returned to the room, Bob had his headphones on and was half-asleep with the ice pack on his eye. I made one last offer to take him to the hospital and he responded with colorful words. I shook my head and climbed into my bunk and went to sleep.

The next morning, I woke up at four-thirty am. We had to be at the out-processing building by seven o'clock. I crawled down off my bunk and pulled the remains of the ice pack off of Bob's eye. With a flashlight, I took a look at his eye. What I saw was not good. It was so very much not good. Bob's eye was

414

swollen shut. It was also the size of a softball and it was any color but that of human flesh. I shook Bob awake right away.

When Bob came to, he sounded off with a groan in agony. I helped him get to his feet and walked with him down to the latrine so he could look at it for himself.

When Bob looked at his eye in the mirror, he turned back at me and spoke. "Well, you weren't kidding around when you said I should go to the hospital. My eye is fucked."

"Bob," I said, "I'm no expert when it comes to eye injuries, but this is bad and you need to get to the hospital as soon as possible. When they ask, you just tell them someone sucker punched you and that's it. They're not even going to care at this point."

Bob nodded and went back to the room to get his shaving kit to get cleaned up.

When I went back to the room to grab my own kit, everyone was looking at Bob's eye. Schlitz was doing his best to hide and then made a run for it to the latrine to avoid the wrath of Blanco and Dodson. SFC Anderson came over, took one look at Bob's eye, and said that Allen had thirty minutes to get cleaned up because he was personally taking him to the hospital. This was the first time we'd heard from Anderson since the night before.

Anderson was true to his word and took Bob to the hospital. When he returned, he told us that it didn't look good. They thought Bob had a detached retina and that they were going to have to do surgery. This meant, of course, that Bob would be held in the hospital and would not be allowed to travel until he was cleared by the doctor.

Without Bob, we started our out-processing.

CHAPTER 51

THE END OF THE LINE

On Wednesday of that week, Bob was released from the hospital and came back to the barracks. The doctors at the hospital had performed surgery to fix his retina and the swelling in his eye was way down. He had to wear an eye patch, however, and with a goofy grin on his face he would randomly point to his patched-over eye. Bob told us that he was going to be held at Dix an extra two weeks until he was cleared to fly. Apparently, a repaired retina cannot take the pressure of a flight for a while.

Schlitz was now staying away from the barracks and away from Bob in general. He would only dip back into the room to sleep at night and then he would be out of the room before we got up in the morning. I was almost certain that at some point Blanco and Dodson were going to rip him to pieces.

Our out-processing experience lasted until Friday. I don't recall much of it, but I do remember one point where they made a group of about fifteen of us sit in a circle with a psychologist. The psychologist may have been a soldier, but she was wearing scrubs with a white lab coat. She appeared to be in her 50s, had graying hair, and wore glasses with a pencil pushed over her ear. She had a kindness about her and it seemed like she really wanted to help people.

The doctor started off the session by asking us how we felt and what our stresses were. Blanco and I were in this group together, and neither of us could keep from laughing at the responses that were hurled back at this psychologist.

The first classic line was when the psychologist pointed to a female E-6 who had just completed a tour of Iraq. I didn't know too much about this woman, but to me she looked like a tough lady that you didn't want to cross. The psychologist asked her how she was feeling.

The staff sergeant responded, "I'll tell you how I feel, I've got two kids at home and a husband that's been cheating on me the whole time I've been gone. The first thing I'm going to do when I get back is cut his balls off and make him eat them!"

I wouldn't have been surprised in the least if she had accomplished this goal. She seemed like the type that meant what she said.

The psychologist then called on another soldier, a male E-7 and asked him how he felt, and if he felt frustrated.

He didn't hold back either when he opened his mouth with, "You know what frustrates me? This kind of bullshit right here. You people don't give a shit what comes out of my mouth or anyone else's mouth here. In six months or sooner I'm going to be right back here at Ft. Dix heading on another deployment. You know why? It's because it's what I do. You sit here and talk about feelings and thoughts, while I blow shit the fuck up down range. So, let's cut the bullshit. Let me get the fuck out of here, rest for my six months, and then I'll be more than happy to go right back to blowing shit the fuck up."

This wasn't going well for the psychologist.

A third soldier was called on, this time a young E-4. He was asked if he had any regrets from his tour and how he felt about those regrets.

The specialist responded with, "I'm infantry. The only thing I regret is not killing more of those mother fuckers shooting at my friends and me."

The psychologist pretty much gave up at this point and Blanco and I had tears rolling down our cheeks. We were laughing so hard at the harsh coldness of the responses.

The people in this room with us were the finest America had to offer. They had just given up over a year of their lives, they had faced hell in terrible combat zones, and they wanted nothing more than to go right back to it. They all had my full respect and admiration.

Early that Friday morning, we awoke and cleaned up. We dressed in civilian clothes as we didn't travel in uniform, if it could be avoided, back then. We pulled our sheets, packed up our bags, and headed down to the duty sergeant's office. We turned in our sheets, dropped our bags in the day room, and then headed to get some breakfast when the chow hall opened.

Bob came down in uniform not too much later. He shook hands with us, wished us a good trip, and sat with us until our shuttle showed up. He did not shake hands with Schlitz and only glared at him with his good eye. Soon enough our shuttle showed up and we loaded our gear and then climbed aboard. I told Bob that I'd see him in two weeks, and he informed me that I'd be buying the first round at Q. I agreed.

I had a feeling of relief and accomplishment as our bus made its way to the expressway and toward Philadelphia. The only thing that bothered me was that Bob would not be traveling back with us. On that bus ride we all talked about the first things we were going to do when we got home, where we would go, and all of the fun we were going to have. Schlitz stayed pretty quiet, realizing he was only minutes away from escaping an ass-kicking.

When we got to Philadelphia, we loaded our bags on a cart and made our way toward our gate. Schlitz would not be coming with us back to Illinois, he would be flying directly to Minnesota. SFC Anderson and I shook hands with him, Blanco and Dodson did not. This was the last time I'd ever see Schlitz.

We checked in with our airline and made our way to our gate. The remaining four members of DET 4 climbed aboard a plane about an hour later and landed in Chicago just a few hours later.

At the airport a lieutenant from our unit met us with a van and drove us back to the unit. We were surprised when a general and his staff were there to greet us! There was also a party being set up on our behalf in the dining facility.

When the four of us entered the office area of the unit, all of the full-time soldiers came out to shake our hands and welcome us home. One of these full timers, a man by the name of SGT MacArthur, gave me a big hug. Mac and I were friends and had worked together on a lot of things in the unit over the last couple of years. He was a good man and I was glad to see him.

The four of us were then taken to another area where a man from the local American Legion started giving us a speech about what to expect when returning home. This man was doing a good thing, but it just wasn't the right time and place. We were being held here listening to him while our families, which we hadn't seen in many months, were filing into the dining facility.

I regret doing this, but I cut the man off and said, "Sir, we all appreciate you coming out here to talk to us today, but we've all been through this before and we all know the drill. Thank you very much for your time, but we'd really like to be done here so we can go and see our families."

I thought this would be it, but then another lieutenant came into the office and started handing out paperwork for us to fill out. This wasn't the simple two-to-three-minute-type paperwork, but this was hour-long-paperwork. These papers were the forms for leave and laundry allotment payments that we earned and had accumulated while on active duty. We were all NCOs in this room, and we knew how to do this paperwork and we didn't need someone guiding us through it step by step. My blood was getting hot now and so was that of everyone else as this lieutenant kept talking on and on.

I finally spoke up and said, "Sir, we'd all really like to go see our families. We know how to do this paperwork and we'll do it on our own."

As I said this, an operations captain by the name of CPT McBride came into the room. I had known CPT McBride for four years at this point and he and I had worked together many times including in Afghanistan on my first tour. He was a good man, I liked him a lot, and he liked me. We shook hands and he congratulated us all and welcomed us home. He had come to find out what the hold-up was and why we weren't joining the general, his staff, and our families in the dining facility.

I explained to CPT McBride what was going on, and he shook his head.

McBride looked at the lieutenant and said, "Lieutenant, these men can do this paperwork anytime. Let's release them here and let them see their families for goodness sake."

The lieutenant was a little taken aback and looked back at us saying, "If you think you know how to do this, then fine. Just pay attention to where to mail it in."

With that, we left the office and headed to the dining facility. We saluted and shook hands with the general and his staff, who were waiting outside to greet us. As we entered the dining facility, there was a loud cheer from the active duty staff from the unit and our families. There were a lot of handshakes, hugs, and kisses that morning. As is Army tradition, we made sure to introduce each other to our families.

The general then called us to the front and cut a classy speech. He put great emphasis on the fact that we had volunteered for our duty and that we had served our tour of duty with great honor and distinction. He also recognized the families that were present and the hardships they endured with their loved ones gone. The general ended his speech by saying that the Army was the greatest in the world not because of our technology and equipment, but because of men like us that made sacrifices in service. His closing words were met with a standing ovation, which embarrassed all four of us.

After the general's speech, there was cake and coffee and we all stood around chatting. I didn't notice it at first, but my Dad had left where we were sitting and had walked up to the general. I saw my Dad shake hands with him, and then they entered into a conversation that lasted well over ten minutes. Eventually, they shook hands again, the general patted my Dad on the back, and then my Dad came over and sat back down with us.

I asked my Dad what he was talking about for so long with the general, and he responded, "Did you notice that the general had a 4th Infantry Division combat patch?"

I responded that I had, but that I'd assumed it was from Iraq.

My Dad went on, "No, he's my age and he was in Vietnam the exact same time as I was with the 4th Infantry Division. It turns out we weren't too far from each other at all! It was nice to see someone still in from that era."

We stayed at this little party for about another hour and then I shook hands with and hugged SFC Anderson, Dodson, and Blanco. I loaded up my duffel bags in my parents' SUV, climbed in, and we headed the forty miles home.

Ghazni,
Afghanistan
September,
2005

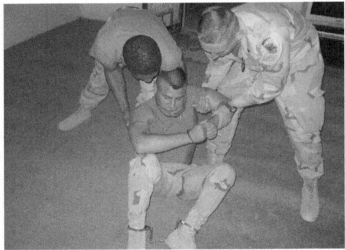

Mobile
Training
Team
August, 2005

We had a barbecue outside of the Kandahar Field Detention Site in October, 2005.

Bob and Ryan celebrate
a birthday on the
second tour.

This is the front of SSG Scofield's lighter. His wife sent me these pictures after he passed away, telling me that Papa Sco treasured this lighter.

This is the back of the lighter.

PART THREE:

THE AFTERMATH

CHAPTER 52

HOME

Being home after this tour was a lot different than the last time. I no longer felt guilty about being home, I no longer felt uncomfortable, and I no longer felt like I had anything to prove. I felt at peace. By the time I was due to go back to drill with the unit, I would only have roughly eight months left on my eight-year contract with the Army.

I spent a lot of time with my friends enjoying the beautiful summer days and partying hard during the summer nights. After a few days of being home, I traveled down to my union school and turned in my paperwork. I had brought back t-shirts and gifts from Afghanistan and they were all thrilled to receive the gifts. There were a lot of handshakes and hugs at the union school and I had a private chat with the coordinator. I told him I wasn't planning to go back to work until October. I said I needed some time to clear my head and I didn't want to rush back. The coordinator understood and said it was a good plan.

Bob returned home two weeks later with nothing more than a little bruising remaining under his eye. I picked him up that night and we went to Q and partied hard. Rest assured, I bought the first round, as promised.

Out of the norm for us, Bob and I started talking about our plans for the future. I told Bob that I did not plan on re-enlisting and that when my contract was up, I was going to get out. I explained that I loved the Army and always would, but things were just getting too difficult now with my career. I had missed almost three years of my five-year apprenticeship, and I really had to focus on my job and to get caught up. I also talked about how MSG Maddon wanted me to attend all these schools and that he had these big plans for me, but that I just couldn't afford to take off two weeks of work at a time. I would eventually lose my job.

Bob understood, but he was disappointed.

He said, "You're a good NCO. You should stay in and make it work. A lot of the soldiers look up to you and think highly of you. You have a lot to offer, man, think about it."

I appreciated what Bob was saying, but my mind was made up. I had to focus on my career now.

Bob's plans were to never get out. All he wanted to do was stay in.

"Bob," I said, "What are you going to do about work? You didn't have a job before we left. Are you going to try and find something?"

Bob shook his head no. "I'm going to go to some schools here that the unit is offering, I can pick up funeral details, and I'll also still work for Dave."

The funeral details Bob was talking about were just that. If you were a reservist or a member of the Guard, you could earn money by doing funeral details for deceased veterans. Not only was it a paycheck, but it was a very honorable thing to be a part of. Bob enjoyed doing them because he felt it was his way to pay back deceased veterans.

Not too long after Bob returned home, a terrible tragedy struck. Bob's step-dad, Dave, who had recently turned fifty, passed away suddenly of a heart attack. It was absolutely horrible. When Bob told me the day after, I came to his house and visited his mother and spent some time with Bob and his younger brother and sister.

Bob and I never talked about feelings, but I could see that this was taking its toll on him. This was a horrible, tragic event. Dave was a great guy and this was just an awful loss.

On the night of the wake, I came home from work, got cleaned up, and put a suit on. I had flowers sent to the family on behalf of my own family, and I drove over to the chapel in Westmont. I paid my respects and then sat down with Bob for a long time as friends, family, and co-workers of Dave's passed through. After a couple of hours, Bob told me he was hungry and asked me if I could give him a ride to get something to eat.

We climbed into my truck and started driving back to Darien because Bob wanted to get a cheeseburger at Q. While driving, he asked me to take a detour and stop at some baseball fields in Westmont. We sat there for a good fifteen minutes as Bob stared out the window at the fields. I turned the engine off, rolled down the windows, and smoked a cigarette. It was none of my business to ask what was going through Bob's mind, all I could do was be there to support him. When Bob decided it was time to leave, he let me know that these fields were where he'd first met Dave.

I took Bob back to Darien and we sat down at Q and ate cheeseburgers and had a few beers. We didn't speak much, we didn't have to, and the mood was somber. Bob and I had been through hard times before, but nothing as horrible as this. I really felt terrible for him and his family.

We picked up some food to-go from a local restaurant and brought it back to the funeral home for his mother, younger brother, and sister. I stayed with Bob the rest of the night until shortly before the chapel closed. I paid my respects again to Bob and his family, and I went home, leaving them in privacy for the closing moments of the wake.

Unfortunately, I didn't attend the funeral the next day because I had just returned back to work the week before and couldn't ask for time off so soon. I regret that. I should have been there with Bob.

CHAPTER 53

LIFE MARCHES ON

I was back to work with the company that had hired me just before I left for Afghanistan in March, 2005. The superintendent had told me to call him when I was ready to come back to work and he would make sure there was a spot for me. When I called him, he was true to his word and put me back to work right away.

I was assigned to a jobsite that was seventy miles one way from my home with a six o'clock in the morning start. I was up at four o'clock each day to be on the road by four-thirty am to make it to the jobsite on time. We were building a brand-new high school from scratch. The building was in the middle of corn fields and was easy to drive by if you weren't paying attention. I made sure I left with plenty of time every day. It was better to be early than to ever risk being late!

The foreman of the job was a big, powerfully built man named Lenny. Lenny was in his late 30s, but smoked and drank very hard and he was already graying and looked like a man in his 50s. Lenny had a great sense of humor, but he was disappointed with my skill set considering what year I was in my apprenticeship. I was disappointed in my own skill set too, but I was three years behind everyone else and I was doing my best to catch up.

Lenny liked to give me a hard time and ride me. This wasn't anything I wasn't used to. There was nothing that Lenny, or any other foreman, could do or say to me that hadn't already been done. I worked hard for Lenny on this job, but I just didn't have the experience yet. I would hear Lenny talking negatively of me to the other apprentices and to the journeymen on the job. I heard one of the other apprentices and one of the journeymen, both whom I had worked with before, stick up for me.

One day, after lunch, I asked if I could speak with Lenny privately. Lenny nodded his approval of the impromptu chat.

"Lenny," I said, "I know you're not happy with my work. You think I'm overpaid for my lack of skills at this stage of my apprenticeship. You also think I'm slow and that I make too many mistakes."

Lenny chimed in, "That's right, I do."

"Well, I get it Lenny and I get that you think I slow down your job," I continued. "What I can tell you, though, is that I'm going to keep showing up here every day hustling and working my ass off for you. I'm going to continue learning and continue getting better every day. You have me working with people here who are finally teaching me and not just using me as meat. Give me a chance here, Lenny, and I won't let you down."

Lenny seemed to really appreciate my little speech. He said, "Okay, Brad. You got it. I'll give you a shot, but if I don't think it's going to work out, I'm going to talk to Ron about sending you down the road."

Ron was our company's superintendent. I responded to Lenny, "That's fair, Lenny, and I understand how this works. Thanks for the opportunity."

I continued showing up to the job site early and opening up the toolboxes and preparing the equipment. I worked every minute of overtime that was offered to me and slowly, but surely, I started to learn new skills and I started to steadily improve.

When the first wave of layoffs came after Christmas that year, I wasn't one of them. I was earning Lenny's respect and the respect of the other workers.

Outside of work, life had changed with Bob and me. Bob was not able to hang out as often as he used to due to helping to care for his younger brother and sister. Bob was stepping up and looking out for his family, and I fully supported what he was doing. We would still get together, just not as often.

What happened a few months later came as a complete and total shocker to me, however. Bob suddenly had a girlfriend! After never seeing Bob date or get involved with any woman, he now had a Czech girlfriend whose name I couldn't pronounce. I nicknamed her "Yuschmenka."

Bob was now spending a lot of time with Yuschmenka, and he even moved in with her in Orland Park, which was about fifteen miles from where we lived. I couldn't believe this was happening so quickly!

Some more time went by and I purchased my first home in March, 2007. I had a lot of parties and a lot of fun in that townhouse over the course of the next few months. Although we talked on the phone, Bob did not have a vehicle, so he rarely came back to Darien. If he did come back to Darien, it was usually with Yuschmenka to spend time with his mom and young siblings. I would never see Bob when he came into town, so I never met his girlfriend.

One night in May, 2007, I was sitting at the bar about nine o'clock with a friend of mine named Chris. Chris and I had already been putting drinks away for a couple of hours when my phone rang, and it was Bob. I answered the phone.

"Drake," Bob said. "I need you to come get me."

"Wait, what?" was my reply.

"Yeah, can you come out to Orland Park and get me?"

I was puzzled. "Right now, Bob? Yeah, sure. Where are you?"

Bob gave me an address and half-assed driving directions. Luckily, my friend Chris had grown up in that area and he agreed to come with me. I cruised out to Orland as quickly as I could, and we were able to find the apartment complex.

As we were pulling into the complex, I heard two thuds hit the open bed of my pickup truck. Then I saw a body running up to the side of the truck and reaching for the door handle. I slammed on the brakes, realizing that it was Bob, and that he had just thrown two duffel bags in the bed of my truck. My friend Chris opened the door, climbed into the back seat, and Bob hopped into the passenger seat, slamming the door quickly behind him.

"Just go!" Bob exclaimed. I didn't ask any questions as I turned the truck around and took off out of the parking lot. I kept an eye out for armed, Czech gangsters who may have been shooting at Bob. Fortunately, I didn't see any.

I never asked Bob what happened because he wouldn't have told me anyway. We went back to Q where we closed the place out. I then dropped Bob off at his mom's house after he declined to stay at my townhouse.

It appeared Bob was single again.

CHAPTER 54

DUTY CALLS

My contract with the Army was set to expire on December 19, 2007. I had not drilled with the unit since my return from Afghanistan in late August, 2006. The company I was working for was booming at the time and we were working 6-7 days a week, every week since I returned back to work in October.

I had called the unit and spoken to the new commander and I explained my predicament with doing the weekend drills. He was an understanding man and told me that he would be able to excuse me for absences, but at some point, he would need me to come in on extended duty and make up the lost time. I told him I could do that, and I would do that, before my contract expired.

So be it that in October, 2007, I received a call from the commander's office ordering me to come in and make up my time on extended duty. My union, my employer, and I all received formal letters calling me to duty to make up my absences. My union was totally supportive, my employer had no choice but to let me off, and the Army had done a good job of giving them, and me, plenty of notice. There were no issues at all, all parties understood.

My company, the HHC, was being deployed to Iraq and was getting ready to start the mobilization process in November. I reported to Arlington

Heights for the month of October and worked a full day, each day. I worked as a clerk for the commander, I helped organize supply cages, I painted an office, and I ran weapons and equipment to the government repair shop.

The government repair shop was about fifty miles away from where the unit was. I was given instructions by the commander one evening to come to the unit at six o'clock in the morning the next day, draw a weapon and a vehicle, and then take the weapons that needed repairs to the shop. I didn't ask any questions, and I did exactly as I was instructed.

The next morning, I was at the arms room at five-forty-five am and I drew a pistol and two magazines. I then drew a government van from the motor pool, made sure the van was full of fuel, and then I loaded up some crates of weapons into the van. With that, I hit the road and drove the weapons to the repair shop. I made it there in good time with zero issues considering the heavy Chicago-area traffic.

While loading the crates into the repair shop and dealing with paperwork, the civilian working the front desk told me that there was a phone call for me. I walked over to the phone and answered.

On the other end of the line was the supply sergeant for the company, an E-7, and she was irate. "Why are you down at the repair shop, SGT Drake? You shouldn't be down there by yourself! You should have taken someone else with you for the drop-off!"

I let her finish yelling at me and then I got back in the now-empty van and made the drive back to the unit. When I got back to the unit, I returned the van, turned in my weapon, and then I walked to the supply sergeant's office to turn in the paperwork from the repair shop.

When I got to the office there was a second E-7 female sergeant there along with the supply sergeant. They both wore faces of anger. I stepped inside the office, dropped the paperwork on the desk, and without being told to, I just snapped to parade rest to take what was coming my way.

Both sergeants first class proceeded to spend the next ten minutes straight blasting me for taking a vehicle with weapons without having someone else in the vehicle with me. They started playing "what-if" scenarios and my aggravation began to grow. I could take an ass-chewing better than anyone, but if pushed too hard I would eventually push back. These too were beginning to push too hard. I couldn't help but notice that neither sergeant had a patch on their right shoulder, either. Both were also well overweight, and neither of them had been there when I had gotten there that morning. This meant that they weren't even working full days.

I decided I'd had about enough of the ass-chewing and that it was time to fire back.

SFC Mitchell, the supply sergeant, had just thrown another "what-if" my way with, "What if you had to use the bathroom? Were you going to leave those weapons unattended in the vehicle?"

I kept my position of parade rest with my eyes staring straight ahead as I responded, "I wouldn't have had to stop to use the latrine. I wouldn't have had to worry about any of the problems you mentioned. I'm a professional. The commander gave me a direct order last night and I carried out that order without question. I completed my mission. That's why people like me fight in wars and people like you stay here."

With that, I broke parade rest and left the office. The two sergeants yelled for me to get back in the office, but instead I walked outside to smoke a cigarette.

About twenty minutes later I was working in the commander's office on some paperwork, when the First Sergeant approached me, pointed at me, and then pointed toward an office in the corner of the room.

"My office. Now." He said as he walked straight back to his office. I followed him in and closed the door behind me. I knew to close the door because I knew what was coming. I stood before his desk at parade rest, staring straight at the wall behind the first sergeant.

He said, "What in the hell just happened with the supply sergeant and the motor pool sergeant?"

I explained to the first sergeant what had taken place and exactly what I had said to them. The stern, fixed look on his face broke and a smile came across his lips. I had only known this first sergeant a few days at this point since I had been gone from the unit for so long. He didn't know me either, so I continued, with a straight-face, to stare at the wall ahead.

"Sergeant Drake," he began, "you did what you were ordered to do, yes, but you should have had someone else with you as protocol requires. Your exchange with the two senior sergeants ends here in this office. You cannot speak to senior NCOs like that no matter how true what you said is. Now go ahead and get out of here and keep doing a good job."

"Yes, First Sergeant," I replied as I moved quickly out of his office. As I left, he was laughing and shaking his head.

I continued on with my duties for the rest of the month, doing every task that I was ordered to do. I enjoyed the work and it was a nice change of pace from freezing outside building piping systems every day. I dare say that I was starting to reconsider my decision to not re-enlist.

At the end of the month, the commander dismissed me, as promised on his formal memo that had been mailed. He stood up and shook my hand and wished me the best of luck in the future. The young captain asked me, one-time, if I would consider taking an extension and going on the tour to Iraq with them.

I paused before I spoke, because I had really been considering it in the days before this. I liked being in the flow of things with the Army again, and I felt that it was something I was very good at.

"Sir," I said, "I'm humbled that you would ask me to go on the tour with you. Unfortunately, I'm just so far behind in my civilian career that I really need to stay focused on it. I hope you understand and don't take this decline of your offer as any form of disrespect."

He said he understood. As I left the office that day, for the last time ever, I shook hands with all of the staff there and I wished them the best of luck on the tour. I did not have to shake hands with the two female E-7s because neither of them would be going on the tour.

CHAPTER 55

THE BEGINNING OF A PROBLEM

Bob and I rarely had beers in the evening anymore at this point. Things had changed in our friendship. It wasn't anything bad, but we were starting to separate and go our own ways in life. I was really focused on my career and Bob was really focused on taking advantage of opportunities with the Reserves. Despite us being on the exact same path for so many years, we were now traveling different ways. We were still good friends, we still got together and partied, we still talked on the phone several times a week, but it just wasn't how it used to be.

One Friday night in early November, 2007, I was up at Q drinking with some other friends. I hadn't seen Bob in a while, and I couldn't believe my eyes when I saw him come walking into the bar with Jamie Hasenfang! I hadn't seen Jamie in three-and-a-half years at this point and I didn't even know that Bob and she had been in communication.

It was around nine o'clock at night and I had already been up at the bar way too long. Not to mention I had to work the next morning. I walked over to the table that Bob and Jamie had sat down at, said my hellos, and then proceeded to crash their date for the next hour. I could tell by the look on Jamie's face, she wasn't pleased.

The next day, a Saturday, I called Bob on my way home from work. I told Bob how good it was to see Jamie the night before and that I had no idea they had been seeing one another. Bob told me he had been traveling to see Jamie for a while and that she would travel to see him also. Again, Bob and I were still good friends, but we just weren't as tight as we used to be.

"Oh," Bob said, "and Jamie says I can't take her to Q anymore."

I'm sure that my drunken display the evening before to two people who were stone sober, probably wasn't a good look for Jamie who was in from out of town. I didn't blame her in the least!

A couple of weeks later, Bob called me on a Friday night. He asked if I wanted to get a few drinks. I said sure, I picked him up, and then we drove over to Q and sat in our old spot. We talked about Afghanistan and we talked about his upcoming deployment to Iraq.

As the HHC's next deployment got closer and closer, I started to get a conflicted feeling in my gut. As a matter of fact, it was turning into pure agony for me. I deep-down felt that I needed to go on this tour with Bob, Ryan, Lester, and all our old friends who were still in the unit. I felt such loyalty to them that I felt that I was turning my back on them by not going. My time at the unit helping out during the pre-mob had started this feeling. As time went on, it just kept getting stronger and stronger.

The problem, I knew, was that if I went on this tour with them, I would lose another year plus of my apprenticeship and I would be even further behind in my training. This would have a negative effect on my civilian career long-term. I also owned a home and a mortgage now. How could I just leave my townhome vacant for a year?

The only way I knew how to handle this agony was to drink. And drink heavily, I did. It turned me into a wreck as this feeling of letting down my friends tore deeper and deeper into me.

By the time Bob and I were having this conversation, I was horribly conflicted inside and suffering immensely from it.

"We're leaving for Ft. Dix tomorrow night. I've got to be at the unit by six o'clock at night. Can you give me a ride up there?" Bob asked. He had a serious look on his face as he looked at me.

I was honored that Bob would ask me this. He could have asked anyone, but he asked me. I was as honored to do this as I was to pin him his E-5 rank two years before.

"Sure, Bob," I responded. "I'll be at your house at four-thirty."

I didn't sleep well that night. The agony of not going with my friends on this tour was weighing heavily on me. Without him saying it, I knew Bob wanted me to come with him for another run. Without me saying it, Bob knew deep down that I also wanted to come with him for another run.

I felt horrible the next day as I left my home and drove to Bob's house. Just like a hundred times before, the garage door opened, and Bob came walking out with his duffel bags. He tossed them into the bed of my truck, climbed in, and he had a shiny CD in his hand. Without saying anything, Bob put the CD in and we began our ride to the unit.

We didn't speak much as we blasted the music and smoked cigarettes. When we got to the unit, I parked in the lot where others had already gathered.

Bob and I stayed in my truck, dropped the tailgate, and we sat there for a while smoking cigarettes and taking in the scenery. I was feeling sick as I shook hands and gave hugs to old friends that passed by on their way to load gear up onto busses. Several times they joked that I could climb on the bus with them. Only they weren't joking. They wanted me to come with them. I wanted so badly to be going with them too, yet I knew I couldn't.

As I glanced around, there were full families clutching their adult children and saying goodbye to them. Even though I'd lived it, it hit me differently this time being on the outside and looking in. I felt awful for those families. It was even worse to see GI parents kissing their children and hugging them goodbye. The children didn't know what was happening and they were sobbing uncontrollably.

Finally, around five-thirty that night, Bob hopped off the tailgate. We shook hands and I thought I was going to vomit. I was in so much agony. Bob was leaving and I should be right there with him. We were best friends, we were a team, and we should be doing this together. Oh, was it a horrible feeling!

As Bob and I shook hands, I said to him, "Bob, please keep an eye on all these kids. Do what you can to make sure they all come home, will you?"

Bob looked me dead in the eye with his jaw clenched when he responded, "Every last one of them."

We then hugged each other and I think Bob knew I was on the verge of losing it right then and there. I helped him get his duffel bags out of the bed of my truck, and I climbed back in my cab. I watched Bob join the others loading gear and then I watched them take their place in their formation.

I couldn't take anymore, and I pulled out of the lot and headed back to the expressway.

While driving south down I-355, I finally exploded. I pulled over to the side of the road and put my emergency flashers on. It had started to rain, and the wipers were clearing the water hitting my windshield, but nothing was clearing the water leaving my face inside the cab of that truck. I was bawling my eyes out, screaming, and punching the seat of my truck. I was unhinged as the agony building for so long had finally blown off.

If I turn around and head back, I could catch the end of the formation. They would take me.

I could cut my hair and shave when we got to Ft. Fix. They would get me uniforms and gear.

Another tour would be nothing, I could do this. They'd take me if I asked.

Bob needs me, and I need him! I'm letting him down by not going!

After several minutes of these thoughts exploding out of me, I eventually put my truck in drive and drove the rest of the way home in a mixed state of depression, worry, and the feeling that I'd just made the worst mistake of my life.

CHAPTER 56

A YEAR OF AGONY

Up until this point in 2007, I would only go to the bar directly after work one day a week. I would meet some friends of mine on Fridays after work for beers and we would call this "After Work Beer Friday."

By December, 2007, "After Work Beer Friday" became "After Work Beer Every Day." I felt absolutely awful about abandoning my friends and not going to Iraq with them. No matter how much I reminded myself that I had done the right thing, in my heart I knew that I had made a drastic mistake. I felt that I had turned my back on the people that I was closest to. It was a horrible feeling and my only way to cope with it was to drink as many Budweisers as I possibly could.

I can tell you that I had a problem with alcohol from the first time I drank it. I liked alcohol way more than a normal person. I liked the way it made me feel, I liked how it relaxed me, and I liked the social environment it usually provided. While I liked drinking in general, I absolutely loved Budweiser. Budweiser never lied to me, Budweiser never cheated on me, and we had the absolute perfect relationship of mutual adoration and affection.

I would go to the bar every day after work like clockwork. Every day I would drink my three to four pints of Budweiser, pay my tab, and go home. While I was at the bar with other tradesmen and regulars, the agony of not being with my friends would go away for a couple of hours. While drinking, I felt free from the horrible feeling of not being who I should be. In my mind and in my heart, I felt that I should still be a soldier.

Although I was doing very well for myself financially as a pipefitter, drove a nice truck, had a great home in a great neighborhood, and had a good and loving family; it just wasn't enough. I desperately missed the camaraderie of the military and missed being with my friends. I felt out of place, I felt trapped to my mortgage, and I felt trapped to the job I needed to pay for it. Although I enjoyed the technical side of my work, I didn't enjoy the commute and long hours associated with it. I was tired, physically beat up, and worn out in my mid-20s.

I did my best during this time period to shut out Afghanistan and to ignore anything to do with Iraq. I felt really bad for those men and women who were being maimed and killed in the two wars. It weighed on me and I felt horribly guilty that I wasn't still doing my part. Because of this, I didn't want to hear about the wars and I didn't want to read about the wars. Every time I'd try to watch something on the wars, I'd get extremely angry and be mad at myself for being home and not doing my job for the Army.

I felt even more uncomfortable when someone would want to talk to me about my experiences or when someone would point me out as someone who had served. People would thank me for my service, and I'd get upset inside. Who the hell was I to be thanked? Good men and women were getting blown up every day while I was back home living on easy street! I didn't like the attention and I didn't feel comfortable with it at all.

If I got drunk enough, I'd tell you that we were all living in "fantasy land" and the real world was taking place in the middle east.

This was not a healthy cycle and I was doing a lot of damage to myself mentally and physically. I had quickly gone from a strong and confident young man, to one that was now bitter and full of anger. I developed a negative attitude because I was unhappy.

Although I always tried to keep a smile on my face while pushing through life, inside I was suffering from depression compounded tenfold by the nicotine and alcohol that I was abusing my body with. I was a functioning alcoholic, of course. I always made it to work, no matter what. In fact, I put my job before everything in my life. I missed many opportunities to take trips with my family and friends, choosing instead to continue my routine of working and drinking. I still made it to social settings and family functions, but I would often skate out early from these events. I just was not comfortable in my own skin and wanted to escape with alcohol.

Although my depression and drinking never affected my job, it certainly affected my relationships with women. I cannot begin to tell you how many women came and went during this time. Things would start out great, and then they'd go running for the hills when they realized how unhappy and how miserable I was. In all fairness, most of them were bar flies looking for someone to finance their good time anyway. Some were really good women, however, and my poor choices in attitude and lifestyle caused me to miss out on some great opportunities and experiences.

I hadn't heard from Bob Allen in months and all I knew was that he was in the Iraq theater. I thought about the guy every day and worried about him and the others. I was sitting in the bar at about four-thirty in the afternoon on a sunny March day in 2008. I had already put down my fill of pints and was getting ready to head home when, all of a sudden, Bob came walking in and sat down next to me at the bar. I was thrilled to see him, and we shook hands and I gave him a big hug.

Bob looked at me oddly with a smile and said, "You look like a homeless guy."

It was true, I had grown my hair out longer than ever and sported a full beard. Although I always kept my beard well groomed, Bob hated long hair and hated facial hair. Anyone that had a beard, to Bob, was a "homeless guy."

"And what the fuck is with your hair?" he continued. "Are you some kind of lefty hippy now?"

Bob said this last part with a chuckle as he fired up a Marlboro Red cigarette. I put my arm around him again and called over the bartender for drinks. I bought a round for the half-dozen of us sitting in the bar. I was so happy to see Bob!

Bob was home on leave for two weeks and he looked good. He was fit, slim, and had a brightness about him. Unfortunately, Bob wanted me to stay after the one drink and keep going with him, but I couldn't. I had to work the next morning and I knew if I kept going with Bob, I would be too hungover to work. After drinking with Bob for five years at this point, I knew I could get myself in trouble very quickly. He understood and we made plans to get together the next day.

As agreed, we met at Q the next day when I got home from work and Bob showed me pictures of Iraq and filled me in on what was going on over there and what they were doing. He also surprised me when he told me, "I bought an engagement ring and I'm going to ask Jamie to marry me."

"You're going to what?" I said as I nearly spit my beer out.

He responded, "It's for real, man. I'm going to ask her to marry me."

I took a sip of my pint, struggling to comprehend how things had moved this quickly. Maybe they hadn't moved too quickly and maybe I just didn't understand the depth of the relationship.

I couldn't help myself when I said, "Bob, what has changed here? A few years ago, Jamie rejected you. You stayed in pursuit, you turned away every woman but one, you went back into pursuit, and things worked out?"

Confidently, Bob replied, "I told her how I felt about her. She never knew how I felt."

I wanted to applaud that Bob had finally exposed his feelings to another human being! I was happy for him, and proud of him, and I hoped that she would say yes. In honor of Bob's new-found happiness, I actually did a shot with him at the bar. I refrained from doing ten more with him, but I did put down more pints than my usual limit.

Bob and I hung around the bar for a few more hours that day, but I had to leave because I knew I could get carried away with Bob and not be able to work in the morning. We shook hands and hugged each other goodbye. Bob told me he wouldn't be around for the rest of his leave, he planned to spend it with Jamie. I told him I understood, and I let him know how good it was to see him. He said the same.

After Bob left on leave, I felt better about things and I wasn't so worried about him anymore. Bob had found his way and I was happy that he was happy. He was also having great success with the Army, just like he always had. Bob had taken on some serious leadership roles and he had grown into the great NCO I always knew he could be. Man, was I proud of him. On the other hand, I still stayed in my cocoon of negativity and depression. In my mind I should have been there with Bob in the pictures he was showing me. It should have been another chapter in our book of adventures.

In early December, 2008, the HHC returned from Iraq after a nearly 10-month tour down range. I was thrilled they were back home safe and healthy.

CHAPTER 57

WEDDINGS AND GREAT PARTIES

My heavy drinking and depression continued in life and time moved very quickly during these days. I bounced from job site to job site, working all over northern Illinois and southeastern Wisconsin. Sometimes I found myself working two separate jobs in a single 24-hour period.

I had turned out as a journeyman in mid-2008, finally completing the five-year apprenticeship I had started over six years before. My skills were still slightly behind for a journeyman, but I was a dependable hand and had earned my place with my company. I found myself working for the same bosses on different jobs. That meant they were picking me to be on their crews because they liked what I brought to the table.

I even picked up a specialized certification that allowed me to work with medical gasses in hospitals. Not a lot of pipefitters at that time carried this certification and it was required in order to braze medical gas piping.

With a new certification came new opportunities with my company and I took advantage of them. Sometimes for weeks in a row I would work a regular 8-hour shift on a jobsite during the day. Remember, I'd always have a far commute so an eight-hour day was really a ten to an eleven-hour day. I'd then go home and sleep for a few hours or I'd drive directly to a hospital where we had another job going on. I'd then work at the hospital and do medical gas piping for another six-to-eight hours at night.

I was making really big money with all of the overtime I was earning, but I was also spending a lot of it on gasoline, eating out, my drinking, and sometimes I'd be working so many hours that I'd have to pay someone to clean my house and do my laundry. I usually only had one day off a week and sometimes I wouldn't have any depending on how much work my company had.

A bright light came into my world at this period of time when I started playing men's league hockey. It was an absolute blast. I was able to combine two things I really enjoyed and that was drinking and playing hockey. I had a lot of fun and made some good memories, despite still being a miserable and depressed person.

In mid-2009, Bob and Jamie got married in a beautiful ceremony in Galena, Illinois. I wasn't there. In one of the most selfish things I'd ever done in my life, I declined Bob's invitation to stand up in his wedding.

Bob had contacted me a few months before the wedding and asked me to stand up in the wedding party. I told him that I was honored he asked me, but I hesitated when he told me that it was going to be a military wedding and that he wanted me to wear a dress uniform. I explained to Bob that I was overweight at this point and my uniform wouldn't fit. I also wasn't crazy about cutting my long hair or shaving. Bob was adamant about me standing with him when he got married and I told him that I'd have to think about the uniform part.

The more I thought about it, the more I wanted to run away from it. In my selfish, depressed, mindset I felt that I had no business wearing a uniform again with these men and women who had done so much more than me. I no longer felt worthy to wear that uniform because I had turned my back on my friends when I should have been there with them on the third tour. Even though it was perfectly legal for me to wear a uniform since I had been honorably discharged, I was no longer good enough to wear one, in my mind.

I was also afraid. I was afraid that I would drink too much and do and say something stupid. I respected Bob and Jamie so much and I was terrified this would happen. I was having a harder and harder time controlling my drinking by mid-2009. I knew that by early evening, I had to have at least four-to-six beers in me, or I was going to be on edge.

All of this selfish, sick garbage in my head caused me to turn down the invitation to be a part of the happiest day of my military best friend's life.

Bob, being Bob, took my decline of his offer, and his wedding, in stride.

A few months after Bob and Jamie got married, Nicole Ward and Ryan Suthard got married. Ryan had been Bob's best man at his wedding and now Bob was serving as Ryan's best man. The Suthard wedding was the fourth wedding of couples from our original company that served in Afghanistan from 2003-2004.

I tried really hard to talk myself out of going to the Suthards' wedding too. I gave myself a million reasons that I couldn't go. I would once again have to be around the people that I had no right to be around because I had turned my back on them. Somehow, I talked myself into going. I think during this horrible, dark period, I was able to convince myself to go to this one wedding because the reception was being held in the same place as the hotel. I could drink as much as I wanted to, and then I could walk directly to my hotel room any time that I wanted to. With this sick mindset I was in, that gave me the comfort and courage to attend.

The Suthards' wedding was a beautiful ceremony. Bob and Jamie had held nothing against me for not attending their wedding, and they both greeted me with hugs. I still held it against myself anyway, because in my head I was a horrible person for not being at their wedding. I also got to see a lot of folks from the first tour that I hadn't seen in years. It was great to catch up with them! Being around everyone again started to make me feel a bit normal, but it was only a brief feeling.

After the wedding reception ended, a bunch of us went to the hotel bar to continue drinking. While there, I was sitting at the bar next to Jamie having a serious conversation. Well, as serious of a conversation as you can have while you're seeing three of the individual that you're speaking with in front of you at the same time. As the three Jamies and I were talking, I saw a young woman in a red dress making faces like she was going to vomit. The woman was close behind Jamie and I told Jamie to watch herself. Just as Jamie moved out of the way, the woman in the red dress vomited on the floor right next to Jamie's chair.

Casually, the woman grabbed a bunch of napkins and threw them on the vomit. She then ordered another drink.

The rest of the people at the reception weren't doing much better. Ryan, the groom, was being held up by two friends and being escorted around the party. He would yell out, "Drink!" and one of his handlers would pour his drink into his mouth. He would then yell out, "Cigarette!" and another handler would put his cigarette in his mouth so he could take a drag.

It was a great wedding that temporarily lifted my depression.

Not too long after the Suthard wedding, I got a call from Bob Allen on a Sunday afternoon when I was sitting at the bar. Bob was calling to tell me that he was driving into Illinois from New York and he would be staying at his mother's house in Darien for a few days to celebrate the 4th of July.

Early in 2009, Bob and Jamie had moved to New York. Bob had taken an AGR job with a Reserve unit which was located in Queens, New York. Bob had referred to Queens as an "open sewer" and in our phone calls he would tell me the stories of not being able to sleep at night because of feral cats everywhere having loud feral cat sex all night long.

Bob would also tell me about his new barber in Queens. The closest barbershop to Bob's apartment was a Russian-owned shop. When Bob described how the men looked and dressed in the shop, it was every Eastern European stereotype coming to life. Bob's specific barber, Sergei, was in his early 50s and had served in Afghanistan in the Soviet Army. He wore track suits with polo shirts underneath, he wore dress shoes, and he sported bad jewelry. He was also a chain smoker that would illegally smoke in his shop while cutting hair. Bob told me how he would practice Pashto with Sergei, who spoke broken Pashto, and how Sergei would try and teach Bob Russian.

Sergei's biggest enemy was Mahmoud who owned the grocery store across the street. Mahmoud was an Afghan Pashtun and Sergei would refer to him as "The Taliban." Bob would tell stories about how Sergei would see Mahmoud come outside his shop and Sergei would walk outside to scream and yell at him in broken English, Russian, and broken Pashto. Mahmoud, in turn, would scream at Sergei in broken English, broken Russian, and Pashto.

Apparently, Mahmoud even went to the FBI and made claims that Sergei was an undercover agent of the KGB. Sergei then informed the FBI that it was really Mahmoud who was undercover! According to Sergei's testimony to the FBI, Mahmoud was Taliban through and through. He could prove it! Sergei's cousin, Mikhael, knew a cousin of Mahmoud's in Staten Island that knew a Taliban member, who told him Mahmoud was a secret operative.

This hilarious story didn't end there. Sergei and Mahmoud would take it even further. Mahmoud would throw his rotting produce against Sergei's shop's windows, staining them. Sergei, in turn, would walk across the street, open the door to the store, and throw his garbage out on the floor.

Going back to the Sunday afternoon phone call, Bob invited me over to his mom's place the next day, Monday, for an all-day 3rd of July party. The jobsite I was on at the time had shut down that Monday, so I told Bob I'd be there, and it sounded like it was going to be a lot of fun.

During this time, I no longer trusted myself drinking. Due to this, I avoided driving my truck whenever I drank. So, I bought a bicycle and I used to ride my bike to and from the bar when the weather was nice. The bar didn't mind, and they'd even keep it in the back for me while I was there. The bike kept me away from DUIs and provided some exercise at the same time.

For Bob's 3rd of July party, I loaded a backpack full of a case and a half of Budweiser and took off for his mom's house at about two o'clock that afternoon. Bob's mom still lived at the same location, but I lived on the other side of town now. It was a good three-mile ride, but it was no problem for me because I was cycling a lot in those days. I wheeled up to the house about a half hour later and walked inside. Nicole and Ryan were there and so was Jamie with Bob. I said hello to everyone and then Bob led Ryan and I outside while the two ladies stayed inside.

Bob had quite the setup going already. He had a large pop up screen assembled with a projector, he had some tables set up, he had a grill ready, and he had coolers and ice ready to go. I put my beers on ice, and we started drinking. Well, Bob and Ryan started. I had already been at the bar earlier in the afternoon. Within a couple of hours, a lot of Bob's other friends started showing up. It was a group of guys that I hadn't seen in years, since the days when Bob and I used to hang out at Q every night. It was great to see them all!

I'm not sure where the ladies went that evening, but we didn't see them for the rest of the night. This party turned into a rage in no time! Bob's friends had brought burgers, sausages, a Jack Daniel's shot machine that plugged in and kept the whiskey cold, and they had even brought a full computer setup to hook up to the projector. They also brought firewood for a bonfire. This turned into one hell of a party!

As the hours went on, we watched Predator and some other movies, and we also watched the entire Alice in Chains Unplugged concert. Bob and I jammed out the whole time, it was just like the good old days of Q. Ryan and I had a few long private conversations too. I let Ryan behind the wall a little bit about how weird I felt with everyone, how I felt that I had let everyone down. Ryan let me know that under no circumstances did anyone ever think that was the case and that

I had nothing to be upset about. I didn't listen, of course.

The party kept going that night. Before I knew it, all of my Budweisers were gone and I was now drinking shots of Jack Daniel's with Bob, Ryan, and everyone else. We kept eating too. Sausages, then burgers, then more sausages. We were telling stories about Afghanistan, about each other, and laughing the whole night away. Man, was it good to be back together with Bob and Ryan and having fun like this again!

I was having so much fun that I forgot that I had to be up at 7 o'clock the next morning so that I could march in the 4th of July Parade with the VFW. As we continued to drink and laugh, I happened to say, "Well boys, I'm going to have to get out of here soon. It's got to be about midnight."

My statement was met with a loud laugh from Bob, who replied, "Midnight? It's almost four in the morning!" Everybody exploded in laughter except for me. I pulled out my flip phone and checked the time and they were absolutely right – it was nearing four am!

I decided it was time to leave the party so that I could make my obligation in the morning. I said goodbye to everyone and came to Bob last. Bob was never one to show emotion, but this night he did.

Bob put his arms around me in a big hug and said, "We really went through a lot of shit together, man. You were a good NCO and always looked out for me. I never told you this before, but I love you like you were my own brother."

This was odd from Bob, drinking or not, and really out of character. I was surprised by him revealing his emotions. I returned Bob's sentiments as I told him, "Bob, you were the best soldier that I ever saw. We were a great team together. I can't put into words how much I care about you and how much I love you. You are my brother."

After this red-eyed, drunken exchange, I hopped on my bicycle and peddled off. I wiped out three times on the ride home including crashing into a bush where I thought I broke my wrist. I slept for an hour and a half on my bathroom floor before I marched with the VFW two hours later, still drunk as a skunk.

I didn't know it at the time, but the early hours of 4th of July, 2009 would be the last time I'd ever see Bob in person. I'm glad we had the exchange we had.

CHAPTER 58

THE DARKNESS

The years kept rolling on and life kept changing. In 2010, I lost my job as a pipefitter in one of the worst economic recessions in the history of the United States. For six months I searched for a job in my field and could not get one. I finally ended up taking a job in the public sector with a 60% pay cut.

Although the pay was low in my new job, I was promoted twice quickly. With overtime, I could keep my head above water. My commute now was around a mile one way to work, I was out of the elements for the most part, and my hardest day in my new career was my easiest day pipefitting. I also made myself available for every minute of overtime including snowplowing and working overnight security. I made ends meet and I was learning a whole new field.

Professionally, I was as good as I always was. I was a dedicated employee and I never let any of my personal issues get in the way of my work. I had learned that a long time ago. When you go to work, you give your very best day in and day out and you leave your issues at the door. You are being paid to do a job, so do it! My love affair with Budweiser never interfered with my work, nor did my feelings of depression. My work ethic was always top notch and that's what helped me to quickly achieve success in my new field.

Women came and went, as usual, and life kept moving forward. In my new job I was given a great opportunity to coach gymnastics, a sport that I was so good at in high school. This was a bright spot in life for me. I really enjoyed working with these kids and helping them. Although I was appalled at the difference in the fitness levels and maturity of these kids as compared to when I was in school just twelve years before, it was a lot of fun to work with them. In my new job I worked hundreds of hours of overtime a year in addition to coaching. I was rarely at home. In fact, when I wasn't working or coaching, I was usually at the bar, and then I'd head home to sleep. Like I said, nothing had changed with my work ethic, it was just a different job.

Bob Allen had gotten promoted to Sergeant First Class and was now living with Jamie in upstate New York where Bob worked as a career counselor for a Reserve unit there. He lived on West Point itself. Bob and I would talk on the phone every few weeks, we'd keep up with each other on social media, and he'd always want me to come out and visit. With my obligations to my job, I never took him up on his offer.

Ryan Suthard, Andrew Blanco, and Lester Dodson continued to do tour after tour overseas. The three of us didn't speak often, but we kept up on social media. I was so proud of them for what they continued to do, and I continued to feel awful that I wasn't still doing it with them. Between their tours, and when we could, we would get together. I would feel like the odd man out when they'd tell their stories, but it still felt really good to be together again.

By the end of 2013, I was convinced that I was going to work in this job for the rest of my life. Things were going very well professionally. I also met a new girl who had started working at Q as a bartender. Her name was Rachel.

Rachel was not my usual type of woman. She had light skin and red hair, two things I'm usually not attracted to. Rachel was about 5 feet 2 inches tall and she was muscular, like a female gymnast. She also had a very pretty face with a wonderful smile. One thing led to another, and Rachel and I were an item.

Rachel was very private. It would take a lot to get information from her about her background. Rachel came from a military family. Her father was a retired aviation Colonel and had served in Vietnam, the Gulf War, Afghanistan, and Iraq. Her brother had served as an infantryman on two tours of Iraq.

Rachel claimed that she had emancipated herself from her parents at sixteen when her Dad was transferred from Illinois to another state with his military duties. Rachel also claimed that she had attended college and had a degree in metallurgy. Over time, I learned that what she had said about her Dad was true, but a lot of her other stories would vary. For example, the college that she attended changed from Texas to Illinois a few times. She had also claimed she was on the independent circuit for high end gymnastics in the style of Cirque du Soleil. Yet, the dates that she gave for traveling the circuit were untrue as she was working at a bar full time in the next town over. A lot of things just didn't add up.

During the period that Rachel and I first started dating, we had opened up our own VFW building in Darien. It took many months and a lot of work as we converted a nail salon into a bar. When we needed a bartender, Rachel agreed to work for us on her days off from Q. Rachel was a natural charmer and got along with everyone in the post.

Rachel and I ended up being together for about nine months before things cooled off and just got, altogether, strange with her. We would talk to each other and see each other every day, even if it was only for 15 minutes or so. During the last few weeks of our relationship, Rachel wouldn't return calls, or I wouldn't see her at all. There was never an explanation or a reason, there was just nothing. Finally, we talked, and decided to call it quits on our thing.

Two weeks later I went on to find out that Rachel had a side project for the last two months that we had been together. There was a meat market next to the VFW and sometimes when I'd stop in the VFW after work, I'd see this skinny kid named Roger who worked at the meat market hanging around the bar talking to Rachel. It turned out that Rachel and Roger had a fling going for months while Rachel and I still had our relationship going.

It didn't end there. I confirmed there was at least one other side project that Rachel had during our relationship. Rachel, when I confronted her about these infidelities, denied that any of this had happened. I also went on to learn that a lot of things that Rachel had told me about herself were false. Rachel was not at all who I thought she was this whole time. This was devastating to me since I had put great trust in Rachel and had really let my guard down for the first time in a very long time.

If this wasn't bad enough, my great job had now turned into an absolute disaster. A new board had been elected to oversee our operation, and they decided that they wanted to cut costs. They hired a new chief financial officer to do their bidding. He immediately cut our overtime and started giving it to outsourced workers while forcing us to train them to take our work. Also, when one of our workers would leave, they would be replaced by an outsourced contractor.

In the course of two months, I had lost my girlfriend and my dream job had become a nightmare. I had always enjoyed going to work every day, but now I dreaded walking into the place each morning. Every day felt like I was being punched in the face as we would learn what was being taken away from us next.

I continued to maintain my high work ethic, but after work I lost total control over my drinking. I was now drinking a full case of Budweiser every night. I felt awful every day as my hands and feet started to bother me, I was putting on weight, and I was absolutely depressed and miserable with life. I developed a horribly negative attitude, a short temper, and I even got into a couple of fights at the bar.

During this awful time period, I was sitting at the bar one Saturday night at about ten o'clock. Rachel was working, I couldn't avoid her, and my blood was boiling every time I had to look at her. I had an empty stool open next to me and a middle-aged black man that I had never seen before sat down next to me. He was extremely clean cut, with a kind face, and he was dressed nicely in slacks and a shirt. He and I got to talking, and I felt obliged to tell this man my story. I caught him up to speed on all that was going on as we bought each other drinks. This man listened to me patiently, taking in all the negativity that was coming out of my mouth.

"My man," he said. "Do you know what your problem is?"

I knew what my problem was. It started with where I was sitting and what I was drinking, but I instead chose to shake my head no.

"You are standing in the darkness when there is a room with light right next door. You are choosing the darkness." He said as he looked me straight in the eye with conviction.

"What are you talking about?" I said as I tried to brush him off.

"You are a blessed man with good health, a strong body, and a great deal of life experience at a young age. You are choosing this negative route and you don't have to. Do you think you're the first man to live this way or to feel this way? Pick up the Bible some time, my man. You will find stories of men that were horrible human beings that stepped into the light, that was right next door, and changed."

I was intrigued by what this man was telling me, but I was still skeptical. I asked him to go on.

"I'm a Christian minister, my man. I'm a preacher. I don't care if you're a Christian or what you are. I deal with people like you on a daily basis. I've seen it and heard it a hundred times. You will continue in darkness until you choose to step into the light. Let me tell you how this works, my man. I was driving home tonight after a Bible study. I had no intentions to stop up here. As I was driving, something made me turn into this parking lot and sit down here. Do you know what that was?"

I was in shock at what this man was saying to me and all I could muster out was a weak, "No."

"That was Jesus Christ, my man. I have dedicated my life to Jesus Christ and Jesus Christ told me that one of his sheep needed some shepherding tonight. And here I am and now here you are. So, you can take or leave what I'm telling you, it's up to you. It's up to you to continue in the dark, or you can step out into the light and stop all of this."

I didn't know what to say to this man. My ego was preventing me from taking it all in, but I couldn't deny what he was telling me.

After our exchange had concluded, we shook hands, and I left the bar trying to wrap my head around what he was telling me.

CHAPTER 59

THE LIGHT

On December 26, 2014, I was in the basement at work painting the fence of our fitness center. It was only ten o'clock in the morning, but I was dumping sweat and my hands and feet were killing me. My head was pounding still from the case of Budweiser I had drank on Christmas and the pack of cigarettes I had smoked with it. I felt horrible and I looked horrible.

For the past month, what that preacher had said to me at Q had been rattling around in my brain. My ego had built a wall up to prevent what he was telling me to fully sink in, but that wall was starting to crumble fast. That preacher had to be right. I was choosing this path of destruction for myself. I was choosing to do what I was doing and to feel what I was feeling. This wasn't the first time I'd heard this either. The words of Father Smith from eight years earlier and his story of "mercy" were also the same message.

As I was taking a quick break and drinking water, while sweat was hitting the floor off of my head, a worker from another department walked by me on his way to use the fitness center. I had become friendly with this man for a few years and I had learned that he was a recovering alcoholic. He had shared some of his story with me before.

I felt this voice in my head tell me to stop him.

"Nick," I said, as he quickly swung around. "Nick, I know you quit drinking some time ago. Look man, I'm in a bad way here and I need to quit. I can't keep living like this. I feel horrible."

Nick took a few minutes to talk to me and asked me what was going on. I told him. Nick asked me what time my lunch break was, and I told him I usually ate at about noon. He told me he was going to get his workout in and then he'd swing by my office at lunch time.

True to his word, Nick came walking into my office at twelve sharp and he had some literature with him about alcoholics anonymous. He didn't preach to me, he didn't pressure me, he just told me that my story was the same as everyone else's and that he, and the others, were there to talk when I needed their help. He also handed me his business card with his personal number on it.

That afternoon I didn't go to the bar after work. I kept thinking of Father Smith's words and that preacher's words. I went home and started looking at the literature that Nick had given me. I went on the websites the literature listed and I started to see that there were millions of people out there just like me who were behaving the same way as I was. These people had the exact same problems that I had with alcohol and the exact same horrible attitude about life.

I decided at home, that night, that I was never drinking again. I also did something that night that I hadn't done in years. I went to my bookshelf and I pulled out a Bible. Growing up Catholic and attending religious education as a child, I remembered a teacher telling us that he would randomly pick a page from the New Testament and read it. I did just that and the reading that came up was

Acts 16.

Paul and Silas had been put in prison, but while praying, and singing hymns to God, an earthquake occurred and opened the doors of the jail, freeing them. Reading this that night hit me as hard as if someone had struck me across the face with a sledgehammer. These men were in prison facing the worst of all consequences, death by execution, but were now being freed by God because of their faith. *I was also in a prison, but now, I too, was being freed by God.*

That night changed things for me permanently. I could no longer deny that the cause of all my years of depression and heavy drinking were because of a lack of faith. I was choosing to do this to myself, instead of simply looking for mercy. That weekend I attended mass for the first time in years and I kept going back. I also started studying the daily readings of the church each day. Reading by reading along with independent research and prayer helped me to start understanding the Bible more and more. Exactly what that preacher had told me was accurate. Exactly what Father Smith had told me was accurate. I was a freed man now because I stepped out of the darkness and into the light. God was always there speaking to me, I had just been making the choice to not listen.

The first year that I quit drinking was not easy. I had to forget old drinking habits and with those habits included old drinking friends. It could be very lonely at times. When I felt my lowest, I would listen to podcasts from those in recovery or I'd give Nick a call and it would lift my spirits. I also picked up a copy of the alcoholics anonymous Big Book and I followed the steps. Although I never went to an AA meeting, I followed their message and participated with groups online. It really made a positive change.

The human mind gets trained to habit. Habits can be healthy or they can be dangerous. An addiction means the wiring in your brain is off and some people are just more susceptible to it by genetics or their environment. When you decide to break the addiction, you have to break the habit that you've put yourself into. You have to begin the process of retraining your brain. Just like a boxer training for a fight or just like an apprentice plumber training for their job, it takes time. You will make mistakes, you will have to correct those mistakes, and you will have to continue working hard to achieve what you want. In the case of addiction, you want to achieve freedom.

As I worked through the steps and I retrained my brain, slowly, my feelings of guilt and depression were vanishing. My anger was also ceasing to exist. I was starting to feel really good about who I was again. I created new habits of getting up at the same time, regimenting my daily routine, and taking good care of myself.

Throughout new sobriety I had a lot of fun re-discovering old hobbies, picking up old friendships that had been put by the wayside, and seeing and doing things that I hadn't done in years. For example, I had really enjoyed reading books about Cold War history, watching pro wrestling, and watching '80s movies. I had stopped doing all these things over the years, choosing instead to focus on Budweiser. I started doing these things again and much more, including getting myself into a great fitness program. It was a wonderful feeling to re-discover things that I had always enjoyed doing and to rebuild my body.

Less than a year after quitting drinking, I even quit smoking. I used the same strength and principles that I'd used to quit drinking.

One year of sobriety turned into two years of sobriety. I kept growing spiritually, I kept taking in new experiences, and I kept building a more positive attitude. I even changed jobs and moved to another public entity where I felt appreciated. I also took things with my faith a step further and started working with children by teaching religious education on Saturday nights. I was helping these 7th and 8th graders with their faith, but really, they were helping me.

I helped these kids understand the Bible by tying in the history of Ancient Rome, Ancient Egypt, and the ancient world which applied to parts of the scripture. These kids were now understanding the context of the times and they were understanding how significant the events taking place in the Bible were. As they were encouraged, I was encouraged. As they learned, I learned. We grew together in faith.

Two years of sobriety turned into three years of sobriety. During this time, I kept reconnecting with old military friends. Ryan Suthard and I started talking more often. Lester Dodson, Andrew Blanco, and I also started exchanging phone calls more frequently. Bob and I were talking more than we had talked in years. It was a very positive time.

The black cloud that had been over me for so long had now vanished. Talking to Bob and the others on a regular basis had finally put away that ridiculous "I'm not good enough" feeling. I had my self-confidence back, I had my physical strength back, and I felt the best I'd ever felt in my life.

CHAPTER 60

THE PHONE CALL

In early June, 2018, I was in an important work conference and I missed a phone call. When I was leaving the conference, I saw that Ryan Suthard had called. This was not common for Ryan to call during the work day, so my concerns were raised. As I was walking out of the building, I called Ryan back. Ryan had called to let me know that Bob had been hospitalized in Hawaii, his most recent duty station. Bob had some serious health issues that were going on and Ryan said he would keep me up to date on Bob's recovery.

I had asked Ryan if it was okay that I contacted Bob or Jamie directly, but Ryan said it was best to give them privacy. I asked Ryan if he would please keep me posted on the situation and to let me know if we needed to make a trip out there. Ryan said he would keep me apprised of the situation.

Ryan continued to call me every other day or so to give me an update. After about a week, Ryan let me know that Bob had turned the corner and would be leaving the hospital soon. He said it'd be okay at this time to give Bob a call.

Bob and I played phone tag for a couple of weeks after he was released from the hospital. It was the early summer, which was my busiest time for work, and the time difference between Hawaii and Illinois didn't help us in connecting.

Finally, we connected one Saturday evening and we chatted for a few minutes. I had caught Bob at a bad time. Bob said that he was working on a model and was running to the hobby shop to get some more glue. I could hear the wind rushing through his open windows as his vehicle was driving down the road. I told him I was just calling to check on him, to see how he was doing, and I told him that we could talk another time if he'd like. Bob said he'd give me a call back the next day.

A week went by and I still hadn't heard back from him. After church on the evening of Saturday, June 30, I decided that I would reach out to Bob the next day at five o'clock in the evening to try and catch up on our chat. That would be early afternoon his time in Hawaii and it would be the perfect time to connect. I wanted to see how his health was doing, if he had fully recovered, and to tell him all about this Captain America comic book series I had picked up recently. Bob had also sent me an article that Friday on social media about a guy that had collected thousands of Teenage Mutant Ninja Turtle figures from the '80s and early '90s. I wanted to talk to him about the article.

The next day, Sunday, July 1, I finished eating lunch at one o'clock in the afternoon, when my phone rang. It was Ryan calling and I figured it would be like any other call.

"Hey Ryan," I said. "What's up?"

Ryan's tone was the lowest and most serious I'd ever heard. "Brad," he said, "I've got some really bad news. Jamie called Nicole just a little while ago to let us know that Bob passed away from what appears to be a heart attack."

I didn't want to believe what I was hearing. I also didn't know what to say, and I hesitated with a response.

I finally muttered out, "Ryan, that's horrible to hear, just horrible. Thank you for letting me know, I'll start making phone calls and I'll let the others know." Before I hung up, Ryan and I agreed to talk again later that day.

I was now in deceased-family member mode, and I sat down at my kitchen table and began to call the others from DET 4, our friends from the first tour, and Bob's friends that were still living in the area. The calls were short, filled with sadness, and to the point. Everyone was in shock.

One of my calls that afternoon was to Ivan Beal. While talking with Ivan, I was overcome with emotion remembering us drinking with Bob that time in the American Legion in Sparta. In mid-conversation, my voice broke and I told Ivan that I had to call him back. It had finally hit me, and my heart sunk to a terrible low. I walked to my bedroom, where I sat on the floor and started sobbing uncontrollably. All of the good times Bob and I had together came pouring out of my mind. I kept seeing Bob's laughing face in my head and my heart kept flooding me with sadness that I'd never see that face again. I suddenly felt that there was a hole in my heart where a powerful pillar had once stood helping to hold it up. That was Bob's pillar. He was a part of me.

Bob was as important to me as my own blood family and his friendship was a part of my everyday life. Thinking of what life would be like without Bob in it was an awful realization. To this very day and since 2003, I have thought about Bob every single day.

When the tears stopped flowing and I regained my composure, I called Ivan back. We finished our conversation. When I hung up, I immediately turned on my stereo and began playing the Alice in Chains Unplugged album. I was taken back to the earliest days of my friendship with Bob, when we'd sit in Q and enjoy that album over pitchers of beer on Saturday and Sunday afternoons.

I sat in silence on my couch as the memories kept coming back. I sat there laughing, then crying, then laughing again, remembering all the times together with Bob. After about an hour, I couldn't stand sitting around at home anymore. I drove to Q, where Bob and I had spent hundreds of evenings together. I saw a few old friends there and let them know what had happened. I sat at the end of the bar, where Bob and I had always sat, and I remembered what our friendship was like for all those years, and how much fun we had together. I made my way over to the jukebox and played the entire Alice in Chains Unplugged album. As I drank Coca-Colas and listened to the music, images of Bob sitting next to me popped into my head. The memories were crystal clear as I could see him sitting there, Marlboro Red in hand, tipping back his pint glass and enjoying the music right with me.

I felt the worst for Jamie and for Bob's mother, Jean. Jamie had lost her husband and Jean had lost her oldest son. I couldn't even imagine the pain that they were suffering through. I knew at some point I had to reach out to both of them, and I had to find the right words to say.

The next night, Monday night, I had a very vivid dream. I was walking on a mountain ridge on a worn, well-traveled path. From the way the stones looked and the color of the terrain, I knew I was walking in Afghanistan again. The path was traveling on an incline, and when I reached the top there was a man standing with his back to me. He was wearing old Army woodland BDUs, the same uniforms we wore until 2006.

As I approached, the man turned around and it was Bob Allen. Bob saw me, recognized me, and gave me a big smile. As I approached closer, I saw that Bob was wearing his E-7 rank on his woodland BDUs, he had his 10th Mountain Combat patch on, and he was fit and in good shape. His face was his current age, but he had his hair in a flat top, the way he had kept it for most of our second tour together. Bob looked healthy, he looked good, and he was happy to see me.

Despite being in a dream, I could feel the heat of the sun on me and there was also a slight breeze. From the breeze, Bob's thin hair moved a little bit in his flat top. I could also hear some water running in the background indicating we were close to a river or to a stream.

I was so happy to see Bob and I was so happy to see how good he looked.

"Bob," I said. "How are you, are you okay?"

He continued smiling as he replied, "Yeah Brad, I'm fine. I feel great."

I walked up closer and we shook hands and I put my arm on his shoulder, feeling so relieved to see him. We didn't say anything for a moment and just held onto each other's hands in our handshake. I gripped his shoulder hard with my hand, thrilled to be in contact with him.

Bob then made a wisecrack, but I don't recall what it was. I started laughing, he was laughing, and then I woke up in my bed laughing. I sat straight up in my bed when I woke, realizing suddenly that I was no longer on the mountain and it was just me, alone, in my bedroom. In the early hours of that morning, I felt some relief from the aching in my heart. I felt that Bob was okay.

CHAPTER 61

REMEMBERING BOB

Ryan Suthard and I went to visit Bob's mother, Jean Drenth, on the Thursday after Bob's passing. We expressed our condolences and we sat and talked with Jean for a while. At that time, it didn't seem likely that services would be held on the mainland for Bob, so the three of us agreed that we needed to do something for Bob's friends and family in the area.

Ryan and I started calling local American Legion halls and VFW halls to try and rent something for later in the month. Unfortunately, nobody was able to accommodate us on such short notice. A friend of mine suggested giving Q a call to see if they could help us. Q had a band room that they would rent out for parties and events.

Sure enough, Q was willing to bump another rental and to let us have our memorial service in the band room. I also made catering arrangements through them and Q went all out to help us. The owner remembered Bob, he was sad to hear of his passing, and he was more than willing to help us do a proper send-off for him.

On Sunday, July 27, 2018, we held a memorial for Bob that we called Remembering Bob. Over 180 people were present, including a very large contingent of current and former soldiers that had served with Bob. We had tables setup with pictures of Bob, and I had my favorite picture of him blown up and placed on an easel in the center of the room. It was a picture that I had taken of Bob before we did our first ever mission in Afghanistan in 2003. Bob was posing with his beloved M-249 SAW, at his very best, and in his prime.

I gave a speech telling the folks present about my friendship with Bob, about how loyal of a friend he was, and how he was the best soldier I'd ever seen. I also made a reference to the song "Rooster" by the band Alice in Chains. There is a line in the song where Layne Staley sings out, "Walking tall, machine gun man." I shared with the crowd about how those words would ring through my head every time Bob and I did a road march together and how he'd be lugging along his M-249. I ended by saying that's how I would always remember Bob, he would always be walking tall, machine gun man.

Ryan cut a magnificent speech where he talked about Bob's qualities as a human being, how dedicated he was to his craft as a soldier, and about how he and Bob had grown through the years to become the best of friends. It was a powerful speech and Ryan ended it with a toast.

Before the ceremony started that day, I made sure to take a picture of Bob and set it up at the end of the bar in the back of the room. It was the position of the bar where Bob would always sit so that he could watch all the exits. I also had a pint poured and a shot placed in front of this picture. I let the crowd know that if Bob was there that day, that's where he'd be sitting, and that's what he'd be drinking.

It was great to see the turnout for Bob. Old soldiers came from all over, many from out of state, to pay their respects, and it was wonderful to get everyone together again. It was exactly how Bob would have wanted it. He would have wanted laughter, jokes, and a party. We gave him just that.

During the ceremony, I asked Lester Dodson to call a final formation for all of us that had previously served with Bob. We all lined up in a formation just like we used to, at close intervals. Lester then turned the formation over to our old First Sergeant from our first tour. Sergeant Major Cooper had lost nothing as his booming voice commanded his formation to salute. And salute we did.

That afternoon and evening caused a lot of old friendships to be renewed and all of us living in the area made a vow to get together as often as possible. We've all kept to our word and we continue to get together. At first it was every six months and now it is every three months. We're a family again.

I wrote a letter after the memorial thanking Q for their kindness and hospitality and I also left them a picture of Bob and asked that they put it up in the bar. Bob really loved that place and I felt it'd only be appropriate for his memory to live on there.

After months of not seeing the picture put up anywhere, I was pleasantly surprised to find that they had framed the photo with my letter and put it on permanent display in the bar. It was a very nice tribute. Usually on Saturdays, after church, I'll swing by the old bar for a cheeseburger and to see some old friends. I sit at the end of the bar like Bob and I used to and the old memories will always come back to me. Before I leave, I make sure to visit his picture and pay my respects.

I still think of Bob every day. My thoughts follow a cycle of laughing, sadness, and then laughing again. I miss my friend.

I am thankful, however, for the years we had together. I'm thankful for the adventures that we had together, the obstacles we overcame together, and the great friendship we shared. Few people have gotten to experience the kind of close friendship that Bob and I had, and we were very lucky. There is a void in my heart with Bob gone that will always be there, but there is also a joy and happiness from our friendship that will always remain.

I have a picture of Bob in my home. He is smiling while the door of a Blackhawk helicopter is opened next to him. The landscape of Afghanistan is behind him on a beautiful summer day in 2003. I remember when the picture was taken, and I remember the hot Afghan summer air whipping through the helicopter that day. I glance at that picture often and it takes me right back to those happy times.

I have another picture in my office at work of a bunch of us together at Ft. McCoy at the end of our first tour. We're all too thin, we're all so young, and we all had our whole lives ahead of us. In the picture I've got my left arm hanging on Bob's right shoulder. It's a rare picture where we're all smiling.

Sometimes, visitors to my office will ask me about the picture. I always grin as I point out all my old friends in the photo. Usually, I will happily tell the visitor some stories about Bob, but there's always a little sadness in my voice too. After I put the photo back behind my desk and the visitor leaves, I usually have to take a few minutes to collect myself and make sure tears don't come out of my eyes. I miss those days and I miss my friend.

Bob Allen stood for something in his life. He had the courage to put on the uniform and he dedicated his life to the Army, to service to this country. In a time when being in the military wasn't popular with our generation, Bob served with pride. Bob did three tours of duty in combat zones and achieved more in seventeen years of service than most do. He was a loyal, good, soldier that never hesitated to protect or help a fellow soldier.

Bob was also a true friend. It could be hard to earn his trust and to earn his friendship, but once you did; you were his friend forever and he never forgot about you.

Most importantly, Bob got the girl. He was a devoted, faithful husband, and was madly in love with Jamie. Theirs was a true love story from the beginning.

Many years from now, I hope, the OIC of this universe is going to tell me that the road march of this life is concluding.

I'll receive orders that I need to make it to the landing zone to catch trans out. It'll be dark that night, but close to dawn. It'll be the perfect time for the pickup. Darkness is always followed by light.

When I reach the LZ, I'll hear the chopper in the distance, searching for contact. I'll pop a smoke canister so the pilot can spot me more easily.

I'll crouch down as the Blackhawk swoops in, blasting me with the air and dust pushed up from its propellers. I won't be able to hear a thing because the engines will drown out any sound.

I'll make my way to the helicopter, hunched over just in case the wind should pick up and bend a prop my way.

The crew chief will have had the side door opened already, anticipating this pickup.

When I climb in through the door, I know Bob will be there with a smile on his face, and his hand extended out to grasp mine. I'll take his hand and smile back. That's when I'll know my life's mission is complete.

A shot and a
beer for my
old friend at his
memorial.
It was at the end
of the bar, where
he always sat.
July, 2018

SGM Cooper (Ret.),
our former 1SG,
has us at attention.
Moments later we
would give Bob
his final salute.
July, 2018

SGM Cooper (Ret.), formerly our company 1SG, and I. He made the trip a long way for Bob's memorial and this was the first time we'd seen each other since 2004.

July, 2018

Jason "Doc" Cain, Lester Dodson, Ryan Suthard, and I reunited for the first time since 2006. The four fingers went up for DET 4.

July, 2018

Jamie (Hasenfang) Allen and I serve as Godparents to Nicole (Ward) and Ryan Suthard's little girl. It was a great honor to step in for Bob.
August, 2019

Ryan Suthard, Andrew Blanco, and I. The four
fingers go up when DET 4 rides. July, 2019

Jessie Antia and I
at a reunion. Jessie
was the toughest lady
MP that I ever
worked with.

July, 2019

Veterans Day 2018
My Family
(Left to Right)

Uncle George T. Lyons
(USMC)

Brad Drake
(USA)
Afghanistan

My Dad, Jim Drake
(USA)
Vietnam

Uncle Rich Vachata
(USA)
Korea

Great Uncle
George Lyons (USA)
World War II

ACRONYM REFERENCE PAGE

AI	Assistant Instructor
AIT	Advanced Individual Training
AT	Annual Training
ASVAB	Armed Services Vocational Aptitude Battery
BDU	Battle Dress Uniform (out of service 2006)
BTIF	Bagram Theater Internment Facility
CDTF	Chemical Defense Training Facility
CIB	Combat Infantryman's Badge
CQ	Charge of Quarters
DCU	Desert Camouflage Uniform
EPW	Enemy Prisoner of War
FCL	Full Combat Load
GI	Government Issue
GI PARTY	Group cleaning of an area
GITMO	Guantanamo Bay, Cuba
KP	Kitchen Patrol / Duty
LZ	Landing Zone
MEPS	Military Entrance Processing Station
MI	Military Intelligence
MP	Military Police
MOS	Military Occupational Service
MWR	Morale, Welfare, Relief

NBC	Nuclear, Biological, Chemical
NCOIC	Non-Commissioned Officer in Charge
OIC	Officer in Charge
PT	Physical Training
PTSD	Post Traumatic Stress Disorder
PX	Post Exchange
QRF	Quick Reaction Force
R&U	Repair & Utilities
RIF	Regional Internment Facility
ROTC	Reserve Officer Training Corps.
SAW	Squad Automatic Weapon
SOG	Sergeant of the Guard
WGM	Waste of Government Money

U. S. ARMY RANK STRUCTURE

Officer Grade	Officer Rank	Abbreviation
O-10	General	GEN
O-9	Lieutenant General	LT GEN
O-8	Major General	MAJ GEN
O-7	Brigadier General	BG GEN
O-6	Colonel	COL
O-5	Lieutenant Colonel	LT COL
O-4	Major	MAJ
O-3	Captain	CPT
O-2	First Lieutenant	1LT
O-1	Second Lieutenant	2LT
Enlisted Grade	Enlisted Rank	Abbreviation
E-9	Command Sergeant Major	CSM
	or Sergeant Major	SM
E-8	First Sergeant or	1SG
	Master Sergeant	MSG
E-7	Sergeant First Class	SFC
E-6	Staff Sergeant	SSG
E-5	Sergeant	SGT
E-4	Specialist	SPC
E-3	Private First Class	PFC
E-2	Private	PV2
E-1	Private	PVT

April, 2004

Brad Drake, Bob Allen, Alan Garretson, Matt Bender,

Ivan Beal, Dennis Rolke, Steve Dinger, and Eddie Balderas.

FOREVER.

Made in the USA
Coppell, TX
07 April 2022

76180798R00272